AT THE
DRAGON'S
GATE

CHARLES FENN

AT THE DRAGON'S GATE

WITH THE OSS IN THE FAR EAST

Naval Institute Press
Annapolis, Maryland

Naval Institute Press
291 Wood Road
Annapolis, MD 21402

All photos are from the author's personal collection.

Library of Congress Cataloging-in-Publication Data
    Fenn, Charles, Captain.
     At the dragon's gate : with the OSS in the Far East / Charles Fenn.
       p. cm.
     ISBN 1-59114-268-7 (alk. paper)
     1. Fenn, Charles, Captain. 2. United States. Office of Strategic Services—Biography. 3. World War, 1939–1945—Secret service—United States. 4. World War, 1939–1945—Military intelligence—United States. 5. World War, 1939–1945—Deception—United States. 6. World War, 1939–1945—Campaigns—China. 7. World War, 1939–1945—Campaigns—Asia, Southeastern. 8. World War, 1939–1945—Personal narratives, American. 9. Psychological warfare—United States—History—20th century. 10. United States. Marine Corps—Officers—Biography. I. Title.
    D810.S8F463 2004
    940.54'8673'092—dc22

                                          2004014326

Printed in the United States of America on acid-free paper ∞
11 10 09 08 07 06 05 04   9 8 7 6 5 4 3 2
First printing

CONTENTS

FOREWORD

I remember the day Charles Fenn walked into our crowded OSS office in Washington, D.C., in 1943. He'd been assigned to the Morale Operations (MO) branch, dealing in subversive propaganda, Office of Strategic Services. Here was a Marine lieutenant from the theater we were targeting: China-Burma-India (CBI). He'd been working with people vital to our mission. He was not afraid to say what he thought, to stand up for his beliefs, however radical. He had been with the Associated Press and knew the media. Eventually he became one of the most effective MO agents in the CBI.

His memoir, *At the Dragon's Gate,* is an absorbing story of one man's crusade on two fronts: subverting the Japanese enemy through propaganda methods and battling the bureaucracy that fettered OSS and most other government agencies in the theater. "Bureaucracy sets in like rigor mortis," he once complained after a particularly audacious MO operation was shot down by top brass.

The CBI theater was fragmented: French and British striving to keep their Asian colonies; Americans opposing the Chinese Communists; and Chinese nationalists fighting the growing Communist insurrection more fiercely than the Japanese invaders. Vietnam, meanwhile, was struggling for political freedom from the French. Fenn met and recruited the man who finally brought that freedom to his country: Ho Chi Minh. Fenn's association with "Uncle Ho" (code name Lucius) is one of the highlights of *At the Dragon's Gate.*

For his wartime service with OSS, Fenn was awarded the U.S. Soldier's Medal for Valor, the Bronze Star, and a citation from General William Donovan, the head of OSS.

In 1948 Fenn returned to London, where he had been born in 1907. He wrote plays for London's Little Theatre and wrote several books on China. Later he also worked with the British Broadcasting Company on the Emmy Award–

winning television documentary *Uncle Sam and Uncle Ho.*

Fenn later retired to Ireland, where he lived in Schull, County Cork, with his family, managing a colorful bed and breakfast, the Standing Stone. For Fenn, it was a green and peaceful spot, far removed, both figuratively and geographically, from the war-torn Far East the author once knew.

His account of his wartime experiences is a witty, insightful story of real-life espionage, another chapter in the history of the OSS, and a passport to another place and time. Enjoy.

Elizabeth McIntosh
West Lock Farm, Virginia
2004

AT THE DRAGON'S GATE

1

FROM WASHINGTON
TO BURMA

Carlyle summarized the politics of nations thus: "Counsellors of state sit plotting and playing their high game of chess whereof the pawns are men." In the ordinary game of chess, a pawn may sometimes hold the king in check. In the high game of international politics, a human pawn may sometimes hold counselors of state in check. Such was briefly my role in World War II.

The chess pawn, being manipulated by the player, has no will of its own. Whether human pawns have any will of their own is a question endlessly debated. In my own case I had little or none; from the beginning I was caught up in the "high game of chess" only by chance and was subsequently manipulated only by further irrelevancies.

In writing this book, I shall hope to be discerning, truthful, interesting, and impartial. I may claim to have one advantage in regard to impartiality; having been born, educated, and briefly employed in England, I immigrated to the United States of America and subsequently became an American citizen. My story begins in 1943 when I returned to New York City after a two-year stretch as an Associated Press war correspondent. I had two objectives: to find a publisher or an agent for a war novel I had been working on and to improve my status with the AP as a mere stringer correspondent despite having covered war fronts in China, Burma, Ceylon, Abyssinia, and Djibouti. I had originally (1940) gone to China as a news photographer for a picture magazine called *Friday,* which rivaled *Life* but was left wing and had a much smaller circulation.

I might describe myself as theoretically left: Shavian inspired and favoring public ownership, equality for women, and racial equality. *Friday* magazine endorsed these concepts but went a step further, supporting the Soviet Union, whereas my own critical enthusiasm had been shaken by Stalin's purges of the thirties, not to mention widespread evidence of other tyranny.

Friday's readership thus comprised not only leftists like myself but those still accepting Stalinism, including a substantial number of Communist Party members. For a large cross section of all these readers, the Soviet-Nazi pact of 1941 was a staggering betrayal. And when *Friday* supported the official Communist Party line of condoning it, they stopped reading the journal. As a result, the paper shortly folded up, leaving me in the middle of China (photographing the Japanese advance) without a job and, as all too often the case, almost broke. Communications were so poor that a couple of months actually went by before I even heard of *Friday's* demise. It took several more months, first to raise the ante and then to make the very complicated journey, via public bus and Chinese army truck, to get back to Chungking in hopes of picking up another job.

I was still looking and feeling thankful you could get a meal in China, albeit largely rice, for the equivalent of five cents, when there came the news of Pearl Harbor. It so happened I was acquainted with the three Army generals composing the so-called American Military Mission who had arrived a few months earlier to liaise with Chiang Kai-shek (throughout this book I will use the Wade-Giles system of romanizing the Chinese written language) in his war of resistance to the Japanese (a subject I shall deal with later). Hearing they were recruiting personnel, I thought that offering my services would nicely combine patriotism with my need for a job. They seemed pleased to take me on, though the remuneration subsequently offered hardly lived up to their smiling welcome. But it did enable me to eat better meals.

Initially, I was asked a great many questions about China: politics, the Chinese people, the war, the top personalities, the administration, and the past, present, and likely future of China, all of which was taken down in shorthand (tape machines, although embryonically invented, were not yet in use). Suddenly, however, I was transferred to the pay department, which consisted of an Army sergeant who did the figure work and a Chinese assistant who mostly ran errands. It seemed the sergeant was needed elsewhere, and there was no one else they could trust to do his job: a meaningless statement because no cash was involved, only paychecks.

It says much for the patience my close association with Chinese people had impressed into my basically fretful nature that I stood three weeks of this otherwise insufferable boredom, and when I resigned, unable to bear any more, the generals, instead of awarding me a medal for heroic service, scowlingly complained that I was letting them down. Perhaps I was lucky the draft did not yet apply.

So now I was free! But, alas, I was shortly broke again. At just about this point, the Japanese invaded Burma. I will never forget how this news on the stuttering radio suddenly set my thoughts racing and how I promptly hired a rickshaw (usually avoided as cruelly exploitative) to the press hotel where Spencer Moosa, the AP man and fortunately a friend of mine, was there in his niche.

So with Lady Luck still throwing me aces, I talked Spencer Moosa into sending me down to get pictures of the Japanese invasion with immediate expenses paid and subsequent payments dependent on results. (I should perhaps explain here that in those days good new photographs were more valued than they are today. Although the top-class cameras of that era, such as Leica, were beautiful pieces of mechanism, they required far more skill to operate effectively than present-day electronically operated cameras. This was also in the days before television made stills of secondary importance.) Travel expenses would be paid, but additional payment would depend on material submitted and approved.

So I subsequently went through two highly dangerous months in Burma with no contract, no salary, and no insurance of any sort (never heard of it) and was lucky to escape getting caught by the Japanese and locked up in a camp or having my head sliced off as a spy. "Where ignorance is bliss, 'tis folly to be wise" was never more true. Because of there being no wired transmission of material, much of mine arrived too late; some was even lost in transit. Nevertheless, bighearted AP sufficiently liked some of what they did get to let me cover other war fronts on the same terms.

But finally, enough was enough. In the middle of Africa, held up for weeks by red tape on my way to the war in Algeria, I was offered a ride on a Liberator returning to the United States. Liberator by name and liberator by deed! Ten days later (on the South Atlantic route to avoid U-boats, flights took that long), I was back home: what joy!

I found my wife, Marion Greenwood, entertaining a few friends, mostly fellow artists. Marion, still young and beautiful, had recently, under the aegis of Diego Rivera, shone in the art world by covering huge Mexican walls with highly competent fresco murals. When Marion asked about my interview with the AP, I saw no reason not to tell her frankly that it had been a washout, and the talk moved on to other topics.

Among the guests was Buckminster Fuller, the architect-engineer who invented, among other significant work, the geodesic dome. He seemed particularly interested that I had been in China and asked several somewhat probing questions. Then, taking me aside, he asked:

"Do I gather you had some·sort of contretemps with AP?"

"You could put it that way."

"So you might be interested in a new job?"

"I might very well be!"

And before he left I had an appointment to meet him in his office at ten o'clock the next morning.

It was that next morning when I learned the following facts: in addition to his usual interests, Bucky was acting as advisor to the Office of Strategic Service, called the OSS (which after the war became the Central Intelligence Agency, or CIA). This clandestine U.S. government agency was the brainchild of William J. Donovan, a millionaire Wall Street lawyer and close friend of President Roosevelt. The agency operated with unlimited funds not accountable to Congress, and its membership was drawn very much from Donovan's lawyer friends and associates, along with politicians, business executives, socialites, and academics in the top bracket. A number of so-called experts or specialists were also brought in, with emphasis on explorers, inventors, linguists, missionaries, observers, overseas businessmen, and journalists.

It was, of course, in this category of "journalist" that Fuller, impressed by my seemingly wide experience in China, thought I might fit. He therefore arranged that I should go down to Washington and meet one of the OSS executives. But before I come to this, it might be useful to consider the origin, purpose, and development of OSS in rather more detail than Fuller revealed at this point.

Wars were originally fought strictly by armies and navies, and the civilian population was affected, if at all, only by the ensuing destruction of property, food, livelihood, and general welfare. This, of course, was at times catastrophically devastating to whole populations, as, for example, during the Napoleonic Wars. But it was only in this century, with the advent of what was originally called the Great War and later World War I, that wars became total, that is, with the whole population regulated in one way or another; if they were not inducted into the armed forces, then they were strictly regulated as to their livelihood, leisure, and subsistence. This extension of warfare was mostly because some European nations, having become increasingly industrialized, overpopulated, expansionist, and competitive, had grabbed off whole chunks of the outside world for their own exploitation ahead of some other European nations who had been initially less organized to grab the spoils worth having.

After a slow start, with the use of methods from the nineteenth century, such as massed infantry attacks whereby men were slaughtered in thousands and whereby cavalry charges slaughtered horses too, war became revolutionized as already described. In addition, the newly invented airplane was utilized, the tank was invented, and with trench warfare becoming the norm, the war was fought largely with shells. Other innovations included the demoralization of the civilian populations by submarines sinking vital food supplies, by slaughter and destruction from air raids, and by propaganda disseminating unpleasant truths as well as lies.

In World War I, both sides adopted certain codes of behavior for propaganda effect, rather than because they approved of such codes, which often interfered with doing the job—that is, either slaughtering the enemy or intimidating him to the point of surrender (a preferred solution because it saved both time and ammunition).

World War II began only eighteen years after the first one ended and was in some respects merely a renewal of it, due largely to the foolish behavior of the Allies in bankrupting Germany with war debts. Out of this disaster had emerged Hitler, a genius with magnetism, energy, and determination, although top-heavily fanatical, which finally led him to overplay his hand to the point of disaster. But meanwhile he inspired his countrymen to subdue the greater part of Europe and to come within an ace of subduing his one surviving opponent, Britain. Parallel with this cataclysm, Japan had achieved an even greater triumph, having shattered the American Navy, overwhelmed all the Allied bases, and occupied most of Asia.

As historian Toynbee emphasized, if an overwhelming challenge does not totally overwhelm, it often inspires the victim to new heights of vigor and success. This was certainly true of America following the Japanese initial onslaught (and even more spectacularly confirmed in German and Japanese postwar recovery). The nation rose to the challenge with an energy, invention, skill, and final success that ultimately made it number one among world powers. All the existing functions in the operation of war were expanded, improved, and speeded up, and some new ones were added.

Among the latter was the Office of Strategic Services, as described earlier. The reasons for the curious mixture in this organization were roughly this: in the USA, equality before the law was not a shibboleth to be lightly dismissed, and the draft then sweeping men below a certain age and physically fit into the military net could not easily be disregarded in favor of wealth, prestige, or political pull. Although OSS was founded for the genuine purpose of serving the war effort, it was inevitable that it would also be used to rescue certain citizens from being drafted into the ranks when it was believed they might be more useful elsewhere, such as in OSS. Although for fear of adverse criticism they must still be drafted, there was no law to say that after some perfunctory training they might not qualify as officers, with rank appropriate to their status in civilian life. This accounted largely for the critical recruitment mentioned above.

I should explain the category of "specialist": explorers would be men of initiative, have traveled alone, be self-reliant, and be able to relate knowledgeably with foreigners. Inventors and technicians would be able to devise gadgets to deceive, frighten, injure, or kill clandestinely. Linguists were necessary not only to coordinate with our allies but to penetrate into and spy upon our enemies. Missionaries would have special knowledge and insight relating to foreign countries as well as personal contact with the inhabitants. Foreign traders and journalists would have similar advantages but in very different environments.

Candidates in all the above-mentioned categories, whether they had been chosen by Donovan and other top figures or had volunteered like myself, were, in these early days, nearly all civilians to start with. They had not yet come up on the draft, they had been found not physically fit for military service, they had been exempted because their occupation was in one way or another useful to the war effort, or simply they had been overseas. (Both these latter exemptions explained my own civilian status.)

OSS candidates about to be drafted might choose to serve in the Army, Navy, or Marines—I myself preferred the more prestigious and selective Marines, not knowing that whereas the Army and Navy required only token training from "specialists," the Marine Corps insisted on a full program for everyone. The strenuous physical regime, augmented by meticulous discipline, was inevitably a challenge to a man aged thirty-six who had not previously been concerned with any physical regime. But I am anticipating the course of events.

Following Buckminster Fuller's recommendation, I proceeded to Washington and was received in the OSS headquarters (an assembly of office buildings only a step up from sheds, which sufficiently reflects the recent birth of the organization) by a congenial, well-informed, and precise Irish American, who, I later on learned, had formerly been—what else indeed?—an eminent lawyer. During the next half hour he probed in some depth my genesis, education, and subsequent careers, with a slant in some questions revealing that although OSS was distinctly elite, selective, right wing, and university educated, the organization realized that "specialists" such as myself might not have all these otherwise desirable attributes. He meant, of course, that OSS would overlook not only my having left school aged only seventeen and gone off to sea as a steward and subsequently been a salesman (an improvement possibly) but also my having worked for *Friday* magazine! However, one must not forget that the Soviet Union was now on our side, and in any case, I had never been a member of the Communist Party. And it could not be denied, he concluded, that my knowledge of China and contacts with Chinese people in so many different fields would be a useful asset in our kind of work.

So I was stamped "okay—subject to a security check," a proviso that in those six words sounded merely routine but in practice took six weeks of undercover probing by security men into every facet of my life both past and present. From a legal point of view, my life was irreproachable. Regarding my leftism, there was almost no evidence of this beyond my assignment with *Friday*.

During this time I had lost my status as a war correspondent and become subject to draft into one of the armed services. OSS personnel who were physically fit but not yet drafted were classified as "specialists" who might enlist into the Army, Navy, or Marines and after training emerge as officers with rank commensurate with their previous qualifications, a classification of dubious propriety because high salaries, impressive background, and influential friends outweighed potential competence. This had the unfortunate result of cluttering up the organization not merely with misfits but with destructive misfits, because high rank gave men special powers to exercise their incompetence. This judgment is based partly on my initial observation, but mostly on my subsequent experience, and it is, of course, only partially applicable, because some OSS personnel rose to leadership by intrinsic merit and right action. Another point to be considered is that we are here concerned with OSS operations in the Far East, an area more difficult for most Americans to operate in than Europe because they knew less about it, found it all very strange, and saw the inhabitants as hardly human!

In choosing to join the Marine Corps rather than the Army or Navy, I was, of course, influenced by knowing it was considered the most elite of the three services. As I had neither social background nor other useful influence, I was given rank commensurate with my earnings as war correspondent, which worked out merely to first lieutenant. I shortly discovered that serving in the Marine Corps offered two disadvantages: one, I had to take the very tough Marine Corps training and, two, promotion was slower than in the Army or Navy.

The Marine Corps training taught me that at the age of thirty-six a man is well past his prime. It also taught me to shoot straight with a variety of weapons, including a Colt .45 pistol, for special competence in which I received a medal as an "expert."

From the Marine Corps camp I was sent to the OSS training school, where I was made acquainted both by instruction and practical operation with the five branches of OSS: Special Operations (SO), Special Intelligence (SI), Counterintelligence (X-2), Research and Development (R&D), and Morale Operations (MO).

SO was concerned with the use of explosives other than in weapons, for example, blowing up buildings, bridges, or aircraft; sinking vessels; destroying enemy installations and equipment; and killing enemy civilians with a poison pill, a small dagger, a sharp pencil point, a single blow, or even a skillfully folded newspaper.

SI dealt with obtaining information through methods outside the military intelligence gleaned by the Army, Navy, and Marines. For example, they obtained information through burglary, theft, pickpocketing, rifling safes, spying, penetrating enemy installations in disguise, and using certain devices such as cameras that resembled matchboxes exactly.

X-2's mission was to combat the enemy's intelligence by penetrating their installation and agents either by traditional means or by our own SI methods.

R&D was to devise new methods of spying, ferreting out, and destroying enemy equivalents of the above and to invent new devices, such as a pocket-sized device for recording conversations. I should note here that somewhat primitive tape recorders had been devised but were not yet in general use.

MO had four goals: (1) to devise all possible ways to deceive the enemy as to one's intentions, capabilities, and timing; (2) to reproduce enemy handouts, leaflets, magazines, newspapers, and photographs in exact facsimile but with subtle changes that were damaging to the enemy, e.g., in a Japanese leaflet urging Chinese civilians not to cooperate with the Americans, to threaten penalties so severe they suggested the Japanese were the real enemy of the Chinese. This briefly stated example is inadequate to establish the effectiveness of this kind of deceit in actual practice; (3) to devise and spread rumors likely to have a demoralizing effect on the enemy; and (4) to spread reports via agents, gossip, the media, and broadcasts with subtle lies either misleading the enemy and hostile neutrals or causing division within or between them.

Our initiation into this MO activity had actually begun the moment of entry to the training school. After having been instructed to discard my Marine Corps uniform in favor of civvies, to adopt a pseudonym, and to guard my anonymity throughout, I was further told to carry no evidence (such as letters) that would perhaps reveal my true identity when fellow trainees followed out additional instruction to spy, pickpocket, search clothing, and use all other means to break our "cover." Although all this training was, of course, strictly for war purposes, I was never, in later life, quite as honest and law abiding as I had been brought up to be. For example, I have never since thought twice about reading other people's letters or about opening desk drawers if I felt so inclined. In Hong Kong after VE day I picked the lock of an office formerly occupied by the Japanese to purloin a typewriter that was, strictly speaking, now the property of the Hong Kong government. Some years later I obliged a friend by entering someone's flat through a back window to appropriate a valuable book she claimed was hers. And when a bank on one occasion credited me by error with a large sum of money, I did not notify them and got away with keeping it. These peccadilloes I would never have been guilty of before OSS. I mention them merely to illustrate that not all the wounds of war are caused by missiles.

Both one's natural aptitude and previous occupation affected one's inclination and skill in shining in any particular branches of OSS work, and it was perhaps inevitable that I should do best in MO activities and was therefore directed to report to that department in the Far Eastern section where my personal experience lay. This had only just been set up and consisted of eight men, half of whom were in uniform, and two women, both civilians.

The commanding officer (CO), Herbert Little, formerly a lawyer but now with the rank of major, was friendly, cultivated, and enthusiastic. But like many of the key men in OSS, he had been appointed by his lawyer pal Donovan and had no background in or knowledge of Far Eastern affairs except what he was now gathering from books or from the two or three members of his staff who had experience in or knowledge of that area. Because I alone had served in Burma (and was acquainted with the then-famous General Stilwell), I was put in charge of Burma operations with one of the women, Betty MacDougal (later to rise to the top echelons in OSS affairs), as my assistant.

A few weeks after this appointment, Major Little, whom I was invited to call Herb, handed me a folder marked "Top Secret." "Nobody else is to see it in any circumstances, not even Betty," he said. I now found myself inspecting with a certain awed incredulity the "Overall Plan for Burma, Code name Daisy," with full details describing how the SO and SI sections of OSS would aid British ground forces and the U.S. Army, Air Force, and Navy in a combined operation to win back Burma.

"Implement this with your own scheme for MO operations and let me have it as soon as possible!"

For several minutes I sat at my desk in a state of euphoria. From being a stringer war correspondent I now found myself called upon to play a vital role in the war effort! When the dizzy spell had passed, I went to work with a zestful confidence that what I set down would actually contribute to winning back Burma. I devised a string of rumors, e.g., "The Japanese raping of Burmese women has grown to such proportions that Burmese protesters set fire to a Japanese HQ and the Japanese executed two of the offenders, thus seriously damaging the existing friendly relations." (This was one of many rumors I successfully promulgated when later operating a real MO campaign in Burma.) The existence of several different tribespeople (e.g., Kachins and Karens) who bitterly opposed the Burmese for exploiting this habitat gave excellent chances for fomenting further resentment by creating fake Japanese leaflets openly friendly but subtly insulting, deceiving, or attacking or by faking divisive propaganda between the various tribes and the Japanese.

After handing my "implementation" to Little, I daily expected to be called to a top-echelon conference at which zero hour for D-day–Burma would be disclosed and the overall plan put into execution. Alas, I never heard another word about this "Top Secret—Overall Plan for Burma, Code name Daisy." It was locked away in the office safe, and I fear it remained "top secret" forever.

My disillusionment from this episode was shortly offset by the prospect of genuine action. Chiang Kai-shek, the military dictator in China, who had long suspected OSS might circumvent his total control, had at last been prevailed upon by Roosevelt to accept some initial representatives.

To represent the MO branch, Major Little decided to go himself. But as he knew nothing about China he believed it would be advisable to have me go along, too. Before I deal with this, it might be useful to explain briefly the China background, because China is the main scene of all that follows.

In 1912, the Manchu Dynasty, which had ruled China for three centuries, at last collapsed. After some years of chaos, an exceptional leader, Sun Yat-sen, briefly gave China the nearest approach to democracy and social reform it has ever enjoyed, but upon his death in 1925, the country was again torn apart by civil war. Two main rivals emerged: the Communists, largely inspired by the recently established Soviet Union, and the so-called Nationalists, a combination of the army with leading bankers led by a clever and supremely ambitious warlord, Chiang Kai-shek. Having outmaneuvered the Communists and driven them into distant exile, he established himself as president of China and generalissimo of the army. Meanwhile, to ensure his alliance with the principal

Chinese banking house, the Soongo, he married one of the three daughters. This woman, known as Madame Chiang, contributed not only the banking link but two other supremely useful assets: one, her magnetic personality and beauty, implemented by drive, ambition, and fluent English, and, two, her enthusiastic support of the Christian religion (shared by all members of the Soong family).

Several additional factors helped the Chiang hierarchy win the sympathy, admiration, and—above all—financial aid of America. China had been the only large non-Western state to remain free from colonial rule and therefore open to American missionaries who, to gain sympathy, support, and funds, had waged skillful campaigns enhancing the virtues of the Chinese people. This had resulted in a special relationship between the two countries. The overthrow of the monarchy and establishment of a republic under the admired Sun Yat-sen won further American approval. Finally, the Japanese invasion, with its barbaric destruction, slaughter, and cruelty, was fully publicized by the newly invented radio broadcasting then sweeping America.

All this created a nationwide American endorsement of the Nationalist Party, led by what was thought to be a heroic military leader and his incomparable wife struggling to save their country from being overwhelmed by a ruthless enemy, but was in reality an alliance of top bankers and a military dictator to amass wealth and deposit it safely abroad. Two enemies somewhat impeded this objective—the Japanese army by military invasion and the Chinese Communists by militant political rivalry. The Nationalists publicized their resistance to the Japanese, thereby winning American support, but in reality concentrated rather more on resisting the Chinese Communists: it was believed that a division of spoils—territory, trade, exploitation—could be made with the Japanese, whereas the Communists were dedicated to total takeover (as, indeed, ultimately proved true).

Little and I flew out east, not as OSS personnel, because this was supposed to be secret, but—dressed to the nines—as Major Little, U.S. Army, and First Lieutenant Fenn, U.S. Marines, duly armed with Colt automatics, Leica cameras, leather dispatch cases, khaki flight bags, and favorable air priorities.

Because the Pacific route was blocked by the Japanese navy and the North Atlantic of that era presented an excessive long hop for the planes, our route out east went via South America and Central Africa. We thus touched down at Miami, Trinidad, Brazil, Ascension Island, Accra, Kano, Khartoum, Karachi, and

Delhi. Even on a favorable priority this took eight days, transport planes still being too few to carry all those awaiting flights. But despite wartime exigencies we were everywhere well looked after, free to move about, and paid the generous travel expenses Uncle Sam hands out under the name of per diem to all personnel employed on his behalf. This "package tour" was consequently one of the best I have ever had. It was also surprising to me, and even more so to native Americans, to find all this route largely controlled by the British even at this late stage, despite World War I having reduced Britain from virtual supremacy among nations to equality with the USA, and in Delhi (and, for that matter, in all of India) the British ruled with an authority that more and more infuriated the Americans, who could not equal (never mind exceed, as they felt they should!) such innate superiority. The British also benefited from two years' prior battle experience, so they seemed to know, and mostly did know, more about everything relative to the Far East as well as to the war than the Americans. But our relations with the French were, of course, far worse. The first barrier was language: very few Americans knew French; not many French at that period knew English. But the worst barrier came through the fold up of the French army on the western front and the subsequent cooperation with Hitler, which inflicted on many Frenchmen a compulsion to cover guilt with either indifference or resentment.

My Marine Corps orders directed me to travel "anywhere in the China-Burma-India (CBI) war zone" that "duty required," which certainly gave me a free hand. On arrival at Delhi, however, we were instructed to report to the OSS headquarters for onward routing. This was located in a large Edwardian house formerly occupied by British business tycoons who were now on active service. This comparatively luxurious living in India, which lasted almost intact throughout the war, was the heritage of Britain's conquest and long occupation of a country where a small proportion of the huge poverty-stricken population had been autocrats living in utmost splendor. When in Rome do as the Romans do, and although the Americans were not to the manner born, they were apt pupils and saw no reason to deprive themselves. This measure of integration by no means erased their ambivalent feelings of inferiority-superiority with regard to the British nor their equally confused attitude toward the Indians, whether the nabobs, whose dolce far niente life they despised yet were happy to share, or the masses, whose cringing subservience they deplored but willingly learned to exploit. The British raj was still resplendent, and Americans were not reluctant to take advantage of the gracious living thus provided, including a diet of steaks, chicken curries, and cheap (although limited) booze, plus having a host of

Indian servants ready to salaam and dancing every evening with the Anglo-Indian women employed as office staff.

We were shortly informed that there was a holdup on our China mission because Tai Li, the head of Chiang's notorious secret police, opposed OSS's intention to operate with Communists as well as with Nationalists. This was not, of course, because OSS leaned toward the left—quite the reverse. But we had finally learned to accept the fact, however reluctantly, that the Soviets had long since been our allies. We had also discovered, with even more reluctance, that the Chinese Communists were not only more vigorously opposing the Japanese but appeared to be more efficient and reliable than the Nationalists. This was partly because the Nationalists were mostly conscripts, ill fed, ill led, and left confused about whom or what they were fighting for and even about who was the real enemy, because they were often required to fight the Communists instead of the Japanese. The Chinese Communists, on the other hand, were self-enlisted, devoted to their cause and to their leaders, and got subsistence from peasants who partly shared their beliefs. They had two enemies: the Japanese and the Chinese Nationalists. They considered the former the greater immediate threat. Observing this, America decided to exploit it, even while being strictly anti-Communist. Because these Chinese Communists numbered at most a few tens of thousands in a population of several hundred million, we believed they offered no great threat to the Chiang Kai-shek Nationalists to whom we gave support that was perhaps a million times greater. This colossal mismanagement cost us vast expenditure of money, materials, and human effort. When we repeated the error in Vietnam we added fifty thousand American lives to an even greater expenditure of money, materials, and human effort. The irony of these errors is that time and inconsistency has since destroyed or transformed the Communist regime without a shot being fired.

While waiting for this holdup to be sorted out, we occupied our time pleasantly and usefully with the British equivalent of OSS, the Special Operations Executive (SOE), where Professor J. D. Bernal and Peter Fleming were always ready to talk to us about the theories, plans, methods, and accomplishments of the SOE. Bernal, a famous Anglo-Irish physicist, was a dedicated Communist but yet a trusted advisor to Earl Mountbatten—a revealing commentary on the political complexities of the period. Fleming was a British travel writer much admired for his incisive accounts of adventure travel. On this visit we were made particularly aware how far the theoretical potentials of clandestine warfare can be made practical and effective and where the limitations lie.

This was by no means the last time I found that although the Americans were inclined to be impatient and even antagonistic in relations with the British, we usually received generous cooperation from them. This was no doubt partly because the British realized that only American finance, equipment, and manpower, plus the enthusiasm and energy of those who come fresh to the task, could bring final victory. It was not that the British came only cap in hand, however; we leaned heavily on their knowledge and experience, as well as on their facilities.

Fleming shortly arranged for us to fly down to Ceylon to initiate MO work with Mountbatten at his Southeast Asia command in Kandy. This delightful hill town set beside a lake in tropical uplands was then still unspoiled, and as I had friends there from war correspondent days, our all-too-short stay was almost another holiday.

Admiral Mountbatten had now been appointed commander-in-chief of the Southeast Asia war zone and was on his way to Kandy, which was to be his initial headquarters. As it happened, I had already met him in China when I had photographed him for *Friday* magazine. As always, Mountbatten was impeccably dressed, except that his tie was slightly ruffled, which I thought would dismay him if recorded in a photograph. So, somewhat apologetically, I suggested he might like to straighten it.

"Yes, indeed!" said Mountbatten, doing so with a smile. "Was it Beau Brummel who said that a well-tied tie is the first serious step in life?"

"Actually, sir, it was Oscar Wilde," I remarked, having been lucky enough one time to buy Wilde's collected works in a secondhand bookshop.

Mountbatten had already favored me with a smile. He now gave me a look that almost said, "All men are brothers." I was pleased about that. Some big shots would more likely have resented my familiarity.

At this second meeting Mountbatten registered our first encounter by asking, "Haven't we met somewhere before?" And when I reminded him of the occasion, he remarked, deadpan, "I've come up in the world since then. These days, my ties are always straight." Indeed, as a human being, Mountbatten had charm; as a leader in a vital war zone the best one could say was that he was honest, well intentioned, and persevering; the worst was that he typified British tradition, convention, and noblesse oblige at a time when the world required leaders who could adapt to the most momentous changes since Napoleon and, we hoped, replace chaos with at least some sort of order. Did anyone achieve that stature? Roosevelt, Churchill, de Gaulle, Stalin? And in a rather different category, what about Ghandi? Alas! What "great man" really survives the rust of time?

Problems with Chiang Kai-shek being still unresolved, we were now instructed to proceed to Assam, on the Burmese border, and visit OSS "Detachment 101," presently working with the British army staging a counterattack against the Japanese occupying Burma. A year earlier, when the Japanese had overrun the British colony and seized the valuable oil fields, I had been attached as a war correspondent to the British army defending the colony, so this zone was to be my present field of operations while Little, after a "look-see," went on to speed up our MO clearance into China.

En route to Assam we were held up in Calcutta by bad flying weather. This city, although not sharing Delhi's elegance and amenities, was another live-it-up spot for privileged Westerners "passing through" (as against having to live there in sweltering heat and no escape). Among my come-and-go acquaintances was a certain Margot M., so essentially bright and attractive that she usually entertained visitors more VIP than mere reporters or first lieutenants. Thus recently she received U.S. vice president Wallace, who was en route to visit Generalissimo Chiang Kai-shek. I must here mention that OSS training included the oft-reiterated injunction to benefit from every contact, no matter how trivial, by discreet probing: even the most trivial gossip might be deftly guided into revealing another fragment of a significant jigsaw. But all I got about VP Wallace was that Margot had cooked his favorite meal of curried prawns.

"How did you happen to know it was his favorite meal?" I inquired.

"Mountbatten tipped me off. Actually, it was Mountbatten who told Wallace about me."

"And who told Mountbatten about you?" I asked with a smile.

"I met him at a 'do' in aid of the British Red Cross. Of course, he was the guest of honor—big deal! But when someone introduced us, he chatted away as if we were old friends. That's part of his genuine charm. It's a pity charm doesn't win wars," she added, with the suggestion of a sigh. That single phrase confirmed what I had feared might be my own somewhat biased judgment.

Finally arriving at Detachment 101, we met the commanding officer, Lieutenant Colonel Ray Peers. A West Point officer, young and alert, he wanted us to get to work immediately: "And not on mere plans but on action!" OSS here was confined so far to SO (sabotage) and SI (intelligence). Peers knew nothing about MO but seemed keen to get it operating.

This liaison having been established, Little decided to fly on to Chungking in an effort to break the deadlock. I was to stay on in Assam and get MO launched prior to the arrival of additional MO personnel, by which time it was hoped we would be cleared for me to get MO launched in China. "Some men are born great, some achieve greatness, and some have greatness thrust upon them." I must admit this suited my temperament rather well. And in addition to being more or less my own boss, I was now in the most pleasant environment since . . . well, probably since my weeks in Ceylon . . . was that only eighteen months earlier?

Although not quite in the same class as that delightful island, this area of Assam, despite being called the front line, was more than just pleasant, being unspoiled, semitropical, and set high enough up in the mountains to lessen the heat. The prevailing lush jungle had been cleared here and there in favor of tea plantations, which of all forms of cultivation must be given the prize for charm, thanks to the shining green bushes interspersed with shade trees and adorned here and there with rows of leaf-plucking women in costumes so bright you would think they were dressed for a musical. In the jungle, meanwhile, one could often glimpse colorful birds and snakes and at dusk a feline or two, notably tigers.

Wresting myself from such distractions, I got to work on MO with the limited means at my disposal. One method requiring nothing beyond ingenuity was devising and spreading rumors calculated to deceive, mislead, puzzle, or frighten the enemy or the natives who might be helping him. Other rumors might aim at stirring up native hostility against the enemy or enlisting their sympathy and even support for our own side.

One might voice such rumors anywhere and to anyone, but it was, of course, something of an art to introduce them casually but effectively. The test of their effectiveness was to have them come back to you. The first one that qualified was told to me by an RAF pilot about two weeks after I had first spread it: "The Japs are paying their Burmese laborers in opium because the Jap issue of currency is becoming worthless." As both these details had a germ of truth, this rumor was rather effective.

I had no facilities to print leaflets or manufacture "deceptive devices," but I shortly discovered that in a neighboring town, two former newspaper colleagues, Vic Ranken and Ralph Bergstresser, were running the local American Office of War Information (OWI). They readily agreed to print up secretly for me some "black" leaflets, that is, counterfeiting those produced by the Japanese or their puppets and superficially pro-Japanese but containing material insidiously anti-Japanese in effect. For example, one exactly imitating the style of those put out by the Japanese high command in Rangoon, and purporting to be issued by them, exhorted the Burmese population to harass the Chins (a minority racial group in north-central Burma) on the grounds that they were helping the British restore British rule. A similar leaflet addressed to the Chins urged them to harass the Burmese for the same reason. The anti-Burmese leaflets addressed to the Chins were distributed clandestinely to the Burmese, and the others went to the Chins, thus infuriating both groups against the backstabbing Japanese, who openly protested friendship. These leaflets had to be compiled not only in the native language—Burmese, Kachin, Karen, and so on—but in the exact format of genuine Japanese leaflets. To meet this challenge I was, after tracking down some Japanese leaflets, entirely indebted to my friends in OWI.

The distribution of such leaflets required visits to the forward posts inside Burma, where natives working either for Detachment 101 or for the British could circulate them clandestinely. These journeys, although to some extent dangerous, had their enjoyable aspect, because the little planes we flew in had open cockpits affording the single passenger a wide view all round, and as we usually flew at low altitudes the landscape was intimately revealed. The field unit at destination consisted of two or three Allied personnel plus a few loyal Burmese or friendly tribesmen such as Shans or Kachins.

The atmosphere in such units depended largely on the particular CO. If he was reasonable, efficient, courageous, tolerant, and fair minded, one might hope to find freedom, pride, and good fellowship. But if he was insecure, bad tempered, or inept, the camp was invariably unhappy or even chaotic. Fatal errors were often made in the choice of forward leaders. It was assumed that the conditions of isolated units called for tough young men who could not only stand up physically to the hardships of the jungle but also, as and when required, boss the natives working for them. Certainly the exigencies of jungle life did call for endurance. But it was loneliness rather than hardship that broke men down. The tough young men went to pieces because they lacked inner resilience. Others withstood the loneliness but made themselves hated through racial arrogance or even brutality. At one camp I visited, the British CO, a former oil employee given rank as captain, personally executed with a Japanese sword a Burmese accused of spying. He added to the horror of this scene by making a frightful hash of it. This was the first occasion, but by no means the last, when I saw that when a man's life is turned upside down and excessive responsibilities are thrust upon him, he either breaks down or seeks refuge in violence.

On another occasion I had the rare experience of sighting a Japanese fighter plane, probably a Zero. These vast spaces of mostly jungle were largely no-man's-land, and neither the Japanese nor ourselves had enough planes to be often in evidence. When I saw this one I assumed we were sitting ducks—and without even a parachute to bail out with! Apparently sensing my fear, the pilot yelled above the engine's roar, "Don't worry—this little crate can crawl around in narrow circles so no fighter plane can get a bead on us!" But my heart did not stop racing until the Zero was safely out of sight.

My next scare was all too real. The pilot had failed to locate the jungle airstrip, and our fuel was finally exhausted, so we had to land on a sand bank. This shook up both the plane and occupants considerably. The pilot was able to send off a signal, but it was almost dark before a British launch collected us. Then we spent hours battling against the river, while rain came down in torrents. This is known as "plumbing the depths of misery."

A third mishap happened near the camp. In a disused warehouse two miles from base, I was teaching a group of Burmese recruits to use fully automatic rifles. This, of course, was outside my own schedule. But one discovered that even apart from any basic desire to be useful, the reward of such volunteer effort would be the gratitude and even delight of the recipients, who were more often exploited than helped.

For the sessions I had with this group, I usually walked to the warehouse along the disused railroad track running alongside the dirt road, which was then three inches deep in mud. One evening when returning to base my leg went into a gap between the sleepers with such a crack that I thought the bone was broken. A swelling on the shin grew as large as a baseball, and any movement caused excruciating pain. Because it was already pitch dark and the road was seldom used, I was in a bad way. As a signal, I fired off my revolver in six spaced-out shots, but after a full half hour with no response I gave up hope. The vehicle that ultimately arrived had come that way by chance. Back at base, the doctor said that although my leg was not broken, there had been a severe internal hemorrhage, and I was subsequently laid up for a week. Danger is at least exciting and usually fast. Boredom drags its weary length along to an exit door it never seems to reach.

A wire now came from Little, already back in Washington, instructing me to proceed to China and start our MO work there in the southeastern war zone. Peers was very indignant at my leaving him so soon and, as a very senior officer, almost ordered me to stay. It is difficult to serve two masters. I subsequently discovered that in OSS, one was sometimes called to serve half a dozen.

It was not only loyalty to Little that prompted me to leave. The pleasant locale of 101 was offset by the prevailing military regime: so many of the personnel were American Army, and Peers directed the camp with a military precision that very soon conflicted with my first impression of being my own boss!

Furthermore, I was never in harmony with the Burmese, who were for more than a century the victims of colonial domination and often either subservient and withdrawn or hostile and exhibitionist. With the Chinese, on the other hand, I almost always felt at ease. Although sometimes irrational, incomprehensible, and even inscrutable, they were almost never subservient, boastful, or two-faced. I had consequently made many friends among them, with whom I now hoped to renew contact and enlist a few in helping me to promote MO. In these Burmese outposts where I was presently operating, I usually had to work with bored Americans or weary British. The resulting apathy was not their fault. Rain, heat, deprivation, loneliness, and monotony were worse enemies than the Japanese. And, too, many of the men in these forward units had been wrongly chosen. It had been assumed that these hard and isolated conditions called for physically tough young men who could stand up to the challenge of the jungle and who could, as and when required, take charge of and utilize the natives. But young and inexperienced personnel not only lacked inner resilience but also the know-how of controlling the Burmese, Karens, Kachins, and other hill tribes upon whose cooperation they depended. Being now thirty-six years old, and having had a wealth of experience in so many environments, I was often tempted to advise them. Fortunately, I was also wise enough to know that advice is the last thing wanted by men breaking down under pressure.

Fortunately, all I usually required of them was to distribute the leaflets I previously described. These could be scattered by any plane bombing, attacking, or reconnoitering in areas appropriate to the particular leaflets or, failing that (because there were few enough Allied planes operating anywhere at this early stage of the war!), through what we hoped were pro-Allied natives distributing them around surreptitiously. The objective was, of course, to fake the implied source of the leaflets—always a difficult task. I also, of course, enlisted their help in circulating rumors and in sending fake messages over the air in code that might be decoded without too much difficulty and that might usefully deceive the Japanese or harm them in some small way.

At the airfield bad weather over the Himalayas kept us for three days and nights confined to the sweltering hostel, with no transport, nothing to read, and nothing else to do except play poker and from time to time open cans of warm ration beer. This beer sent jets of foam over everything and everybody, so we lived in a fugue of stale beer. I reiterate such laments not really to lament but to stress the importance of finding ways to avoid or lessen the debilitating "nonaction" in a war.

Waiting to ferry the backlog of personnel and equipment over "the Hump" (a nickname for the Himalayas) were five DC-3s. This two-engine plane, although a step up from the time-honored DC-2, needed every last ounce of power to surmount these formidable peaks, especially when loaded to the limit. There were rumors indeed and even assertions that sometimes they did not make it.

The roller-coaster flight, when we finally took off, was certainly no joyride. Because there was no pressurizing, we took intermittent whiffs of oxygen. To fall asleep could, unless someone noticed, prove fatal. Actually, nobody died, although most personnel got so sick they wished they had. In the cubbyhole serving as a toilet, a small cup attached to a tube presented difficulty even to males whenever the plane lurched, but when the Red Cross nurse traveling with us had to use it, she left the deck awash and then had to face some GI wisecracks.

As we came down over Kunming, dawn was already turning the sky violet, and the sun came up amid a scattering of fair-weather clouds. How joyful it seemed, after Assam's sweltering heat and our appalling flight, to step out into the bracing air of Kunming, a semitropical city set six thousand feet high amid lakes and mountains and enjoying almost perfect weather!

It was therefore with a buoyant heart that I hurried to the hostel to eat one of those breakfasts for which the Kunming airfield was famous: four fried eggs (albeit small) and ample Stateside bacon served up by a Chinese with one of those grinning, good-humored faces that leave permanent photographic memories. Bliss was it in that dawn to be alive, and to be fairly young was very heavenly. But when subsequently reporting at the check-in counter, I fell out of paradise with a thud: of the five planes that had left Assam, only two had reached Kunming; the other three had simply vanished in the storm. I went off to the transportation office feeling just that little bit less sure of my charmed life.

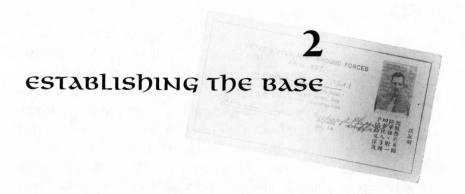

2

ESTABLISHING THE BASE

In Kunming, OSS had acquired a well-built house formerly belonging to an oil company. The eleven members installed therein included an elderly CO, Lieutenant Colonel Robert Hall (formerly a geography professor at the University of Michigan), a major, two captains, one lieutenant, a naval commander, an ensign, and four civilians. We all sat democratically at one long table and ate warmed-up rations or local products badly cooked in European style. Nobody would risk allowing the Chinese cook to prepare delicious Chinese-style food for fear of getting dysentery, typhoid, cholera, and tapeworms, not to mention the risk of ultimate starvation.

I shared a room with Captain Tolman, in charge of Research and Development, who was fond of demonstrating antipersonnel devices such as propelling pencils that exploded when you twisted the lead, chocolates laced with poison whose efficiency he demonstrated on rats (always in plentiful supply), and flashlamps that winked on and off (then an innovation). "If we float them down river into Japanese-occupied territory, they'll scare the hell out of the Japs."

All these showed promise, but what interested me most was his description of a gadget called a "tape recorder": "Sound is registered on metallic tape instead of on phonograph records so that you can get the contents of several records on a disk of tape not much larger than a silver dollar. But the real advantage," Tolman continued eagerly, "lies in the extreme accuracy of the recording: no scratch whatever and absolute pitch. It runs off a small battery so silently that an agent could, for instance, set one going in the Jap headquarters and record all their conversations without them knowing anything was there! Really fab!"

"It certainly sounds great. When can I get some?"

But alas, the war was over before we got any useful supply (or even any supply) of such gadgets. This deprivation of matériel was typical of the problem here in China, which the GIs rightly called "the arse hole of the war." China had, of course, always been remote and largely neglected except for the treaty ports— Hong Kong, Shanghai, Tientsin, and Hanchow. When the Japanese invaded and occupied those points of entry, China was shut off as if by a Far Eastern version of Stalin's iron curtain, because mountains, deserts, jungles, and rivers, combined with vast distances, closed off other access. This isolation was remedied for a while by establishing a supply route through Burma—the once-famous Burma Road, whereby men and materials shipped to the port of Rangoon were forwarded by rail to Mandalay in central Burma and onward by a two-thousand-mile trek through jungles and wildernesses over mountains eight thousand feet high and so at last into China.

When the Japanese succeeded in closing the road, China became isolated except for contact by air, always inadequate and often vulnerable (as I had just discovered). Other than military aircraft and the extensive personnel required to fly and service them, only special priority brought anything over "the Hump." Although that term "special priority" was somewhat nebulous, it did exact a strict limit to the total weight of men and matériel that the available planes could deliver.

Another limitation was the vast distance across China. With the Japanese having seized (in addition to the treaty ports already mentioned) a few hundred miles of coast, Chiang Kai-shek had set up his new capital in Chungking, some five hundred miles farther west. Meanwhile, the American Fourteenth Air Force (which constituted the only armed service of the Allies) had set up its headquarters base in Kunming, some seven hundred miles southwest of the Japanese advance. Travel by air was, as already stressed, very limited. Travel by corrugated dirt roads might take days. I was now to experience the formidable challenge of this particular marathon!

I intended to set up my base of operations in Kweilin, in central China, the forward base of operation of the Fourteenth Air Force and some fifty miles from the Japanese frontline. Transportation to Kweilin was very hard to procure. But I was fortunate enough to know General Chennault, the Fourteenth Air Force commander, quite well, having covered the exploits of his famous "Flying Tigers" for several weeks as an AP war correspondent.

This group played such a significant role in the China-Japan confrontation that it might be useful to explain its origin. In attacking China (largely for exploitation of ores, metals, fuel, and other vital products) Japan had a vastly superior army and weapons, plus complete control of the air, because China had neither an air force nor air defenses. The fundamental partiality of America for China and the nationwide resentment against reported Japanese brutalities prompted President Roosevelt to seek ways of aiding or relieving the Chinese. Thus a group of American pilots, both civil and Air Force, was enlisted as paid volunteers to go out to China and fly combat plane in attacks against the Japanese. Their selected commander, Claire L. Chennault, had served in World War I under famous airman Billy Mitchell, one of the first pilots to employ air tactics, as distinct from combats limited to individual planes. "Tactics" meant involving three or more pilots who cooperated in attack, defense, maneuver, evasion, and subterfuge with, for example, emphasis on getting superior height and the sun behind when attacking. So with fifty Curtis fighters (that is, the Flying Tigers), Chennault almost cleared the Chinese skies of Japanese aircraft, which had formerly bombed and ground strafed at will, never bothering with tactics because the Chinese had no aircraft and almost no air defense.

Chennault was a striking example of how to live life to the full if you are not too weighed down by convention, high principles, and who your friends are. So he not only went to the top as an Air Force commander, but by skillful maneuvering with Chiang and his banking associates was equally successful in postwar commercial aviation (and got out before they collapsed). Nor did he ever neglect to exploit those pleasures of life other leaders so often pass by (but are they high-minded or merely prudish?).

Thus, for example, on this occasion, after checking at the outer office with Doreen, a pretty Eurasian girl from Flying Tigers days, I was shown into Chennault's private office, where a young woman I did not know—American, tall, lean, and boyish—sat taking notes. A third female—pure Chinese, but dressed in a WAC's uniform curiously adorned with pearl buttons—brought in coffee. Chennault behaved as though he had less contact with any of these females than with the cocker spaniel who gazed at him with luminous eyes.

Always alert for any project that would widen his own sphere of influence, Chennault was immediately interested in my plan to enlist some of my Chinese friends as agents and do the kind of MO work I had done in Burma, and he promised his active cooperation in every possible way—except, of course, in the way I then needed, namely, a plane ride to Kweilin. It seemed that in respect to transportation, I could do him a favor. A convoy of Fourteenth Air Force vehicles waiting to be driven down to Kweilin, along with forty personnel, needed a leader familiar with this route, someone reliable who knew some Chinese.

"As I recall," said Chennault blandly, "you convoyed trucks for the Chinese Red Cross one time, so this job would be right up your alley!"

There was, of course, no way out of this. Apart from the personal angle, OSS could not afford to refuse Chennault a favor, because he was not only the most famous Westerner to have come to China since Marco Polo but also the key to all air transport. So I had to hide my annoyance at being given this tedious, time-wasting job.

At the last moment, because of problems about billeting en route, the convoy was divided into two, with one-half given over to an Air Force officer unfamiliar with the route, knowing no Chinese, and—as events proved—of total unreliability. In my own allocation I was given the additional burden of transporting five nuns who were joining a mission hospital down the line. Fortunately, they were all unattractive.

Our route went over a dirt road snaking through several mountain passes. At the end of each day's drive, we got beds in Chinese inns and a meal of warmed-up rations. The men refused to believe that Chinese food was not only delicious but so safe to eat that I had lived on it for eighteen months. Nor could I be aloof by eating on my own. These men were all "specialists" in something or other and very conscious of having been snatched from their independent status as garage mechanics, radio salesmen, and post office clerks and made into plain GIs. In time of war, democracy is a terrible burden.

On the third day, high in the Kweichow mountains, rain came down in torrents, and the road became one long slither of mud. Driving a jeep in the lead was the top sergeant with one of the nuns as a passenger. I myself drove another jeep as rear guard. We were coming down the hairpins of a mountain pass when I saw the far-off sergeant's jeep go into a skid and roll off down the slope. Because jeeps had only canvas tops I thought both occupants would inevitably be killed. But when I clambered down I found them still breathing although groaning with pain. My medical kit contained no morphine, and I dared not give them oral painkillers for fear of their internal injuries.

After we had half-carried, half-hauled them up the slope, I drove the shattered pair fifty agonizing miles to the nearest hospital. In addition to various other injuries, the sergeant had broken his spleen, an injury that subsequently proved fatal. The nun had several broken bones plus a double fracture of the spine. Although permanently crippled, she nevertheless survived.

Meanwhile, my team, with the help of thirty coolies, had hauled the precious jeep up the mountainside. Apart from the demolished hood and a few dents, it seemed almost undamaged, and the gallant engine started up with only a few coughs. The accident, however, made us a day behind schedule, so the other convoy, although stringently ordered to keep a day behind, now forged ahead, and during the remaining days of our journey bedeviled every mile with drunkenness, whoring, and indiscriminate shooting: an appalling example of how a sprinkling of GIs, not circumscribed by discipline and hating their fate in having been torn away from Stateside joys and Mom's loving care, could create a mayhem that goaded the Chinese population into a fury that subjected our own team following behind to constant abuse and often a volley of stones. Luckily, my own boys behaved pretty well, despite their aching homesickness at being deprived in this filthy, primitive, and comfortless land of even such basic necessities as movies, hot dogs, real dames, baseball, corner drugstores, Cokes, and double maple-and-walnut sundaes with genuine whipped cream and hot chocolate sauce.

In Kweilin the OSS commanding officer, Lieutenant Colonel Wilfred Smith, another Michigan professor and son of a China missionary and thus considered to be doubly qualified, was busily winning the war single-handed: a disease endemic among OSS personnel who had had greatness thrust upon them. Escaping from his jaunty self-assurance, I took a room in a Chinese inn and began contacting former Chinese friends to build up a network of agents. I soon enough found two former acquaintances who were studying at the university. Like almost everything in China's interior, this institution had been, thanks to the Japanese invasion, cut off from funds and important equipment. Food for both staff and students was sadly inadequate. Heating in the cold winter months was at best a few sticks of charcoal.

Fu-tong and Gerald (many Chinese who have learned some English or had contacts with England or America like to adopt English-style names) Chen were therefore not reluctant to join up with me and help with what I assured them was useful war work. When I explained in some detail what was involved, they could not wait to get started! This ready response to the challenge of new ideas and responsibilities is typical of so many Chinese who are not ground down in mere toil and perhaps accounts for their almost invariable success abroad.

While exploring Kweilin for further contacts, I also enjoyed its attractions. Picturesquely set amid the sugar-loaf peaks so often featured in Chinese paintings, it offered a diversity of architecture, shops, markets, and cosmopolitan refugees from all quarters, plus the added sophistication of a university town. Refugees also were the pretty "flowers" (high-class prostitutes) who had fled here from the conquered treaty ports, and innumerable opium dens offered cheerful hospitality day and night to the weary, the lonely, and the oppressed. A similar friendly welcome might be savored in the bathhouses where, for a pittance, one might enjoy a private room complete with couch, tea, sunflower seeds, hot water, soap, towel, and the services of a boy to "crack" your fingers and toes, a therapeutic treatment singularly soothing.

During my war-correspondent days I would often escape the grind of war-torn China by seeking refuge in bathhouses, tea houses, opium dens, and sing-song girls' parlors. Although prostitutes were also available in some of these establishments, this was subsidiary to the genuine provision of the stated purpose: a warm bath, steam room, foot massage, tea drinking, gambling, smoking opium, and girls singing, playing dulcimers, telling stories, cracking jokes, or merely looking decorative: an exploitation of the female sex not to be condoned, but short of the millennium, an improvement on the Western equivalent.

Partly to offset the spread of venereal disease among service personnel and partly in the hope, however vain, of presenting a moral, disciplined, and well-behaved image to the Chinese population, these houses of relaxation (all lumped together, however innocent, as brothels) had recently been put out of bounds and were continually patrolled by military police. Offenders discovered therein were reported to their commanding officers and duly disciplined.

I was caught rather often in bathhouses and similar establishments. Colonel Smith tore his hair. "That's two weeks running your name has headed the list!"

I politely explained that these places offered the best chance of spreading rumors (which was indeed partly true).

"Every night of the week?" exclaimed Smith. Adjutant Mykland, always heavily sarcastic, dubbed me "Fearless Fenn," a pejorative that earned me snide witticisms until a spate of newcomers arriving in the camp assumed it was a tribute to my exploits in the field. I was torn between enjoying this and guilt at its falsity!

It was in a bathhouse where I encountered a former friend, Rewi Alley, who ran the Chinese Industrial Co-operatives (CIC). This left-wing organization managed to operate in the teeth of Chiang Kai-shek's right-wing dictatorship because their production, although very small and primitive, contributed to China's limping economy. Rewi also worked closely with the Chinese Red Cross, another left-of-center outfit useful to Chiang in salvaging some of his own war casualties. On behalf of these two groups I had driven a truckload of medical supplies from the Burma Road terminus to the CIC base up north (since my contribution not only was in a good cause but also offered good photographic material). I therefore felt justified in asking Rewi's help in finding agents. He found me three good ones and lent me a truck to get my team down toward the frontier with Japanese-occupied China. Because any form of transport in these forward areas was almost impossible to get, Colonel Smith assumed that I and my "gang" had stolen this truck from the Chinese army, which added to my "fearless" reputation.

As a training and operations base I had chosen Patpo, a small town on the Wan-lo River, some thirty miles above Japanese lines. U.S. personnel were precluded from going inside Japanese lines because any non-Chinese would immediately be detected and shot for spying. One therefore had to stay this side of the frontier and utilize Chinese agents for infiltration.

My team was composed of three CIC men, a high-school teacher, two refugee students, and a driver-mechanic, all Chinese, of course. Colonel Smith urged that, in addition to my MO work, I get "special intelligence" for the Air Force: weather reports, targets, Japanese defenses, troop movements, and, above all, weather reports, without which the planes dare not fly.

"But what about our own SI?" I asked in some surprise.

"Okay, but we can never get enough info."

Indeed, as time went on I began to feel that however effective MO might be, SI was far more essential.

At the last minute, Smith also asked me to take a Special Operations officer, Lieutenant Devine, plus two cases of "plastic" explosives (the term "plastic" was given to a light detonation explosive recently invented) to block a railroad tunnel on the route we were following. U.S. Army Intelligence had reported that the Japanese intended to advance to this point and then capture and use this railroad for a further advance. Hence the SO intended to block it.

At this request (almost an order) I almost rebelled. First SI work, now SO! But then it occurred to me that it might be a rather intriguing distraction. So off we all went.

After driving for five or six hours we detoured a mile or two along a track through the rice fields and reached the tunnel escarpment just as the sun was going down. The railroad was one track and long-since disused, the Chinese having blocked it much earlier against the Japanese advance.

We helped Devine tamp plastic into a crevice of the rocky roof. Then, having trailed a coil of fuse wire to a sheltered spot, he touched it off. The explosion sounded louder than a thunderclap, and a shower of debris flew out of the tunnel opening. We ran back to the site fully expecting that half the mountain would have fallen in. Alas! Everything looked much as before, except for a large crater in the roof, the debris from which had mostly blown out of the entrance.

"I kinda thought it would need more plastic," lamented Devine, "but that was all we had." This was a typical plaint. Everything had to be flown over that formidable "Hump," so there was never enough. But I rather thought that Devine should have known his operation would not be effective.

Driving at night on a lumpy dirt road with inadequate lights was too hazardous. So, having slept under the stars, we drove on at dawn and reached Patpo by midafternoon. All accommodations being crowded with refugees, we installed ourselves on a junk that had formerly plied the opium trade with Canton and, the weather continuing to be fine, slept on deck. With the river water lapping beneath, the occasional plaint of the owner's one-stringed fiddle, the strumming of cicadas in the adjacent bamboo, and the drowsy redolence of opium still pervading the boat, those few nights beneath a crescent moon shine out amid the troubled war years like a stained glass window in a very gloomy church.

Meanwhile, however, we got a small house built on a plot amid eucalyptus trees, which the owner sold us for a trifle, knowing he would get a free house when the war was over. Our four-room dwelling, built from timber framing and bamboo matting, with a solid wood floor and tiled roof, cost the equivalent of U.S.$500. Of course, we had neither electricity nor plumbing, and the lavatory was merely a dug pit with an adjacent wooden tub for washing. For lighting, I was thankful enough to find a small kerosene lamp and a quart of oil. But this was luxury compared with the prevailing shacks and squalor. I mention these details only to illustrate the privation extant everywhere in China except among the Chinese lords, the mandarins, the foreign enclaves (whether business, political, or religious), and all the American bases. Yet in Western eyes, most of even these were considered to be "making do."

My plan was that three of the team members who knew that area would infiltrate into the Japanese-occupied areas and with the help of friends, relatives, or carefully chosen locals gather intelligence for the Fourteenth Air Force, circulate rumors, distribute black propaganda, and employ the few deceptive devices I had collected from Tolman. Because we had no radios we had to organize couriers between these agents and our base. The most useful men for this job were those already trading between occupied and unoccupied China (a traffic encouraged by the Japanese as being useful for their own commercial ends). The problem was, of course, who to trust. I found by experience that those who called themselves Communists, whether party members or merely sympathizers, were the most trustworthy, willing to help, and efficient, being mostly young, as well as sincere and intensely anti-Japanese. It was, of course, such earnest youngsters, plus equally earnest students and long-exploited peasants, who swelled the ranks of Mao's veterans and helped him to overcome Chiang's vast armies, despite America's constantly increasing help with money and matériel.

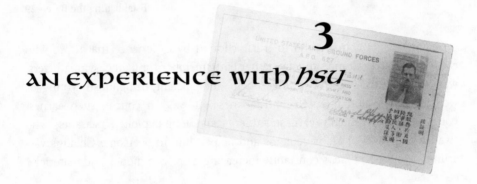

AN EXPERIENCE WITH *hsu*

With the Patpo base established, our agents dispatched down the line, and a courier service linking up all operations, I felt justified in returning to Detachment 101 as promised to Peers. It was not only this obligation that prompted my return. I was also feeling frustrated by having had no backup for our Patpo operation from either Kunming or Washington: no supplies, no personnel, no funds, and only one letter from Little, full of eulogy for my work in Burma and calling me the "Lawrence of China" (an allusion to the still-famous Lawrence of Arabia who had stirred the Arabs in the Middle East to revolt against the pro-German Turks). This absurd tag, although meant as a compliment, was worse than Mykland's "Fearless Fenn," meant as a smear. So having appointed one of the CIC men as deputy CO, I got a ride to Kweilin on a Chinese army truck carrying two dozen sick or wounded soldiers from down the line. It seemed that the Japanese had already begun their new push to seize the railroad and possibly Kweilin. Chiang's troops had made some resistance but were now in retreat.

These wounded in their padded cotton uniforms looked like stuffed dolls that had seen better days. There were also three generals aboard (in an army of two million there were, of course, a lot of generals). Wearing uniforms adorned with Sam Browne belts and medals, they smoked Lucky Strike cigarettes throughout the journey.

There was, on the other hand, a curious social equality between these generals and those wounded who were well enough to talk. They chatted amicably and shared melon seeds and once even cigarettes. And although it could not be said, as of Napoleon's army, that every soldier carried in his knapsack a field marshal's baton, the Chinese saying that in the end of his bamboo carrying pole, every coolie carries a lottery ticket with prizes of wealth, power, influence, and status had an element of truth. "The General is lucky now; tomorrow it may be my turn." Although political democracy does not exist (either then or today), human democracy often does.

The generals warned me that the Japanese intended to push on to Kweilin and seize the U.S. airbase, which had been slowly but surely expanding the attacks on Japanese targets. Indeed, on reaching Kweilin I found large elements of the population already beginning to panic. American institutions such as the consulate, the Red Cross, and the oil and tobacco companies were already pulling out, and the military units were preparing to follow. Not surprisingly, the Chinese called the exodus "ratting," whereupon our own people retorted that they themselves had invited the collapse through inertia. Even words such as "cowardice" and "collusion" were bandied about. Although there was an element of truth in this, the Chinese were naturally furious to be defamed by foreigners who, apart from Chennault's fighter pilots, had done nothing to stem the Japanese advance. There were, indeed, thousands of well-armed service personnel posted all over China who had never fired a shot except at birds. This was not because they lacked enterprise or valor but because they were all service personnel, not fighting troops. But the Chinese never understood this, and that was why the rot really took hold.

Until this period, Americans had easily been the most popular of all the foreign groups, being considered essentially noncolonial and nonexploiting. But now the gloss wore off. When some Americans openly declared that "the slope-heads have no guts to fight," the furious Chinese retaliated that the Americans never fired a shot except at crows. Meanwhile, the vast cash flow in salaries, victualling, per diem, housing, and general maintenance had caused severe shortages, leaping inflation, and wholesale black marketing that benefited a minority of predatory Chinese while wrecking the livelihood of the masses. Kweilin's happy atmosphere was thus destroyed. Five thousand determined, experienced, well-led, and utterly ruthless Japanese soldiers would now turn fifty thousand pathetic Chinese soldiers, three thousand well-armed GIs, several hundred Western civilians, and a large proportion of the city's one million inhabitants into a scrambling mob.

Amid this scene of dissolution I experienced another striking example of Confucian *hsu*. (Inadequately translated "reciprocity," this concept denotes that the heart is always sending out waves, and if you meet someone on your own wavelength you find immediate "reciprocity.") One morning while still angling for a flight to Kunming, I went into the OSS dining room for a cup of the brew

they called coffee (effectively destroyed by the Chinese cook from beans imported from Indochina). The time being midmorning, the room was empty except
for two strangers, an oddly dissimilar pair, one being a tall Westerner and the
other an exceptionally short Chinese, both wearing civilian khaki. As the other
tables had been cleared, the Chinese mess boy gestured for me to sit with them.

Although very different, both men had features suggesting quality, intellect,
and purpose. I could also sense that they were studying me with equal interest.
But it was with the tall Westerner that I experienced immediate hsu.

Our initial conversation was of course limited to trivialities: the undercover
nature of my work necessarily made me cautious in talking to strangers. They
were similarly reticent. But in the twenty minutes that we sat there, I did learn
the following: the Westerner, named Laurie Gordon, was Canadian; his companion, Tan, was Chinese American; and they were somehow connected with
French Indochina (comprising the present Vietnam, plus Laos and Cambodia).
When I said goodbye to this pair I little suspected that this encounter would rad-
ically change the course of my present occupation!

The following day the rumor of a Japanese takeover became a reality. The
last of the Americans and a few lucky Chinese sped off in vehicles just ahead of
the invading Japanese troops and were soon bogged down among thousands of
other Chinese crowding the one road going west. I was more fortunate. A pilot
I knew from the old days gave me a ride in the last DC-2 flying back to
Kunming.

Everything was stable in that happy haven—everything, that is, except OSS
headquarters, which was now so inundated with newcomers that I could no
longer get even a bed. Rather than stay in the Army hostel five miles out of town,
I secured a berth in the local base of the British-American Tobacco Company
(BAT). (They were not yet abhorred, the deadly effects of tobacco not having
then been exposed.)

It now appeared that Hall was against my going back to 101. "The fact is,
Charles, Colonel Peers is mad at you for walking out on him and doesn't want
you back. Whereas I have a special mission for you here. I know you have a lot
of useful contacts around Kunming, so I want you to hunt around and find us
something suitable for larger headquarters, such as a school, factory, or mission
compound. Buy or rent—price no object. Okay?"

My orders might have taken me to 101 without Hall's consent, but crossing
up a CO cannot be undertaken lightly. Besides which, it might have been true
that Peers did not want me back, nor was I that anxious to go back to Assam in

the coming heat of summer. Although this new assignment was another time-wasting, out-of-channels job, it at least would not prove unpleasant. The Kunming scene vied with Kweilin in colorful amenities and was a great deal better in terms of climate.

To contact old friends was a pleasure rather than a chore. Among these was Ralph Bergstresser, who had helped me get the leaflets printed at Detachment 101. Ralph told me that Vic Ranken, who had also helped there, had recently crashed behind Japanese lines while distributing his own leaflets. "He and the pilot started to walk out. But rain, hunger, and injuries received from the crash were too much for Vic, and he died en route." It was another small shock to the faith I had in my own charmed life.

As for the building, Ralph knew just the thing. "It's a large half-completed hospital in the center of town. The doctor who launched it has run out of funds, so I'm sure he'd want to sell it." And he gave me the address. After I had organized the purchase of the hospital, Hall rigorously excluded me from everything connected with its completion as OSS headquarters, and he subsequently claimed full credit for having engineered this coup. I was, nevertheless, still kept on a string, with various excuses offered for the continuing delay. I finally concluded that he simply liked having me around as a knowledgeable and discreet cicerone in visiting opium dens, bathhouses, and brothels—not because he smoked opium, took baths, or screwed whores (at least, not overtly) but because he liked the illicit adventure. His own particular gambit was to play with one of his many handguns in front of the girls: a phallic symbol that satisfactorily scared them out of their wits, particularly when the evening wore on and he got drunker and drunker. Some creatures survive being taken out of their natural environment and put into zoos or circuses; there are others, such as pandas and gorillas, that very soon go into decline. In this instance, an elderly university professor was the victim of confinement in a very different sort of zoo.

The new headquarters was soon so full of newcomers that I no longer recognized a tenth of the occupants. Major Faxon, fat and fifty, had now been put in charge of MO. He had been for many years a *taipan* in China (that is, head of a foreign business). This eminence had earned him not only the rank of major but the self-importance characteristic of old China hands. Hall directed me to hand over to him all my Patpo operations, together with the agents. Not one of them subsequently had a good word for their new CO, although they were too polite to say anything worse than that he was ignorant, inefficient, bad tempered, and prematurely senile.

In my opinion there were three main reasons why many OSS leaders were ill chosen. One: a high proportion were lawyers. This profession by no means limited their intelligence or capabilities, but it did too often affect their adaptability. A lawyer's purpose is to interpret the law and use it not for the public good or for any other good, but to serve his client. The goal is to win, regardless of rights and wrongs, true justice, or innocence or guilt. A lawyer is entirely justified in, for example, defending a man he feels pretty sure is a murderer. The end is to win the case, and this end justifies the means. This may work well enough in legal battlefields, but in a real war, although the end of victory is common to all, the complexity of reaching it requires cooperation, insight, tolerance, judgment, and adaptation that transcend individual goals.

Putting lawyers in key wartime roles without retraining was the first mistake. Even worse was the appointment of socialites, politicians, millionaires, business tycoons, and similar dignitaries, some of whom in consideration of their prestige, political pull, wealth, or specialized talents were thus rescued from the draft. (Such patronage was not, of course, limited to OSS, but crept into many wartime institutions.)

The third abuse, perhaps worst of all, was the promotion of civilians to Army and Navy rank considered commensurate with their peacetime status (mostly assessed on their income). This often enabled them to interfere, control, and frustrate those of lesser rank who in this new environment were more knowledgeable, and therefore more efficient, than they were. I must apologize here beating my own drum. Indeed, I must admit some personal prejudice in respect to all these judgments. On the other hand, I may claim to be, on the whole, fair minded, disposed to friendliness, and a fair judge of character. In this latter regard, I was greatly helped by having learned to analyze handwriting. Those who dismiss this technique as spurious, in a class with astrology, palmistry, and fortune-telling, are gravely in error. Having learned it during the war, I have used it ever since, always with reasonable accuracy, if somewhat limited depth—because I cannot claim to be expert.

Ensign Mykland (my "Fearless Fenn" associate) had now been appointed executive officer. Formerly a junior company lawyer, he had a special urge to make you feel ignorant, superfluous, troublesome, and mentally deficient. In this role he was aided by two assistants, both second lieutenants, whom I called the "Kafka boys" because they resembled that pair of clerks in *The Trial*, always up to pointless tricks and able to do you a lot of harm while grinning all over their faces. How thankful I was to escape to the BAT refuge! But one of my "spies" (whom I tried to have everywhere) informed me that this escape gave me another bad mark.

This particular informant was Kasy S., a Eurasian woman married to an American pilot who was usually (and conveniently) on duty elsewhere. Attractive, lively, and amusing, she was also number one on Chennault's list, so although always discreet, she often disclosed something useful. She also had a wide circle of friends, mostly in the upper bracket, who were welcome to call in for a chat in her comfortable house (a comparative rarity even in live-it-up Kunming). On this occasion, for instance, shortly after we had returned from dinner, we were joined by General Carton de Wiart, that romantic diplomat-warrior with the black eye patch, curled moustache, and VC on his breast, whom Churchill had called "the epitome of chivalry and honor" and had sent out to Chiang Kai-shek as his personal emissary at a time when England had little else to send, all money, time, matériel, and human effort being concentrated on the life-and-death struggle on the western front. But what could de Wiart achieve with Chiang, who wanted money, supplies, or fleets of bombing planes to resist the Japanese while he himself finished off the Communists? Roosevelt had sent Vice President Wallace on a similar placatory mission even though the United States was already financing Chiang to the hilt.

This problem of ends and means was one of three facing Allied efforts in China. The second was the immense distances coupled with inadequate transport. The third was the divided objective of Chiang Kai-shek.

When de Wiart had gone, I remarked that it was a pity the American top brass were not equally gracious. But Kasy was quick to retort that de Wiart was a special case. "Generally speaking, the British top brass can be worse than the Americans, because we Chinese"—she thus identified herself—"can put up with bad manners more easily than with the racially superior attitude of so many of the British."

On arriving back at the BAT house, I was told that Miss Doris Lee, "a young Chinese lady," having waited to see me for quite some time, had left her name and address. I subsequently found she was living in a room half-filled with what looked like the contents of a shop: lightbulbs, pencils, notebooks, stationery, cigarettes, candy, flashlamps, batteries, and thermos flasks—some of which I recognized as PX supplies—so would I care to sell any of my own ration—particularly my cigarettes since I didn't smoke? Should I again blame my OSS training for making a deal with Miss Lee? At the time, certainly, it never occurred to me not to.

The report had now circulated that a new OSS overall boss had arrived on a priority plane—a full West Point colonel named Coughlan. And the following morning I received a summons to meet him at the office provided for the visiting top brass.

"Take a seat, lieutenant—or may I call you Fearless?" said the tall, good-looking officer from behind the desk provided in this up-market nest. "Have some coffee?"

Served real Nescafé (in China, still an innovation) with real canned cream, I was made to feel further at ease by the colonel putting his feet up on the desk. Bright sunshine streamed into the room, and through the wide-open window one could see, above the green and yellow roof tiles, a horizon of lavender mountains.

"It sure is great to have this weather!" exclaimed the colonel, happily banging his chest. "I flew in yesterday from Burma. Torrential rain the whole two weeks. Well now, Fearless," he continued, suddenly businesslike, "we have a great new field for you to get busy on! It's with the Gordon group covering Indochina."

"Is that Gordon and Tan?"

"You've hit it. Top priority, believe you me. So how would that suit you?"

"It would suit me all right," I assured him, remembering how much they impressed me, "but how would it suit them? I know nothing about Indochina."

"Hey, now, Fearless, don't start getting modest. From what I've heard, it's out of character." He opened up a map. "I'll explain the setup. You got Annam here in the north, Tonkin in the south, and Cambodia and Laos over here in the west. They call the whole shebang 'French Indochina' or simply FIC. When the French folded up in Europe the Japs walked in and took the lot. We couldn't do a thing about it until last year when we had a few planes to spare for bombing and strafing. But we pretty soon found out there was practically no intelligence on weather, defenses, or targets. The French Military Mission (FMM) operating in China keep up certain contacts with a few Free French inside. But it's only courier stuff and mostly useless by the time we get it. But Gordon's got a couple of agents with transmitters. He works mostly with the British, but he also gives out all his gen [information]—'all' as far as we know—to the Chinese, the French, and the Fourteenth. We wanted to take over the whole operation for OSS full stop, but he wouldn't buy it, insists the success of his operation—and in a small way it sure is successful—depends upon him staying independent. So in the end we agreed to give him backing if he'd take an OSS officer into his group. Well now, Fearless, I'll level with you. Yours was the only name he'd agree to. So is it a deal?"

"Sure, it's a deal, if you say so."

"Good man! So I'll have Gordon contact you."

"Colonel, there's one small favor I'd like to ask."

"Not promotion, I hope. You should never have gone into the Marines. They're hell on promotion."

"Forget the promotion. But would you mind not calling me Fearless?"

"What? I thought everyone called you that. But just as you like. Is it okay if I call you Charles?"

I replied with a salute, accepted the colonel's proffered hand, and went out into the corridor repeating those lines of Shelley's:

> The world's great age begins anew,
> The golden years return . . .

But after the sunshine, rain; after the daydream, reality. On my way to the street a messenger ran up to say that Hall wanted to see me.

He greeted me with a bland smile. "Didn't I always tell you we were keeping something special for you? I told Colonel Coughlan you were just right for this job! But there's one thing you've got to keep in mind. We want to know how Gordon really stands with the other outfits he's hooked up with. Is he maybe a British agent? Or working for the FMM? Or even Tai Li? His radio operator at this end is actually one of Tai Li's men! So get the gen on all this. But play it cool. Gordon's a touchy fellow, and that's putting it mildly."

"He's also pretty smart, I'd say. If I don't play it straight, I'll be out on my ear."

"We're not in OSS to play it straight but to get the job done! I've told you what's required. Now it's up to you. And by the way, here's a letter for you."

During the past few weeks, Hall had been intercepting and opening all our mail, often with subsequent interference. Although this had caused general indignation, nobody had yet figured out what to do about it. The letter Hall gave me now from Herb Little, dated two weeks earlier, had been delayed at least a week.

While waiting to hear from Gordon, various Chinese friends continued to solicit me for jobs. Rather than disappoint them, I sent them on to Faxon, who employed several. The major, a die-hard reactionary, was unaware that some were Communists! Another caller was my former roommate, Captain Tolman, who wanted to launch his scheme for poisoning Japanese officers' cigarettes. "Above the rank of field officer they buy only the best brands, so all we have to do is mix some of our new formula DNH-7 into certain well-known brands for them all to die more or less painlessly before they find out the source."

"But how could you limit the sale to Japanese officers—of whatever rank?"

"No, we couldn't. But that wouldn't matter as long as we get a fair percentage of the top echelon."

Tolman had another scheme for disseminating among both officers and men fake packages of brand-name cigarettes that would explode upon opening the wrapping paper and blow a man's hand off. There was one thing you could say for Tolman—he was full of enthusiasm.

Calling in at Kasy's I was received by her daughter, Doree, who gravely asked what I would like to drink. "There's Seagram's rye, Gordon's gin, orangeade, or beer. Last week we had champagne. But there isn't any left."

"It was a party for General Chennault's birthday," Kasy explained. "Not that he really wanted to have a party—he was still feeling blue after losing Kweilin. That was the Fourteenth Air Force's finest base. It's sad when you think how much he put into it."

And I might have added: especially when you think that he had no one but himself to blame for losing it. Stilwell always said Chennault screwed up in letting his Air Force depend on Chinese troops instead of organizing U.S. ground forces. It was largely over this issue that Stilwell had quarreled with Chiang and was sent home, where, as a consolation prize he was made the first five-star general in American history. There are ironies that "do often lie too deep for tears."*

Coughlan asked me to dinner at the Annamese restaurant. The other guests were Bill Luther of the State Department; a Major Reilly, who liaised with the French Military Mission; and a couple of FMM officers, Major Duval and Captain Lamy. "It's just as well for you to get to know these guys," said Coughlan, " now that you're going to operate in French Indochina. Besides which, after the balls-up in Africa, Washington's dead keen for us to improve Franco-American relations."

The Annamite proprietor of the restaurant asked for our orders in quite good English. But Captain Lamy insisted on ordering in Annamese. Whereupon

---

* William Wordsworth, "Intimations of Immortality."

the proprietor explained in excellent French that although he could speak English, French, and Chinese, he could not speak any Annamese, having come to China when a child. The captain furiously retorted that *ce cochon* (this pig) could certainly speak Annamese if he wanted to! He was only trying to cover up his anti-French bias and so on and so on!

After dinner we went to the Hotel Commerce for coffee and the peppermint liqueurs made there by a French refugee. Although the hotel was now owned by an American missionary doctor and his wife, it still retained some small flavor of a French provincial hotel from the days when Kunming was connected to Hanoi by railroad (now cut near the border).

Sitting at the next table was an American pilot who had in tow the attractive mistress of a war correspondent then off in Burma. Major Reilly was all for inviting her over "even if it means including the goddam pilot!" But Lamy insisted she was pro-Vichy and even pro-Nazi. The major was indignant to have politics thrust between him and such promising material. This account illustrates the difficulty of promoting good relations among the Allies!

At dinner the next day, an OSS officer, formerly a Saigon businessman with a lot of useful contacts in that area, was being sent to the Indochina border to develop an intelligence network. I asked, as if casually, "Would that be anything to do with the Gordon outfit?"

"Oh, no!" said the major brightly. "We want to ease out that lot!"

Coughlan having now flown off to Delhi, there was nothing for it but to write, a risky proceeding now that Hall opened all mail. Having related the interference and frustrations I had been subjected to since coming to China, and adding this further evidence of double-dealing, I asked to be released from my new assignment and transferred to India, Burma, or Ceylon.

To circumvent Hall's censorship I gave this letter to a pilot friend to deliver personally and if possible bring back a reply on his return flight. Two days later I received the following:

Dear Charles:

All that you have said in your letter is true and I think that you are justified in making the request that you have made. You did good work at 101 and you did good work from Kweilin and I did tell you to go back to 101. I am sorry that I didn't make myself more clear; I'll admit that I was in the wrong. I could sum up the past with simply saying that you have done a very good job under very trying circumstances and in return have been treated rather shabbily by me and others.

My asking you to go down with Gordon was not and is not trying to find a job for you or get you out of circulation. It is absolutely essential that I have a man down there who is agreeable to Gordon, and also one whom Gordon will have confidence in. I know that you can fill this bill. It is an important job and it is a must job. There is no place where you are needed half so badly. I do hope you will give it a try for I am not kidding when I say that I need you down there.

This letter, of course, made it impossible for me to refuse the job. Nevertheless, I still had to wait for Gordon to finalize his plans, and while Coughlan was in Delhi, Hall was here, still opening my letters, both private and official. Another one from Little, written weeks earlier, contained a plan whereby I was to run MO-China with Faxon as my assistant! There were other absurd suggestions revealing Little's total ignorance of the true setup. The only way I could give him the true facts was again to use a pilot as a courier. But this letter would have to go all the way to Washington! Just in case it went astray I worded it impersonally and did not sign it.

So off I drove to the airfield with the letter in the pocket of my field-jacket —an outside pocket, there being no inside one. But when I arrived, the letter was missing! After vainly searching the jeep I concluded it had blown away en route. If it were found and opened, the contents, although unsigned, might well bring it onto Hall's desk. It was only after a couple of days with no repercussions that I breathed freely. Gordon now wired me from Delhi that he would be arriving in Kunming as soon as a flight was available, and would I get ready to proceed with him to his base on the Indochina border?

Ravenholt, the UP correspondent just back from Salween, told me that thanks to Stilwell, the Chinese troops down there, having been well led, well fed, well trained, and well armed, had for the first time in the war driven back the Japanese. Everywhere else, said Ravenholt, the Chinese fighting morale was weakened by conflicting purpose. Although the Japanese had to be resisted, the Chinese Communists had to be totally suppressed. Furthermore, amid all the corruption now prevalent, few commanders could resist getting caught up in money making. So the Japanese had advanced more or less as they pleased.

Ravenholt also told me that Teddy White, the *Time* and *Life* correspondent, was in hospital with jaundice. So I took him a few small gifts, including books. He told me that Bill Munday had been killed in Italy. The last time I had seen him was when we drove through that Japanese roadblock in Burma.

Driving home from the hospital I picked up a couple of GIs thumbing a ride.

The road was cluttered with peasants and animals coming back from market. The GIs went off a streak against "all these dumb slope-heads in this arse-hole of creation." Why were we wasting good U.S. money to keep going a bunch of chiselers who were stashing it away in Stateside banks? Scarcely a single Chinese on the whole journey owned much more than the rags on his back.

I stopped at a precious-stone carver's shop to buy a jade bracelet carved in the endless-rope pattern. The carver wanted to tell me something about it, but as I could not understand I asked him to write it down. But he said he could not write. If this "dumb slope-head" had been educated, he might have become as civilized as the two GIs.

A new SI man named Caldwell wanted my help in contacting key Americans in China, such as officials, businessmen, missionaries, or journalists, to organize an intelligence network. When copying names from my address book, I saw that "DEAD" had now been written against five of them.

Colonel Bill Smith told me that he had put my name down for a Bronze Star. He had told me that twice before; I did subsequently get a Bronze Star but not through Smith.

Tolman contributed a new circus act with the help of his pedigree Sealyham dog, which he had trained to press its paw on the lever of a box, thereby ejecting a dog biscuit. When I questioned the practical use of this trick, Tolman threw a scrap of tetrasol (a newly invented high explosive) into the ashtray. It exploded with a blinding flash, and everyone ran for cover. He also told us of the practical use of another gadget: a Chinese man had been crawling through a small gap in the wall of the compound and stealing bits of parked cars. So Tolman had set up in the hole a booby trap he called a castrator. So the Chinese lost part or all of his genitals.

Gordon rang from the airfield to tell me we had seats on the flight to Nanning the next morning. A bare half hour later I was sent for by Hall. As soon as I entered his office, I saw my lost letter lying on his desk! It called Hall, among other pejoratives, "a tin-pot empire-builder fit for the loony bin."

His expression was more in sorrow than in anger. "To think I've always considered you a friend!"

"Well, Colonel, as you've often said yourself, we're no longer playing games in high school."

"Yes, and that's why I'll have to send you to Delhi for court martial."

"I rather think Colonel Coughlan won't agree with you on that." And I handed him the colonel's letter.

After reading it, he stared at me in speechless frustration; he could not bear to let me off the hook, but neither could he bitch up Coughlan's plans. To help him out I looked duly penitent and told him I was very sorry to have stabbed him in the back. In pre-OSS days, I might almost have felt truly sorry for him. We parted with the guarded truce of two dogs sniffing at each other's backsides.

The next morning, while checking in at Operations for the flight to Nanning, I was intercepted by a major who had just flown in. "Charles Fenn, is it? The very man! My name's Monroe. And as you've probably heard, I've been appointed chief of MO-China. So there's quite a lot of background material for us to talk about! And here's a letter from Herb Little. You can read it while I'm tracking down my baggage. Don't go—I'll be right back!"

Little's letter informed me that a certain Major Harley Stevens had now been sent to Chungking to coordinate all OSS work in China and that I was to run MO under his overall direction. "All this has been agreed at top level. So now we're all strictly according to Hoyle!" There wasn't a word about Major Monroe.

Shortly before dying in a mental home, Baudelaire wrote in his journal, "Today I had a strange warning: I felt the wings of insanity brush my mind." Anxious to avoid Baudelaire's fate, I tore up the letter from Little without waiting to talk about quite a lot of background material with Major Monroe and hurried off to meet Gordon.

4
ÐROPPING IN ON
NANNING

Nanning being already threatened by the Japanese advance, there were only three other passengers flying there on the battered DC-2. Scenically, it was a beautiful flight. Yunnan's terra-cotta fields were now checkerboarded with squares of new-sown rice threaded here and there with glistening streams. Around the scattered hamlets, centuries of plodding feet had worn a network of brown paths. Farther south the terrain grew wilder, with rocky shrubland ousting the pattern of rice fields. Dark zigzags of erosion and weed-covered floodlands were suddenly gold plated as the sun came out from behind the clouds.

Dropping from fifteen thousand feet into the semitropical warmth of Nanning, we hurriedly changed into shirts and shorts and checked into the comfortable hostel built by the Japanese when they occupied this area three years earlier. It would all too soon be back in their hands.

Gordon's base was at Lungchow, one hundred miles southwest on the Indochina border. The only route was by sampan up a fast-flowing river and would take a week. After hiring a suitable boat for departure the following day, we went to call on the French Military Mission. "When there's no point in trying to keep a secret," said Gordon, "I always prefer to play an open hand. So they might as well know you're joining the group." But I think he was also pleased to show them his OSS addition. The three French officers were coldly polite until we had a few Indochina rums and the atmosphere warmed up, after which they even asked me to take some mail upriver to their forward camp.

Armed with our own bottle of rum, we then spent the evening in a sampan where the owner's wife served us a delicious meal of river trout garnished with ginger while two girls played zithers and sang. "Who was it said," asked Gordon, "'Give me the luxuries of life, and we will dispense with the necessities'"? In China, one seldom got enough of either.

Early the next morning we got to work buying and loading up stores: rice, pickles, bean curd—plain bean curd—cheese, bananas, peanuts, candied fruits, olives, and "hundred-year-old" eggs, plus straw mats and pillows, oiled silk rain capes, and paper umbrellas. As we pushed off against the swift current, a squadron of Japanese bombers swooped down and gave the environs a pasting.

The river was jammed with boats fleeing from the Japanese takeover farther downriver, some so overloaded with refugees and their belongings that foundering in the swirling current seemed inevitable. Nor was our own boat lightly laden. In addition to our baggage and a pile of stores, the twenty-five-foot-long boat carried the boat owner with his wife and five children, six crewmen, and our two selves. Two "cabins" had been roughly constructed from bamboo mats, one for us and one for all the rest, including the improvised "kitchen." Alongside the gunnel, running the full length of the boat, were broad planks on which the crew walked while poling.

For reasonable safety from bandits we tied up each night near a village. That first night, a group of Miao tribeswomen, their rounded, nut-brown faces shining in the light of a brilliant moon, were singing love songs on one river bank while their gallants on the opposite shore played five-toned flutes. These aborigines, although driven into the hills by the Chinese some two thousand years earlier, had retained their tribal customs and a certain independence. The women wore embroidered dresses and pleated skirts so much in the Magyar style one thought the two races must have shared a common ancestor.

The following morning, long before the sun came up, the crew members were back at their toilsome poling. Even close to the bank the current was swift. They would put their shoulders against one end of their very long poles, touch bottom with the other, and then shove with all their weight while walking from one end of the sampan to the other, meanwhile emitting grunts and groans suggesting their physical anguish. Although I had been long enough in China to be inured to the sufferings of porters, rickshaw men, water-laden women, and children hauling "night soil," these boatmen gave me new pangs. They kept at their toil from dawn to dusk with no break other than to snatch a meal. Five times a day the owner's wife would cook rice, and the boatmen would gobble down a few bowlfuls, supplemented with a mouthful of pickled vegetables and a few scraps of fish. These meals were like a fill-up of gasoline. When the boatmen's flagging efforts registered that the fuel was running out, they would snatch another fill-up and go back to their toil in full vigor.

Whenever the wind was right, the wife, with the help of the children (aged from two to six), would hoist the bamboo-mat sail—although this seemed more decorative than functional. These children always stayed so quiet and well behaved. Certainly there was no noise against which they had to compete: no city hum, engines, traffic, planes, or radios. Did the harmony of the Chinese scene set them an example? Was it their low-calorie diet that kept them so quiet? I was also surprised that they never fell overboard, but Gordon said that children on such boats often did. Then the swift current swept them away to almost certain death.

Explaining further details of his operations, Gordon said he now had a dozen friends in Indochina sending reports: two by radio contact, the others by courier. He had recently sent down six more portable transmitters, the famous B-2 model given him by the British. All his operators down there were volunteers. The political setup in Indochina was roughly this: When the Japanese came in, the French saw no hope of effective resistance. And, of course, they got no outside help. So they thought it better to cooperate and thus at least retain control of local affairs. They had, in fact, been allowed to carry on much as before, while the Japanese concentrated on military posts and exploiting economic resources. They always kept sufficient occupation forces to curb either French or native resistance. Having worked in French Indochina before the Japanese took over and being generally pro-French, Gordon did not mention that in this colony, as in the homeland, a large element of the French had been, if not wholly pro-French, quite willing to cooperate in running the country— barring, of course, any military control. But all his French friends, both inside and outside French Indochina, were strictly pro-Allies. And as a Canadian, Gordon was also in tune with the British and Americans. If he was rather more friendly with the former, this was largely because they were more friendly to him.

"As you probably know already," said Gordon, "the indigenous population consists of Annamites in the north, Tonkinese around the Saigon area down south, and Laotians and Cambodians in the west. All my contacts are either in Annam or Tonkin, sometimes called Cochin-China [the two areas that were later called North Vietnam]. The Annamites have always been the most vigorous in resisting the French. But apart from certain small political groups with Communist or anarchist leanings, there is never any effective resistance.

"The Japs have been satisfied to let the French run the country within the above limits. Although the Allies consider all these French down there to be pro-Vichy, many of them are secretly Gaullists and work with the FMM in Free

China. The head of this group in Chungking, Colonel Garnier, is quite friendly to our group, and we work well together.

"I've got even closer ties with General Chang Fa-kuei, warlord of the Fourth War Area [slightly left wing and not subject to Chiang's dictatorship] bordering Indochina. And in Lungchow I'm working closely with General Chang's political representative, General Wu, whom you'll meet—a delightful fellow.

"Not for the record, Charles, but both the French and the Chinese are reluctant to have the U.S. come in on the Indochina scene. The French, because after the Darlan affair in North Africa, they simply don't trust the Americans. And who can blame them! And the Chinese, because at present they've got all the border areas under their own supervision and don't relish American interference.

"The British interest in the area is limited to overall war strategy. So they're quite agreeable to the Yanks coming in. With the U.S. fleet moving up into the China Sea, this is inevitable. When they get carriers near enough to the coast of Indochina, they'll want to stage raids on Jap installations. So they'll need to know weather, targets, and Jap defenses. That's why Coughlan was told to get into this show and get in fast. The only effective way he could do this was through our setup. Hence his anxiety to bring us together. As for Hall, you can write him off. I happen to know he's already on the skids." (He had, as I learned later, already been ordered home.)

On the third evening of our trip the perennial blue skies were blotted out by purple-black clouds streaked with fiery red, and soon afterward, as we tied up for the night, a cataclysm of thunder and lightning threatened the end of the world and inundated us with lashing rain. Almost within seconds we were soaked to the skin and only just in time got our supplies and equipment covered against the deluge. The river turned to dancing froth, and waterfalls cascading down the banks seemed like a tidal wave that must surely sweep us away. Then the storm was over as suddenly as it began, the rain ceased, the skies cleared, and we were back into a calm and beautiful evening, with the sun going down behind a last gray veil of rain across the distant sugarloaf mountains.

Having beached the boat, we made a bonfire and got dried out, while the boatwoman indefatigably prepared our meal. Sitting there in the firelight drinking Indochina rum, we listened to the frogs singing hymns in praise of rainstorms. Later, in the glow of our pith fragments burning in peanut oil, we enjoyed a meal that tasted better than all the haute cuisine of city life. In honor of the full moon, the children were setting out an altar decorated with red and gold paper cuts, votive offerings of moon cakes, thimble cups of wine, and joss sticks wafting incense. All these children were endearing, but the oldest, aged six, already a competent guardian of the young siblings, so won our hearts that Gordon nicknamed her Circe. We taught them English words, mannerisms such as winking and clicking tongues, bird calls, making kissing noises, as well as tricks with string, paper, cork, and can lids. How they loved it all! No one had ever had the time to play with them before. But the second eldest was, alas, miserably sick with what I diagnosed as dysentery. When I administered kaolin and sulfaguanadine tablets, she managed a grateful smile.

The next morning the river torrent was still too swift for poling, so the crew went ashore with ropes to tug us along. But we were no sooner bouncing off through the stony rapids than the sampan gave a frightful lurch, whereupon the owner went into fits of yelling and jumping, while all five children let out wails of terror. We ourselves were a fraction of a second slower in registering that the tug rope had broken and the sampan was swirling downstream! In that maelstrom we should probably have capsized and drowned had not the boat luckily swung abeam, with the stern momentarily pointing to the bank, which enabled the owner, by leaping into the current, to get a rope looped around the sternpost and, with all the crew pulling hard, thus to avert disaster.

It was typical of their general unconcern that within a minute of this near-calamity everything was back to normal, with the crew tugging and groaning, mother setting out the dishes for our evening meal, and the children gazing longingly at the steaming rice.

We came upon a large ferryboat top-heavy with passengers and a cargo of vegetables, charcoal, bamboo canes, and bundles of hay. Strung out behind were six or seven water buffaloes, only their muzzles and dilated eyes visible amid the torrent. This convoy hurtling downstream shot past us like an express train.

Along the banks clusters of avocets were busily extracting worms from the silt with their scimitar beaks, watched here and there by egrets stretching and shaking their wings toward the sun. Beyond the banks the red soil with its sheen of new-sown rice glistened with a shot-silk richness. But suddenly the bank rose into towering walls of rock, pitted with caves as black as night except where shafts of sunlight lit up their fairy book interiors in startling greens and purples. One of the rowers got a bad chest from not drying himself after the storm. I treated him with sulfadiazine, which made him lose his appetite and thus the ability to pole, but as he believed in the efficiency of the medicine, he soon believed himself better, started eating, and was back at poling. Everyone called "Ai-ya!" and the boatwoman broke an egg into our midday soup.

In an oddment shop in Nanning I had found a copy of *Whitaker's Almanac* dated 1910, which gave Gordon and me long hours of statistical exploration and quiz games, a welcome relief from cards as a method of not always rereading our scanty supply of books. Promptly at six when the sun went down, we made cocktails from rum and pomelo juice or lemonade powder from K-rations, while the boatwoman made our simple meal, usually supplemented with tidbits we had bought in Nanning, and then we would have a grog of Indochina rum and coffee as a nightcap. Life was never better.

Gordon explained about the American group called Air-Ground Aid Services (AGAS) with whom he was working closely. "Their function is mostly the rescue of downed pilots and contact with prisoners of war [POWs], but at all times they collect intelligence—which is, after all, everyone's nagging concern [as I myself had already discovered and concentrated on]. The drill for the pilots is that whenever they have any choice they should land in designated areas. If, for example, the plane isn't shot down into a total nose dive, the pilots can sometimes glide their ships a good long way before they jump. But if they have to land in 'unsafe' areas they should then endeavor to reach a designated 'safe' area, traveling only at night and hiding during daylight hours. Meanwhile, those pilots who had returned to base would have reported that one of their group had baled out, and our agents would have organized fires on the hillsides. Upon approaching such fires the downed pilot should watch for Frenchmen and signal by waving a white handkerchief (which all pilots are instructed to carry). Natives have to be avoided because they have all been offered high rewards by the Japs for turning in pilots whether dead or alive. Rewards are, of course, also offered by the Allies. But the Jap reward is on the spot while the Allied reward is a nebulous five hundred miles away!

"Our biggest hurdle, however, is to get the pilots' cooperation. They all like to think that they themselves will never get shot down—the usual 'charmed life' concept!—so it isn't worthwhile to study maps and memorize the designated areas. Up to now, indeed, shortage of planes has so limited air activity over Indochina that only two pilots have been shot down during our six months' operations. One of these was collected through my own contacts and brought out to China. The other was rescued by the Chinese Fourth War Area group, who also brought him out safely." [At this time Gordon had not heard that a third pilot, named Shaw, had been rescued by an Annamite group known as the Vietminh.]

My diary records:

In the twilight a sharp rain is hitting the water with a kind of crackle and beating a louder tattoo on the bamboo roof. The children are happily sucking sugar cane. From one section Circe has made a noise-maker with which she successfully imitates a crow. Fortunately she soon grows tired of this diversion. After their hasty meal the polers are back to staggering to and fro with their shoulders in the crutch of their poles and guiding themselves with one hand clinging to the improvised rail. Their whining moan trembles between the baying of dogs and the suffering lament of grievously wounded men. I try to expunge from my heart a compassion that would be futile. Yet I long for that moment when darkness will put an end to their toil and groans and we can tie up in quietness on the bank.

When I voice this lament to Gordon, he says that although their labors are as painful as any concentrated labor is likely to be, the noises they make are largely an expression of their energy output. "It's like sea chanties when sailors perform similar muscle-wrenching tasks. I doubt if their sweated toil is worse for the human constitution than our indolence and self-indulgence as we lie here drinking grog."

"Nevertheless," I counter, "they say a coolie wears himself out in ten years."

"Yes, but isn't that more because of short rations, poor diet, cold, wet and the consequent resort to opium?"

As soon as the rain stopped it grew warm again, and we swam from time to time. But the current was still surging, and to avoid getting swept away we were careful either to choose backwaters or to hang on to a rope. The wind being desultory, the sail was seldom used, but used or not, the crew never ceased to labor. Sometimes when their poles would not reach bottom, they could no longer push, and the banks were too rocky for pulling, so two of them would take turns at standing at the stern to row with long, powerful oars. At the end of each stroke they gave a final strong jerk before raising the oar out of the water, and this made the sampan positively leap. I several times tried both poling and rowing but would feel exhausted after a few minutes of either.

At Talu, about halfway on our journey, Frank Tan was waiting to join us. He and Bob Lee, one of my former agents whom I had assigned to GBT (Gordon, Bernard [who would join us in Lungchow], and Tan) work, had been transporting, with the help of coolies and ponies, twenty-seven drums of gasoline to the

GBT depot of Yungli, where Bob had stayed to guard it. Tan's cheerful personality gave us all a boost, but his greatest hit was with the children because he added to mere games the advantage of shared language. But he found their Kwangsi patois somewhat cryptic.

One of the crew who had been doing less and less work finally quit entirely and declared himself sick. In a village where we stopped for the night, he had himself "cupped" by a healer (based on a Chinese healing fable whereby poisons are sucked out of the skin by the application of cups), who left a pattern on his back like a spray of ailanthus leaves. But because he did not look sick and his appetite was not affected in any way, we insisted the owner pay him off and get a substitute. It then turned out that he had paid the owner for a ride to Lungchow and had pretended to work the first few days to put us off the scent. As the owner was otherwise doing a good job, we let him get away with this subterfuge and keep his illicit passenger on board. As Gordon remarked: "Every dog is entitled to one bite!"

Meanwhile, our real patient was getting worse. Finding she now had a temperature of 104°, I concluded she might have typhoid, for which I had no remedy except to give her powdered milk and have her mother prepare something nourishing such as egg custards and chicken broth; however, it was now difficult to make her eat or drink. The poor child would sit there in the back of the boat silent and deathlike, until one of the other children would, alas, start teasing her, whereupon she would soon be shaking with soundless tears that coursed down her shrunken cheeks in endless streams. When I bathed her face and tried to feed her the milk concoction, she would still manage the ghost of a smile before sinking back into an exhausted sleep.

The boatmen figured distances not in linear measurements but in turns of the river, the distance from Nanning to Lungchow being 360 turns. On a good day we would make forty or fifty, on a bad day as little as ten. On one long stretch the current ran so swiftly over rapids that we were a whole day struggling along a single turn. The boards having now grown slimy, the crew kept slipping, and several times one or the other went smack into the current, when only the instant throw of a rope could save the poor fellow from whirling away downstream. This did indeed happen at least once a day on this last stretch, and we would have to shoot back after the struggling victim, lug him aboard, feed him hot grog, and hope for the best. Small wonder that after a trip like this, the crew would need a week to build up sufficient energy to tackle their next journey.

From my diary:

A wondrous sunset tonight, the sky pale green above a horizon of red and gray bands, with the evening star glowing above. I write my notes in the light of China's ubiquitous illumination—a snip of burning pith-wick floating in peanut oil. Meanwhile Gordon is astonishing Tan with my OSS contribution of radio sets, guns, watches, cameras and PX luxuries like candies and powdered coffee.

Since the rains stopped and the current eased off we have been making better time. But there continues to be striking evidence of up-river erosion, the river thick with silt and torn foliage, including whole trees which rush at us like enormous crocodiles, while the boatmen make frantic efforts to get us clear. Here and there the river cuts through walls of gray cliff, gouged out in cellular spirals like gigantic Henry Moores.

The sick girl is now a distressing sight. Several of her teeth have dropped out from the bleeding gums and her hair is coming out in tufts. I feed her pomelo juice, cabbage juice, a crushed vitamin C tablet, but all in vain. Her little brother pulls out more hair as he meticulously ties up what's left with a scrap of dirty ribbon he has picked up somewhere. The girl's face is always salt-caked with tears, and beneath her pitiful rags we can see that her rectum and vagina are red and swollen like wounds. I keep thinking I should give her an overdose of sleeping pills but can't face up to thus killing her.

Several times when stopping for meals, Gordon and I would try fishing. But Chinese fish have learned over millennia of the most intensive fishing in the world how not to get hooked. Only the most exceptional skill and patience can hope to outwit them. At one place when we stopped, however, a fisherman had outwitted three fine specimens of the carp family, which he now offered for sale. When it came to paying he looked at our money with a troubled air: could we not pay him with something tangible, like rice? But it so happened we were now short of rice, with no chance to buy any for a good long stretch. When I successfully paid him with a spare shirt, he went back to his boat looking as though this was the happiest day in his life. And that evening what a feast we had!

The contents of *Whitaker's* being to some extent exhausted, we hit upon a new pastime. By an odd coincidence (but also something that suggested how much we had in common), both Gordon and I had with us an Everyman edition of *Shakespeare's Tragedies,* so the three of us took turns declaiming the various parts. Sometimes the river banks would reverberate with our clamorous delivery so much that the boatmen and anyone else within earshot would gape in mingled bewilderment and laughter.

Because of poor light it was difficult to read after sunset, so we played poker, which I had already taught Gordon and now taught Tan. We played for small stakes, and the winner was then expected to provide some small treat from his stock of rum, candy, or local goodies. Because we went to sleep early, we were always up at the dawn's first glimmer. Needing less-than-average sleep, I often woke even earlier and would lie there working out the constellations or listening to "Eine kleine Nachtmusik" from gurgling water, frogs, insects, and the occasional hoot of a fish owl.

But despite such joys, the last two days of the trip seemed endless, partly because it rained unceasingly and partly because the crewmen were now poling in a dream, with consequent lack of pace. Yet at mealtimes they yammered away as busily as ever. Meanwhile, we talked rather less: spend five days in such close confinement, and one usually talks rather less. "What on earth do the crew find so interesting to talk about?" I asked Tan, having understood almost nothing.

"Always the same fascinating details: food, prices, weather, sickness, women, festivals, and the curious behavior of foreigners."

Strings of motorboats were coming down the river. "They all seem empty," I remarked.

"They've been taking salt to troops up the river," Tan informed us.

"All that salt?" There must have been at least fifteen boats.

"Ten thousand troops need ten tons every month."

"And how much rice?"

"Only enough to feed five thousand."

We play poker hour after hour with endless variations Hoyle never thought of. Tan drinks rather more rum than his two-drink capacity, turns from pale amber to *sang de boeuf*, and raises his bet to a whole dollar. When his full-house-to-an-ace-high is beaten by Gordon's four jacks, we fear he will explode, but he only gives a hoarse yelp like the start of death rattle. . . . There is a spectacular sunset, with red rays striking out into the sky like a gigantic Japanese navy flag.

The sick child died in the night. And there she lay like a rag doll battered with long, rough usage. I could not stop thinking that I might have saved her a week's misery. The weeping mother brought our breakfast muttering, "Sorry, but with one thing and another I've burned the rice." The boatmen, having gobbled down their ration, went back to their moaning toil without even a glance at the dead child.

> To each his suff'rings, all are men,
> Condemn'd alike to groan;
> The tender for another's pain,
> Th' unfeeling for his own.*

*Thomas Gray, "On a Distant Prospect of Eton College."

5

ARRIVING IN LUNGCHOW

As we approached Lungchow, a frontier town some twenty miles from the border with French Indochina, the river banks rose to huge stone cliffs on which a brownish line forty or fifty feet above the present water level marked the height of the floodwaters a few days earlier: a small wonder that we had had to wrestle against swirling currents!

Lungchow had served as the Chinese customs post prior to the Japanese occupation. The fine steel bridge crossing the river that marked the border had been blown up, and the customs post had, of course, been abandoned. Our boat tied up at the foot of some tricky stone steps cut into the massive cliff rising to Gordon's headquarters. In consideration of receiving copies of his Indochina intelligence reports, the Chinese authorities had loaned him the use of a fine brick house formerly the residence of the Chinese customs, with a garden full of tropical shrubs and flowers. What with the luxuriant foliage, the towering cliffs, and the river foaming over variegated rocks, this setting was a veritable Chinese Xanadu.

I was now introduced to the third member of the group, Harry Bernard, an American. Like Gordon, he had worked for Texaco in Indochina. Short on words, he was long on know-how, especially concerning technical matters. The domestic arrangements were in the charge of Madame Tong, a refugee from Indochina. Her daughters, Helen and Janet, did office work, including cryptography. Helen, plain and dumpy, was efficient and genuine. Janet, two or three years younger, was sultrily sexy and inclined to affectation. We all ate together at one round table, the very good Chinese food being served in fine porcelain Gordon had rescued from Indochina.

On the day of our arrival, the cook's daughter was being married, so we were given a feast: fifteen dishes including a suckling pig cooked whole. The bride was all done up in flowered silk, and her hair was jeweled with combs. Joining us for coffee was General Wu, the Fourth War Area political representative. Essentially a debonair young man partly educated in Paris, he sported a narrow-brimmed trilby hat and carried a gold-knobbed cane. He was otherwise quite unassuming, and following Gordon's lead, we were soon on first-name terms.

The next morning disaster struck this happy scene when the boatkeeper's daughter, Li-sun, aged five, picked up one of the detonators used by local fishermen to stun fish. This "toy" exploded and blew off part of her hand. The parents screamed in total panic, but Li-sun calmly told them to fetch Mr. Tan (a great friend of hers)—he would soon cure it! While someone else rushed off to get a doctor, Tan fed her a codeine tablet, and I helped him bandage the pulped flesh with sulfathiazole ointment. When she murmured something to me, Tan translated: "She says you must be careful going up and down the steps." Chinese children often seem curiously adult. Early in life they are, of course, made part of the adult world (or they were at that period): no school, very little play, sharing adult work, and always integrated into the family. This upbringing offered advantages as well as limitations: the children learned the realities of life instead of the myths and distortions of Western "education"; there was no generation gap; and although they missed some childhood fun, they largely missed the pangs of adolescence.

Gordon arranged a visit to the French camp on the other side of the river. Going down the steps I remembered Li-sun's warning and trod carefully. But there were other hazards. Halfway down a piece of overhanging cliff, eroded by the rains and perhaps further shaken by our movement, tore away without warning and went hurtling down with a great whoosh of falling earth and stones, splattering the boat tied up below. We went aboard across a slippery plank; one false step would have thrown us into the racing swirl.

Although the boatman rowed straight for the opposite bank, we were carried a mile downstream, which was fortuitously the exact site of the French camp. At their jetty—a construction of logs in a backwater—their own boat looked sadly neglected but was guarded by a pretty Chinese girl wearing a khaki uniform and smart kepi. "Vive la France!" murmured Gordon as he caught my covert smile.

The camp consisted of a few sheds and a brick house, with furniture in cubist style, lamps with parchment, leather-thonged shades, and carpet in dadaistic scrolls. A huge French tricolor hung above a sideboard displaying ten or a dozen bottles in various stages of emptiness, plus an unopened bottle of

Black Label scotch, which Gordon told me afterward had been going the rounds of the local black market for weeks at a vast price and had doubtless been hurriedly purchased in our honor. In any event, after formal introductions, the cognac, vermouth, anise, Bhyrr, and all the rest were ignored while our hosts ceremoniously opened this virgin bottle and made ready with the Sparklets siphon.

Our hosts were a trio: one captain and two lieutenants. The captain—plump, debonair, and talkative—wore loose balloon-type trousers tied around the ankles. They were indeed all smarter than we were. One lieutenant wore a polished Sam Browne, the other a rosette in his buttonhole and two ribbons on his breast. Their elegant and rapid French was the obligato to this visual presentation.

The following day the young lieutenant, wearing smart riding breeches, visited us with his sergeant carrying a radio, which they asked our help in repairing. Liang, Gordon's Chinese operator, soon detected the fault. Meanwhile, the lieutenant was admiring my Leica, Gordon's fishing rod, and finally the ping-pong table made up from packing cases. "Ah, that scores ten!"

With Tan I went to call on General P'an, the military representative of the Fourth War Area, who was living in a new timber-built house prettily set against the shrub-covered hillside. Like most Chinese habitations, whether upmarket or downmarket, it was almost bare inside; indeed, the main room contained only a table and four hard chairs, with the usual oleographs of Chiang Kai-shek and Sun Yat-sen on the walls.

The "boy" who brought in the tea was wearing a blue silk gown and, fanning himself throughout, explained to General P'an that the hens were not laying because rats sucked their blood by night, so could the honorable American officer please supply some poison? "Buy ten eggs in the village," P'an told him, handing over a ten-dollar "gold unit." This new currency was reputedly backed by receipts from Chinese customs, a government department originally installed by the British customs and considered incorruptible. The "gold units" were supposedly safe against the rampart inflation then debasing regular bills. But the boy had a different opinion.

"Excuse me, honorable Lieutenant General P'an, but the value of the gold units has already declined 30 percent, so this ten-dollar bill will buy only six eggs."

To save face the general told us that this decline was due to the Japanese counterfeiting the gold units in Hanoi and smuggling them into China despite the most careful supervision. But he knew as well as we did that excessive printing of the notes by the Chinese themselves had already made these gold units "rolled gold" (gold plated).

On our way home Tan took me on a detour to look at the remains of the cantilevered bridge that had spanned the river between China and Indochina. The Chinese had blown it up some years earlier, and the two ends now jutted out from the banks like gigantic cranes, with festoons of rusting rods and girders hanging in Daliesque fantasies. "Five years ago," said Tan, as we surveyed this sad wreck, "I sped across that gap in a train that made the whole journey from Hanoi to Kunming in less than twenty-four hours. There were sleeping cars, all done up in red velvet, and a dining car where you could get luxury meals, and champagne for a dollar a bottle! But did we appreciate it? Like hell we did! We only complained about the soot!"

One of Gordon's agents informed us that a pilot named Marshall, shot down near Haiphong (Annam), had been rescued by a Chinese farmer there, and the pair had already crossed into China. They arrived at our camp the following day. The farmer, old, worn, and ragged, was almost childishly delighted to have brought this American pilot safely back to his friends. Marshall, although raggedly bearded and disheveled, looked as carefree as if he had walked in from a picnic. We had no tape recorders then, and I got Marshall's words down in my own rusty shorthand plus Helen Tong's similar effort. Here is the story he gave us:

I was bombing and strafing the airfield in Haiphong. Then I wheeled round to strafe shipping in the harbor—one large vessel and several small ones. After dropping the rest of my bombs, I came down again to strafe the larger vessel. Going into a dive and letting her have it, I felt like on a drunken jag, even though the vessel was belching spurts of flame straight at me. I banked down so low past the hull of the ship that I was looking up at her structure. Just then I felt something shake the plane, and the spinner of the propeller flew past my head, along with several other bits of metal from the nose. Jesus, this was it! But I still kept my cool. Knowing that before bailing out I must get clear of the Haiphong area and hopefully get altitude to take me as far as the mountains, I revved the engine up to all she had, watching the fire take hold of her and start to throw flaming strips back towards me. When I opened the cockpit at a thousand feet, the flames bellowed in, and the plane was already heeling over even as I jumped. Because of this, oh boy! I banged right into the tail, which by this time was almost vertical. Before the chute opened, both me and the plane hurtled down so close together that I finally landed only twenty-five yards from the flaming wreck!

While I drifted down, there was shooting all round, but I hadn't cared much, feeling confident they wouldn't hit me, Christ knows why! Luckily I had landed in brush. Having quickly hidden my parachute I headed fast towards the mountains. It was then 7 A.M. About noon, after slogging it out all morning, I sat down with my back against a rock so that I wouldn't be come upon from behind. All this time I'd been hearing sporadic bursts of tommy-gun fire and the various signals of shouts, whistles, and bugle calls. Then I heard footsteps somewhere on the hillside. But before I had time to pinpoint this, a native boy was standing there gaping at me, not exactly frightened but astonished. I had my hand on my .45 Colt, ready for it. But I soon figured the boy was friendly, got out my walkie-talkie book, and found the words for "friend, American, please help" and so forth. The boy took the book and from it managed to explain it would take forty piastres to get me out to China. As this was only about eight U.S. dollars, I had small hopes! Anyway, I gave him the money, and off he went. When he hadn't come back after several hours, I wrote it off but decided not to move on until darkness fell.

I was just about to get going around 8 P.M. when the boy reappeared with the old man who I called "Pop" right from the start. After stuffin' down some rice they had wrapped up in a banana leaf, we set off walking and kept at it with only brief rests for two whole days and nights, passing through several villages, where I'd pull my hat down well over my eyes and keep going fast. I also pulled out my shirt to cover my belt and pistol and rolled my pants up to the knee. But it must have been clear to everyone that I was a foreigner. And often enough it was touch and go whether we'd be challenged and stopped. When approaching some villages Pop would have me wait outside while he went in and argued or got the lowdown on the village attitude. And sometimes he'd hurry back and quickly drag me off into the hills.

At one point we crossed a dirt road with marks of tires. So I figured I might wait for the next vehicle, kill the driver, and drive it as far as the gas held out. But then I reckoned this would only draw attention to me being in the area. We often got lost trying to find a path around a village. But finally someone would turn up and whistle softly, and this would be a friend of Pop's who would guide us right. I never could figure out how Pop could have all these friends far and wide or why they risked their lives helping us. [Some of them had no doubt discovered that the Japanese were worse masters than the French.]

On the third day another boy joined us as a guide through one area Pop wasn't sure about. That evening at twilight, coming to a village, we suddenly realized the villagers were closing in on us. So I cocked my .45, ready to shoot it out and at least sell my life dearly. But Pop urged me off along a jungle path, where by twisting this way and that we finally shook off our pursuers. But then we hit a real snag. We were constantly wading through streams, and I'd slip and get soaked, and my money was getting so pulped I felt it best to hand it over to the boys, because they hardly ever slipped. But hell, now we lost both boys, so all the money was gone!

While Pop went off to find them I fell asleep. When I woke up it was already pitch dark. I suddenly realized that the jungle all around was twinkling with the torches of a search party, and they were slowly closing in on me! ["Pop" told us later that this was near a village where a downed pilot named Norton had shot a headman and had then been tracked down and was himself shot. This was why here and nowhere else the whole village was out to get Marshall.] I lay there in the brush with my pistol cocked, thinking this was it. The lights crossed and recrossed, some within a few feet while I held my breath! I'd fixed it with Pop that the signal between us would be a grunt from him followed by three claps, and I was to reply with three claps. So during the blackness when I heard a grunt I waited for the claps, but there was only another grunt. The fact was, Pop hadn't dared to clap because the searchers were too near. Anyway, the next thing I knew Pop was tugging at my leg and gesturing for me to take my shoes off; otherwise the villagers would track me by the marks of the shoes.

Then we climbed higher and higher up the mountains until we could see the whole valley honeycombed with moving lights. By running hard we got something of a start, but I suffered not only from my shoeless feet—pretty tough!—but even worse from banging into trees and such; one caught my face—a real shiner. So rather than knock myself out I insisted on lighting a torch, feeling that one more amongst all those already burning could scarcely matter. But to be on the safe side I sent Pop a few steps ahead so that if we ran into anyone it would be Pop who got shot and not me.

We kept going for a further two nights and a day without a scrap to eat, and finally both of us dropped down exhausted. When a native found us lying there, Pop dickered with him about bringing something to eat.

The guy finally fetched two bowls of rice but as we had no money wanted either my watch or my gun. As I wouldn't hand over either, the dickering went on and on, until I felt myself getting light-headed from hunger and exhaustion. Pop seemed to be trying to get my gun away from me to give this guy, and I half made up my mind to shoot the fella and then either tie Pop up to stop him taking the gun away or just shoot him too and put him out of his misery. All this period was hazy in my mind, but it seemed like days and nights went by while we dickered with this native, who kept coming and going and refused to let us have food without payment. So finally I gave him my watch, and he handed over the two bowls he'd all the time been keeping out of reach and went off promising to bring back more but never did.

It was raining nearly all this time, and we made a kind of lean-to. But it hadn't been much good, and Pop decided it was too much of a giveaway, so he tore it down. I lost count of how long we were stuck in this place, but it seemed like forever. [When we subsequently worked out a time chart, it seemed that Marshall had stayed *five days* at this place, and during all that time and the previous thirty-six hours, they had nothing to eat!]

Pop then said, as near as I could gather, that our only hope was to struggle back along the way we had come and either find the boys or some of his relations. So somehow or other we made it back there, Christ knows how, and at last found the boys, who now had a small sackful of rice but only one hundred piastres in cash, having spent all the rest in various payoffs to those who'd helped us.

So after stoking up with rice, we got going again along the same route north, but this time skirting the hostile village. But Pop was now ready to think every man an enemy and drove us forward like on a route march, ignoring anyone who happened to see us, but telling me with one of the English expressions he had now picked up to give them "the old bim-bam" if they started anything. Fortunately, nobody did, although we had one near disaster on a mountainside where we were following a soft buffalo track when I slipped in the mud and would have hurtled five hundred feet down to the valley below if the neck of my shirt hadn't caught on a bough and held me like it was a miracle! And that was when we were within an ace of being saved because on the other side of this mountain was the river marking the border, and even as we came down to it we saw someone waving a white flag, and that turned out to be your contact man—oh boy, what a moment!

Marshall was one of the most voluble young men I have ever met, and when he was not talking about his astonishing tale of survival he was, for instance, expounding aerodynamics, about which he had a good superficial knowledge, telling us colorful anecdotes centering around the hot-dog wagon he ran in Passaic, New Jersey, or relating other adventures of his time in China, such as on his first night flight when, hundreds of miles from base, his radio stopped working.

The countryside below was one vast pit of blackness, and although I could fly in the general direction of base, I might easily overshoot it without getting properly located, and then I'd be really in trouble. So I flew away from base towards the coast, where I knew there would be a string of lights, then turned north and located certain clusters I could identify as particular towns on my map. Then I could head back towards base along a known route and distinguish in the blackness the barest glimmer of a village I'd otherwise have missed but knew it was there because it was marked on the map. It was like those times when you move about in a dark room where you are already familiar with the contours so that even in the total blackness you are able to "see" them and get around safely. So in this way I got back to base and landed three and a quarter hours after takeoff, a record for that particular crate, and everybody had already written me off. It's all a question of keeping your cool. I came out to China in the first Army–Air Force flight, and now there are only two of us left. Don't never give in—that's it. I guess there wasn't once on that long, long trek when I wasn't determined to get back to China. Sometimes I thought—why not lie down and die, but I just couldn't do it, just couldn't do it!

What seemed incredible was that after this nightmare journey the only things wrong with him were sores on his legs and feet, a scar on his face where he had banged into the tree, and a burned patch on his head where he had lain too near a fire. (Indeed, the toe of one of his shoes—which he had carried most of the journey!—had been completely burned off when he had happened to be wearing them. And although his toes were also burned, he had been too exhausted even to wake up!)

The old man's story had its own special interest. Helen took it down and translated it (subject to our small stylistic amendments) as follows:

As soon as the plane came down, word spread like wildfire that the

Japanese were offering huge sums to catch the pilot. So everyone—
Japanese, French, and Annamites—was madly looking for him. But the
fact is, a lot of the Annamites are pro-American, and almost all those like
me who are of Chinese origin know that America is helping China against
the Japanese, so we want to help them. Well, about a year ago some
leaflets written in Chinese were dropped where I live, and they said everyone should help American airmen if they got shot down. So I knew it was
my duty to do that, no matter what. The boy who found Mr. Marshall was
my nephew. He came home around noon that day and told me what had
happened, secretly of course, because we weren't sure who was pro-
American and who wasn't. So we went off without a word to anyone.

As for saying anything to the French, well, as far as I'm concerned,
French and Japanese are much the same, I don't trust any of them.
Although to be fair, you could say things were better with the French.
Since the Japanese took over, taxes are even higher, and they take two-
thirds of our crops instead of only half, and they order us around even
worse than the French. But if it comes to that they order the French
around too! As for all the big rewards they offer, well, in this case they
were offering up to one hundred thousand piastres for Marshall, but
nobody really believed it.

Anyway, I never thought anything about rewards, not from anyone. It
was strictly to help an American I did it for. Not that I didn't hope to get a
bit if I got Mr. Marshall safely out, that's only natural—I mean, that the
Americans would want to show how pleased they were. But that only
struck me later on. What really made me do it was my nature. Most of the
time I'm easygoing, but when I do decide to do something then I stick at
it, simply can't do otherwise. Like the time in my farming when one year I
changed from rice to sugar cane. Well, things didn't work out too well, but
I had to keep at it, had to prove I could make a go of it, and finally I did,
more or less. So once I started I had to keep going with Mr. Marshall, and
now I'm glad I did and really helped the Americans.

As soon as Marshall had arrived we wired Nanning, and they promised to
send an L-5 to pick him up on the strip we had recently drained off and leveled
out. The L-5 took only thirty minutes to cover in a straight flight the 430 turns
of the river that had taken us eleven groaning days! Having landed bumpily but
safely, it whisked Marshall away without his remembering (or bothering?) to say
goodbye to the man who had saved his life. A curious anomaly: one admired his

remarkable fortitude but deplored his total egoism; yet the first depended largely on the second.

When "Pop" learned that Marshall had flown off, he asked with touching
naïveté, "How soon will he be back?" The two boys had now joined him, and
while they were preparing for their long walk back he several times asked the
same question, and we had to make up various lies to explain why Marshall still
had not come back. When we gave the old man five thousand piastres, about
U.S. $200, as his reward, he seemed to think this princely, and it is probably
irrelevant to mention that a pilot was considered to be worth about $50,000. So
before saying goodbye, the old man and the boys went off to the village to buy
new clothes to replace their mud-caked rags. Before they set off home I took the
old man's photograph and asked for his address to send him a copy. Smiling, he
begged to be excused. "To receive a photograph from the Americans would be
to receive a bullet from the Japanese."

6

LIFE IN LUNGCHOW

After this episode GBT relations with the French slid further down the hill: it was Gordon, not the FMM, who had scored by bringing Marshall out. It was Gordon who now had an American officer attached to him. It was Gordon who had built an airstrip, thus invoking further Japanese vengeance. Even the ping-pong table stirred up jealousy!

We were therefore not much surprised when one of the GBT agents coming up to meet Gordon at the frontier was required to have a permit from the French group here in Lungchow. I accompanied a seething Gordon when he went to get this permit, and while it was being made up, we were both subjected to a string of complaints: "Why does the Fourteenth Air Force seldom bomb the targets we designate, such as Japanese troops, equipment, and military installations, but always manage to hit French property? When we informed the Fourteenth of some Japanese ships in Tourane harbor, they waited several days before mounting the raid, by which time the ships had sailed. So they dropped the load just anywhere. Nothing Japanese was damaged, but many Frenchmen were killed!"

"I'm sorry to hear about that," I said. "But on that raid a lot of the dock area and factories were demolished. And that certainly hurt the Japanese more than the French."

"*Vous en pensez* [You think so],, m'sieu?" he asked ironically. "Don't forget those docks and factories are really French property!"

A French priest, Father Maillot, asked my help in getting certain supplies, including radio sets, to operate his own intelligence net. But although we should have gladly complied, Gordon said we would have to refuse because the FMM would have been furious at such competition.

Meanwhile, our relations with the Chinese improved. General Wu came in each evening and was soon enrolled in our poker sessions. Once inside the house (and only there) he was called by his nickname, Jo-Jo, and it was the one place where he could relax and not have to consider maintaining face. With French the common language, an occasional drink, and the friendliness Gordon exuded to people he liked, the general—whose rank was only to give him status and enough pay to keep up appearances—could recapture something of his carefree scholastic days in Paris. As a result of such camaraderie, duly revealed to higher echelons, Gordon's relations with the Chinese were always harmonious. Too often the Americans, and less often the British, allowed their exasperation with these "capricious, inscrutable and even untrustworthy" Asians to impede the total necessity of cooperation, because the Chinese, whether coolie or warlord, could frustrate them with long-practiced ease. This is not because the Chinese are sly, deceitful, or treacherous but because they have long since discovered that, short of war, that is the best way to keep the foreign devils out. But they could not keep the Japanese out, because they are Asian, too.

Helen and Janet would also sometimes join our poker game. As is generally true, our playing was perhaps a good reflection of our characters: Bernard, careful and attentive, was the best player; Gordon, bold and intuitive, often won with poor cards; Tan, erratic and impulsive, invariably overplayed; Jo-Jo, cautious and hesitant, too often played for certainties; Janet invariably got too excited to play good poker; and Helen was soon as good at the game as she was in most other things. Meanwhile, Madame Tong stayed watchfully in the background, not quite sure that her daughters were safe in this gambling environment. We always gave the girls a gambling "allowance." As for Jo-Jo, whose pay was small despite his rank, Gordon suggested we should not try excessively to win against him. Considering his charming nature, this was no hardship. How essential it is to assess the personality as well as the ability of men and women appointed to key positions!

On Sundays the girls, who were brought up Catholics and educated in a French convent in Shanghai, would put on, instead of their usual khaki uniforms, traditional Chinese costumes and accompany their mother to a 6 A.M. Mass in the village. Later in the day we would often take a picnic to a sandy inlet across the river and swim in a backwater. Helen could already swim a little. Gordon was in the process of teaching Janet, who would squeal with simulated fright or coyly protest against Gordon's supporting arm, while Tan, who was infatuated with her, would leap around like a porpoise to hide his jealousy!

The fraternization on evenings and Sundays never affected the disciplined work carried out six days a week. Nor do I recall ever hearing Gordon criticize or reprove without good cause. When he disapproved my choice of Bob Lee, I thought he was prejudiced, but time proved his judgment was better than mine. When he tolerated Tan's infatuation with Janet (which I thought disturbed general discipline), he was right in judging it a passing aberration. When he fraternized with venal Chinese, it was to utilize, not to trust them. And as we shall see later on, when he angrily attacked without apparent good reason a significant proceeding of my own, he later saw equally good reason to condone what proved to be right—if not exactly convenient to his own postwar ends.

We had a visit from a French captain Lemaitre, who had just come upriver from Nanning. Having previously been stationed in Kweilin, Kunming, and Chungking, he was more sophisticated than the other FMM officers stationed here and referred to them as *cette bande de l'autre côté* (that lot from over there) as if renouncing such bourgeois types in favor of our livelier atmosphere. We also had a visit from General Chen, who had been sent by Marshall Chang Fakuei of the Fourth War Area to assess the local military and political situation. He was particularly concerned about whether we were working with the Annamites. Although we could truthfully say we were not, I asked Chen to explain why the Chinese would object if we did.

"They aren't to be trusted. For one thing, they aren't really interested in the war against the Japanese. It's true they're anti-Japanese, but they're equally anti-French. To a lesser extent they're anti-Chinese. So they'd hardly make a loyal ally. I suppose you've already discovered they profess to be pro-American. This is because they hope you'll help them to gain independence when the war is over and we kick the Japanese out. You may be approached by a group known as the Vietminh, which is more or less Communist although they pretend to be strictly Nationalist. They offered to help Marshall Chang against the Japanese if in turn China would help them gain independence after the war. In this instance, the marshall consulted with the generalissimo. But His Excellency was dead against it. Although France is at present a dead duck, it's possible she may stage a comeback. So it wasn't worth offending her for the sake of helping an insignificant group like the Vietminh, who'll probably never amount to anything. But if they should approach you—they claim to be strongly pro-American—don't get taken in, if you'll forgive my saying so. They have a big sales talk but nothing much to sell." (How wrong he was!)

"You needn't worry on that score," said Gordon. "We have no intention of working with any Annamites. I agree with you they're all anti-French and quite untrustworthy." (This was the basis of the disagreement between us that I mentioned earlier.)

As I was more interested in listening and learning than in offering any comment about something I still knew little about, I remained silent. But Chen again pressed me to state the American attitude. As I really did not know what it was, I chose an easy way out. "The Annamites haven't approached us. We don't need them, so we shan't approach them." Chen obviously would have liked a more specific answer.

But Gordon switched the conversation. He told me afterward that the less we said about the Annamites, the better. "Chen might quote something out of context and upset either Marshall Chang or the FMM, both of whom are worried that your people might want to help them. But anyway, you gave the right answer—we don't need them, full stop."

It now became clear that the Japanese, having ringed Nanning, could take it any day and, after this, come up the river and take Lungchow. Gordon had in mind to move his headquarters to Ching Hsi, a few hundred miles farther north and then if necessary move on to Meng Tse, still farther north. In addition to equipment and personnel in Lungchow, there was the problem of moving the twenty-seven drums of gasoline stored in nearby Yungli, which might instead have to be destroyed to prevent its falling into Japanese hands, a prospect that made Gordon sigh and Bernard groan but which I myself thought unimportant, having had too much experience with scorched-earth policies in Burma to be concerned about such trifles. I admit with some shame that what concerned me most was having to leave Lungchow, with its natural beauties of foam-flecked rivers, craggy rocks, sugarloaf mountains, intricate caves and banana palms, hibiscus and flame trees, and the French inheritance of gay pavilions, precarious ladders leading up to watchtowers, stone parapets sea-green with lichen, ancient tombstones overgrown with vines, and arched wooden bridges decaying above the lotus pond.

Taking a walk with Tan before we had to bid it all goodbye, no doubt forever, we first visited the market to buy the luscious papayas and melons one never seemed to tire of. Then I collected from the shoemaker the set of leather cases he had made for my camera equipment with such exquisite stitchery that I almost could not bear to use them. At the shop selling tea, where the decorated containers, each in its own special niche, gleamed like idols, and one central jar, domed and gilded, shone like a buddha, we bought a supply of that special leaf that the officiating priestess, displaying her shining gold teeth, insisted was grown on a hillside so inaccessible that monkeys had to be trained to pick them. In the "chop shop," Tan chose a piece of old ivory and took it next door to have his characters carved thereon. (A "chop shop" is the highly specialized emporium that makes and sells the "chop," or small carved object with which almost all Chinese identify themselves by pressing it into red-inked loose silk as a seal that identifies the owner when stamped on a document.) The craftsman was interested to see my own chop, carved on chalcedony when I first arrived in China. He graciously conceded that, considering the hardness of that stone, it was quite well done. In the butcher's shop down the street, the dismembered carcass of an ox had its tail still attached to prove that the beast was an ox, not a buffalo. In the baker's shop we bought honey-and-almond cakes. The baker was busily making moon cakes for a group he described as "the pirates up the river." It appeared that the previous night the crew of a Chinese junk that had come up from Indochina with a cargo of crepe rubber had robbed a bridal party as well as a house occupied by a French family, "although nobody was hurt." When the baker invited us to come along to meet these pirates who were, he assured us, "a very friendly lot," we said we would be delighted.

The junk was tied up against a long-built wharf beyond the broken bridge. The thirty-ton vessel, some eighty years old, was built from hand-hewn pine and equipped with a small steam engine made in Germany and dated 1908. At the stern stood a pair of brass cannons, the barrels beautifully engraved with Manchurian characters. The five raggedly dressed "pirates" carried Enfield rifles, equally ancient, and the captain, wearing a turban and carrying a Mauser, looked appropriately sinister.

Tea and sunflower seeds were served by a woman I took to be the captain's wife. "Ai-ya, the foreigner speaks wonderful Chinese!" she exclaimed with more politeness than truth. There was only one embarrassing moment. After I had examined the captain's World War I Mauser, he not unreasonably asked to look at my Colt. I thought it best to remove the clip first.

"Ha-ha, he thinks we might shoot him!" exclaimed the captain, and they all joined in his sinister laugh. Of course, when your hosts are called "pirates," it makes you somewhat on edge.

Back at the camp we had a visitor: Simon Yu, a Chinese-Belgian agent of Gordon's. Long famous for his prodigious treks, he had walked nearly two hundred miles from his base near Hanoi, mostly through jungle in the Hundred Thousand Hills of northern Annam (a feat that Gordon claimed to be a record). Speaking fluent French, Simon reported that in the border town of Langson the Japanese were doing a brisk business with Chinese merchants, trading opium against mercury and copper ore. "Thus at one stroke they deal two blows against China, since the opium destroys Chinese health and morals, while the mercury and copper make detonators and bullets to kill them." It was clear from the start that Simon was exceptionally intelligent and knowledgeable. I discovered only later that he was also oversensitive and easily offended. This complexity characterizes many Eurasians, who do not reflect either category of their double ancestry. One may learn how to behave toward a Belgian, one may even delve the mystery of the Chinese ethos, but a mixture of the two often defies analysis.

General Wu called in to consult us about the problem of refugees now flooding over the border from Indochina. It seemed that since Marshall's escape the Japanese were accusing all Chinese living in Annam of being pro-Allied, and the consequent harassment was driving them into China. "This, of course, is causing problems of feeding, housing, and sanitation" (by which he meant that people left to starve could be dangerous). "Yet to stop them coming over would be hard on them (meaning that in process of doing so, we would have to shoot them).

"Nevertheless," put in Simon, "they must be stopped. A lot of them are really spies and fifth columnists preparing the way for a Japanese invasion."

"Besides which," put in Bernard, "if a few genuine refugees do get shot, it will discourage both genuine and false from coming in. And I gather you don't really want either." Bernard was always essentially practical. Jo-Jo seemed relieved to accept what had probably been his own solution to the problem.

Our next visitor was the CO from the French camp, who had his own problems. "Ah, *par exemple* [just imagine]! Now the Japanese are blaming us for Marshall's escape. Ah, *c'est le pompom* [that's the limit]! They've sworn to put paid to both our camps! You can thank us for giving you the tip-off that at any time now . . . !" Just as in a play, the sound effects were right on cue—Z-z-z-z-z-z-z-z came the hum of the deadly Japanese squadron that in another five minutes would wipe us all out. "Ah, *c'est du proper* [that's the payoff]!"

Everyone was diving for cover when Gordon cried, "Hey, take it easy, that's probably a couple of P-40s that have been dropping leaflets over Indochina! They promised on their way back to signal "'Mission Accomplished.'"

We hurried outside to check, and there indeed were the two P-40s diving low and rocking their wings as a signal for "Okay!"

"Ah, *c'est trop fort* [that's going too far]!" cried the captain. "This is sure to bring retaliations!"

"What kind of leaflets?" asked Jo-Jo, who always liked to get things clear.

"Telling the Annamites they can win further rewards by rescuing more American pilots," explained Gordon.

"Ah, *il ne manquait plus que ça* [that's all we need]!" cried the captain, saluting a goodbye with almost whiplike wrath and almost riding off without his kepi.

"One must remember," said Gordon, when things settled down, "he's had a very bad time. Three years in Lungchow without a break and his family in occupied France—who wouldn't be up the wall?"

Another time, when Gordon was out, we had a visit from Captain Lemaitre, calling to say goodbye before going on to Kunming. "What a relief to get away from that gang across the river! And their tempers aren't improved by the fact that they've been ordered to stay on, whereas I'm free to leave! As you can imagine, that really burned them up! Kunming isn't Paris, but it has a lot of charm. And while I'm there this time, I hope to learn some English. Would it be asking too much for an introduction to one of your friends?"

I could not but feel sorry for him. How awful to find your country divided into two camps, where now your enemy might be former associates, friends, and even someone you loved! So I wrote down Kasy's name and address. "One learns better from a woman," I remarked, handing him the slip.

"M'sieu, you read me like a book!"

Jo-Jo returned the next day to tell us that General Chen had decided not only to keep the refugees out but also to resist the threat of Japanese attack by stationing "a strong defensive force" along the frontier. This turned out to be the Peace Preservation Corps, a local militia armed with rifles made in Shanghai circa 1920, plus a few machine guns left over from the Russo-Japanese War of 1905.

A wire came from Faxon asking for details of my arrangements about pay, seniority, and individual potential of the Patpo team. I wired back that all the details were already there on file, whereupon Faxon wired again that the files had been mislaid, so would I give him the details from memory? From memory after several months? Gordon wired Faxon that I was now away on a mission.

"Mac" Sin arrived from Yungli, our subbase down the line where he operated the radio. On loan from the Chinese army, he wore the usual cotton uniform and rope shoes, but sported a U.S. Army carbine slung across his shoulder and a Belgian Browning .32 automatic stuck into his belt. Crazy about weapons, Mac Sin fondled my silenced .22 with popping eyes. When I examined his Browning, I found that the cartridges in the clip were about .33. "It's lucky you never fired one. It would have blown your hand off."

"Really? I suppose that's why this soldier sold it to me cheap," said Mac Sin cheerfully.

He had brought a letter from Bob Lee, the agent I had loaned to GBT to help at Yungli, which, duly translated by Helen, read in part: "My life down here is very restricted. May I have a post where I could utilize my contacts with top Chinese officials?" I believed that through his family he did have such contacts, but Gordon thought he was featherbedding. Subsequent events revealed that we were both right.

Mac's own account of Yungli life was more romantic. "We lived in a pretty bamboo house on an island in the river, and the jungle on the southern bank was full of tigers [meaning wild cats]!" Small and very girlish in his delicacy of movement, he effervesced about anything that pleased him and skipped around the camp like a Chinese Ariel.

Liang, the radio operator permanently stationed in Lungchow, was a very different type, being essentially adult, serious, and intellectual, although he also loved a joke. With the rank of colonel in the Chinese army (from which he was on loan), he had frankly admitted being an emissary of Tai Li. It seemed that when Gordon's own clandestine contacts had ferreted this out, he had thought that having Liang there not only kept the Chinese friendly but also forestalled their surreptitious spying. "Better a devil you know than one you don't know. And in any case, I've nothing to hide, and all intelligence we collect goes equally to all the Allies, including of course the Chinese in the camp. What I do outside the camp, Liang doesn't concern himself with. I had a feeling right from the start that if I played it straight with him, he'd do the same with me. And I think that's how it's worked out." The more I got to know Gordon's associates, the more I approved of both them and him.

OF FRIENDS AND FOES

Around this time our contacts with OSS went sadly adrift. Hall had, as Gordon predicted, gone into limbo; Monroe and Stevens were here, there, or nowhere; Faxon sent questions to which there was no sensible answer; and Mykland, the adjutant, sent directives that Helen called "uninscrutable." There were also several messages from a Lieutenant St. Phalle, who wanted to know, for example, "How often and when the ferry leaves Nanning for Lungchow, what the weather is like, and does one need mosquito nets?" It was Jo-Jo who enlightened us on this particular phantasmagoria.

"He's the nephew of a top French banker and is being sent down here to liaise with the FMM across the river." But surprisingly, we got several messages from the FMM wanting to know who this St. Phalle was and why he was coming to Lungchow. Finally, Jo-Jo told us he had already arrived in Nanning, bringing several radio sets for which he had not received Chinese clearance. "That's a bad mark against him from the outset," complained Jo-Jo.

Gordon finally sent Tan off to Nanning and Kunming to dig up the gen on this curious mix-up. "It will also give Frankie a much-needed break," Gordon confided to me.

While Tan was in Nanning he got friendly with a pilot named Brodsky and perhaps overenthused about our camp, because a few days later an L-5 landed on the strip and out climbed this Lieutenant Brodsky. Gordon was naturally indignant about a visiting plane that drew further Japanese attention without having any object other than amusement. But Brodsky was not the sort to register hints that he take himself off. For a day or two his life-of-the-party personality rather intrigued us. He taught us several useful statistics about poker, although our low stakes soon discouraged his interest. He then introduced other gambling devices; for instance, having marked a chalk ring as a target, he then rather clumsily practiced throwing his knife. Spectators were encouraged to have a go, and he soon had everyone at it. At this point he casually introduced gambling, and as the stakes increased, so did Brodsky's skill, until suddenly he was so expert that he beat everyone. This source of revenue exhausted, he started games of guessing the number of beans in a bottle, peas in a glass, rice in a cup, lotus seeds in a jar, peanuts in a bag, and pomelos in a pail. Here again he would lose the first few times and then, having fanned up the gambling heat, would win the next four in a row.

His repertoire included eating twice as much at a meal as anyone else and finishing off by scooping a handful of peanuts from the dish on the table and throwing the lot into his mouth at one go. He finally shot his bolt through a very different trick. We had as water coolie a pretty girl, Ah Mui, whom Brodsky had his eye on from the moment Helen and Janet brushed him off. On the third morning of his inflicted stay, when Gordon had decided to order him off, we heard a loud female scream from outside followed by an equally loud yell from Brodsky. It turned out that he had made an amorous grab at Ah Mui, who looked as frail as a water lily but whose daily occupation of hauling buckets of water since the age of three had given arms of steel. So she clipped Brodsky such a whack that he flew off without even saying goodbye.

Despite anything Tan could do in Kunming, OSS continued to send the same chaotic wires. A Major Wickham, now in charge of SI, took up hours of Liang's time in receiving, Helen's time in decoding, and my time in elucidating long, complicated questions about Japanese airfields, installations, and troop movements and the political, social, and economic status of the inhabitants in various parts of Indochina where we did not even have agents, never mind any trained in military intelligence. The fact that these wires were addressed to "Glass and Gordon" did not please either Gordon or Fenn, both of whom remembered that Glass was the man OSS sent down to compete with GBT.

Having sent Wickham whatever information we could gather, we then received complaints that we had not given coordinates, although the places named were as well known to those concerned with the area as Brooklyn would be to someone living in Manhattan. A rebuke for not giving full identification of Japanese units would be followed by a lecture on Order of Battle. Theoretically, Wickham was on the right track. Unfortunately, it was a railroad track, and we had only horse carts.

Our agent in Langson sent us a wire that at 3 P.M. on the following day a Japanese general would be arriving there to attend a feast given by the Chinese magistrate. So we wired the Fourteenth to stage a small bombing mission. The agent informed us later that everything worked out nicely. The general and two of his staff had just sat down to the first dish when there came a sound of planes. "Don't be alarmed," he told the other guests. "I mentioned to our air force in Hanoi that I was coming here, and they offered to give us a greeting." This was no sooner said than the first bomb dropped, whereupon everyone rushed for the shelter. Half an hour later they began the meal again, only to be interrupted by the further roar of planes. This time the general was the first to reach the shelter. After crouching there for ten minutes they were told by a Chinese servant that these last planes were Japanese.

We heard on the radio one evening that "for reasons of health," Stilwell had been relieved from the China command and had been replaced by General Wedemeyer. "The Generalissimo insisted on this exchange," Jo-Jo confided, "because Stilwell wouldn't cooperate. But to save his face he will be promoted to five-star general."

"Impossible!" I exclaimed. "No U.S. general ever gets five stars!" This showed my ignorance as well as the efficiency of the Chinese G-2, the Chinese intelligence unit. Stilwell did indeed get his five stars, and he was reported to have commented, "Only five? The Plough [the star constellation made up of seven stars] has seven." Stilwell was famous for his acerbity, which earned him the name of Vinegar Joe. He was equally famous for his terseness. While attached to his command in the Burma war I one day had a half-hour interview, from which I squeezed four hundred words. In his diary published later, Stilwell condensed this interview to two words: "Fenn called."

The Japanese continued to push northward. Our agents informed us that two of their divisions were now crossing from Burma into Laos. "Road building is being pursued with frenzied haste. Hundreds of rafts are being assembled to cross the Mekong. Fifteen new airfields are in the making. The French barracks formerly allowed to control local security are now being occupied by Japanese troops." Hearing the frequent drone of planes and thuds of bombs, we kept ourselves in daily readiness for a fast getaway.

A small steamboat that sometimes plied the river brought one of Gordon's couriers, an old man named Lok, who had been operating in the Nanning area. His silvery hair and wrinkled skin went rather well with a white linen suit so carefully patched and restitched that it looked like a piece of old lace. With Jo-Jo interpreting, Lok explained that although he himself had escaped the Japanese, our main agent there had been caught. Lok had consequently left without funds and had had to beg his way to Nanning, where he had luckily talked the riverboat captain into a C.O.D. passage. So would Mr. Gordon kindly let him have five thousand Chinese dollars to settle this debt? Although this sum equaled only about twelve U.S. dollars, Gordon expressed surprise that the fare had so suddenly doubled. Old Lok then confessed that this was the fare for himself and his wife.

"But I thought your wife was dead?" queried Gordon.

"That's right, she is. But the last time I went into Indochina I met some friends with a daughter still unmarried at the age of twenty-three, so they offered her to me for only five hundred piastres [about twenty U.S. dollars]. As I knew she was a nice, well-mannered girl we got married right away, and I've had her ever since."

Anxious to see this exceptional bargain, we asked him to bring her in. Lok shortly returned with a young woman who was not only attractive but fetchingly modest. Those were the days.

The cook was always promising to find girlfriends for us and always about to produce a couple who never did show up. His usual excuse was that the sort of girls he thought suitable for us were only to be had at fabulous prices, and he could not bear for us to waste our money. So now we were able to show him this very nice girl that Lok had bought for only five hundred piastres. "And that price is freehold!" Bernard pointed out. "So what's all this talk about 'fabulous prices'?" The cook obviously thought he had lost face through Lok's easy purchase, so his only recourse was a stream of invective, which Liang and Simon Yu between them translated something like this: surely we did not want a worn-out public bus (that is, a girl everybody gets on and off in rapid succession) who had been screwed uphill and down dale over half of Tonkin and was no doubt bursting all over with syphilis!

Gordon's main agent, André Lan, wired us from Hanoi that owing to increasing tension he was coming up for consultations and would be accompanied by a Gaullist patriot named de Courcelle, who was on his way to Chungking to liaise with the FMM. As they would now have trouble in getting through Chen's Peace Preservation Corps, Gordon and Simon went down to meet them. Before leaving, Gordon told me, "This involves a certain risk that I might not get back. Harry will of course take over, but I hope you'll go on working with him and help him all you can." I thought that this little speech raised our friendship a degree or two higher.

As things worked out, there were no snags, and he got the two Frenchmen safely to our camp in a mere four days. Our visitors were in curious contrast. De Courcelle, a top banker, essentially looked the part in his tropical-worsted iron-gray suit, despite its evidence of wear: a shortcoming hardly surprising in a country that had now been cut off for three years. André, small and somewhat bony, was dressed in a white shirt and shorts and looked rather like a schoolboy ready for tennis. Even when a typhoon subsequently made it so cold that I had to wear a heavy sweater, he continued to wear this same garb and politely spurned my offer of extra clothing. Gordon confided, "That's his 'formal' garb. When traveling, he wears a khaki shirt and shorts!"

During several interesting talks André told me the following:

When the Japanese first came into Indochina, they took over, amongst other things, the supervision of agriculture and in many areas changed the crop from rice to jute, which was then fetching good prices in the hard-currency markets the Japanese needed. But when the war with America broke out they couldn't any longer export the jute, and many farmers were ruined. This was their first bad mistake. Their second came from introducing the military yen. Because of their usual resistance to change, the native refusal to accept it was so persistent that the Japanese finally had to give it up and thus lost considerable face. The third gaffe came through currency problems. Whenever the Japanese wanted anything—foodstuffs, textiles, ores, labor—they were careful not to commandeer it but to pay full price. This at first stimulated goodwill both from the French and the Annamites. But soon enough everyone realized that the bill was really paid by constantly increasing taxes and other impositions.

One thing in the Japanese favor is that their troops behave better than Western troops, whether French, British, or American. The officers are always strict in enforcing discipline. In general the Annamites prefer the Japanese to the French merely because they so much hate the French.

The Japanese don't interfere between the natives and the French except in freeing the political prisoners because they need the prison space for what they consider more important offenses, such as anti-Japanese behavior or troublemaking, noncooperation, and minor espionage—major spies being shot at once. The Japanese have learned by experience to let the French go on running most administrative functions, since they have the know-how. But they've taken over the more lucrative trades, as well as black marketing. They also get preference in transport and rations and, when wearing a uniform, total priority in everything.

Despite overall acceptance of Japanese control there is always an undercurrent of protest. For example, French youngsters go around altering the pro-Vichy notices. On one that reads, "For Petain—or against France!" they change the "or" into "and." Beneath "The Past is certainly dead!" they write "Vive la Resistance!" No amount of punishment stops this pinpricking. When they claim to have a victory, the Japanese are encouraged to go around singing in the streets. So the Free French proclaim that it's easy to tell when the Japanese are losing by the amount of street singing, and hearing these songs the French will call out, "What! Another Jap defeat!"

Inside various detention camps are a few thousand mixed Australian, British, Dutch, and American prisoners of war—a very few of the latter. I always carry in my car a few tins, packages, and oddments of clothing, and whenever I pass a truckful I manage to throw them something. The prisoners have recognized my car by now, so they elbow the guards aside and usually manage to grab and hide what I throw them. By using the van that delivers rice to the camps, one of my contact men managed to smuggle into one camp a whole machine gun with ammunition, and they're keeping this weapon for an organized getaway. One day when the Japanese guards were searching for letters reported to have been smuggled into the camp, they came upon several rounds of this ammunition. But their one-track minds were fixed upon the letters, so they merely commandeered these bullets without comment!

My diary at this time records the following impression of Gordon's other helpers:

Helen makes up for her plain appearance by being polite, attentive, quick and careful. Janet, although by no means stupid, relies heavily on her sexual charm in an environment essentially masculine. Madame Tong is always dignified, formal, carefully behaved and exceptionally well-informed about world events and places. She has a quick grasp of any problem and when translating goes from Chinese to French or English without a moment's hesitation. Her English is rather vernacular, but Janet and Helen speak a precise literary English that they learned initially in a convent school. When playing poker they intersperse this formal diction with oddly amusing slang like "down and dirty!" "two aces talks!" "three aching aces!" and "fricking slut!" (said innocently). They can now both hold their own with men who consider themselves fairly deft at the game.

Liang, our radio operator, with his long, thin moustache and heavy framed spectacles, looks like a cross between a Japanese academic and a Russian revolutionary. It is this latter strain that prompts us to call him "Liangski." Although he has learned English only since coming with the group, he's already quite expert and uses a lot of slang. But when he gets excited he translates freely from the Chinese, so that a sentence will come out like this: "Her understanding-Morse-code-ability comes like big surprise package!" Like André he has excess nervous energy, with consequent fidgeting, such as tickling his nose, adjusting his glasses and twiddling his fingers as if about to perform a conjuring trick.

Simon Yu, I've now discovered, is Belgian-Chinese-Annamese, and talks all three languages fluently as well as English. He is another high-energy type, whose particular habit is to cross his legs and nervously swing the top one, a habit also common amongst the Chinese and a sure sign of frustration and high tension. Simon doesn't suffer fools gladly and one of his favorite expressions is "balloon man" to describe someone out of whose mouth comes meaningless words.

The cook's wife, who does all the kitchen work and mostly keeps the camp clean, asks for nothing better than to work harder, for the sheer pleasure of doing everything well. When we offered to raise her salary she said she didn't want any more money, but we could buy her a new pair of trousers! When we also bought her a skirt, we got ten times our money's worth in seeing her delight. "It is the giver not the receiver who lays up treasure."

Gordon told me about Tan's infatuation with Janet: "At one time he asked her to marry him. Madame Tong considered this proposal carefully, but finally decided Janet could do better. Frankie was so upset that to help him get over it I had to send him off to India (a live-it-up area for anyone except Indians). But he came back still infatuated. As you may have noticed Janet treats him with a contempt that brings their relationship to the edge of hate. When Frankie sees Janet flirting with anyone, which is not infrequent, even if circumspect, he is likely to start drinking—a remedy he picked up from me on one occasion: the pair of us were off in India when I happened to lose my own girlfriend to an American colonel (in the days when rank meant something). So I said, 'What the hell, let's get drunk!' And we went out and got loaded. This gave Frankie the idea that you could always drown your frustrations in drink. But he can't handle it and his loss of control only increases Janet's disdain. As against this Achilles' heel, Frankie has many excellent qualities, such as drive, enthusiasm, personality and a special expertise in handling the Chinese top brass, whom he knows exactly how to please and flatter. Unfortunately he can be very arrogant with hoi-polloi natives, whether Chinese or Annamite, because he feels himself, as an American, to be superior.

"Harry Bernard, of course, is first-rate: able, conscientious, hard-working and loyal. But he doesn't bother to hide his adverse opinions and his brusque manner sometimes puts people off.

"Your agent, Bob Lee, is a bright, go-ahead boy, but he thinks too much of himself. Because he's better educated he considers himself a cut above most other Chinese and takes a lofty tone to some of those working for us, including Mac Sin, whom he calls 'a little clown.' But Mac is an endearing clown, as clowns always should be, whereas Bob is merely a juggling clown." In this as in so many other assessments Gordon proved to be right. [As an addendum to my diary, I will add here that after the war, Tan and Sin (who wisely romanized his name to Shin!) went to America, married charming women, and had lovely children. Tan made big money in trading enterprises, and Shin made a fortune in property deals.]

A wire from Lieutenant Colonel Jacques de Sibour announced that he had been appointed acting chief of OSS-Kunming pending the arrival of the new chief, Lieutenant Colonel Richard Heppner (the former Major Heppner who had interviewed me in Washington). "Congratulations on your work," the wire concluded. "Request you stay on and keep it up."

"*Toujours la politesse* [Always be polite]," I remarked to Gordon. "Although he's a naturalized American, he's still a Frenchman to the manner born."

"As you're still an Englishman to the manner born!" Gordon countered.

"Sometimes, perhaps. But then I haven't been appointed acting chief. It's a curious appointment when you think that OSS are basically anti-French."

"Anti-everything except feathering their own nest. Which brings me to a subject I've been meaning to talk to you about. OSS congratulates you on your work, and so do I. But I don't congratulate OSS. So far they've taken everything and given almost nothing except backstabbing, with men like Glass and St. Phalle sent down to compete or even spy on us and subvert our agents. André tipped me off to that. Frankly, I've had enough of such double-dealing. So I intend going to Kunming for a showdown. If OSS won't play ball, I intend throwing in my lot with AGAS, who are only too keen to take us on, while allowing us full independence. So perhaps you'd like to come with me and support my facts."

"I've already reported all the facts. But I'll certainly come with you and report them again, if that's what you'd like me to do." OSS had given me nothing but frustration, whereas GBT had treated me squarely all the way through. On the other hand, I was employed by OSS and on that score owed them loyalty. It was because of this dilemma that I thought I had better get detached from OSS and switch my services elsewhere. Should I go to AGAS, perhaps?

A decision once made, Gordon was not the sort to waste time. At dawn the following day we set off in a sampan downriver. It was cool weather, with the breeze whipping spray off the white caps of the river's waves, and the sampan hurtled down the current with thuds and flying spray. We had no need for poling, and the boatmen used oars only for keeping us steady. By the end of the first day we had already covered a third of the journey.

Nanning headquarters had earlier informed me that a pile of my mail that had accumulated over the past six weeks had been put aboard a French sampan going upriver. I was therefore delighted to see a tricolor flying on a sampan tied up at this first stopping place. But the lieutenant on board said my mail was in the sampan ahead of his; we must have passed it earlier that day without noticing. It was six more weeks before I got that mail. In times of war, letters are like drugs to an addict, and to be deprived of the shot you are counting on can be a grievous blow.

Emerging from the deserted landscape along the upper reaches of the river, we sped past inhabited areas where villages perched up above the rocky shoreline were fringed with towering bamboo plumes. Each cluster of houses had its flight of worn steps leading down to the river, up and down which tripped an endless string of figures carrying buckets. Even the smallest tots manipulated their carrying poles as if they were an extension of their arms, with muscles and nerves that reached out to the very tip.

We were again traveling at the time of the full moon, and to get us to Nanning ahead of the invading Japanese, the rowers plied their oars all night, and we shot down like a speedboat. Above the splash of oars and the croaking of frogs there now came the intermittent rumble of guns and bombs.

On arrival we found the roads chaotic with refugees. All the foreign groups had already left, with a vestige of the Fourteenth Air Force taking latecomers on a few final flights. Having no warm clothes, we had a bitterly cold flight, ascending in a mere half hour from Nanning's semitropical heat to ten degrees below zero centigrade at fifteen thousand feet. How exquisite was the warm bright sunshine when landing at Kunming and the hot coffee served by the ever-friendly Chinese at the hostel!

A very different welcome awaited us at OSS headquarters, where Mykland was scarcely willing to find us a meal, never mind a bed. I again had to be beholden to those scourges of the human race, the British-American Tobacco Company. I fear the devil might have a soft sell if he wanted to buy my soul.

First thing the next morning we called on de Sibour, who was full of fair words and friendship as well as several amusing stories such as this one:

When General Donovan found that Chiang Kai-shek was not giving us full cooperation he sent as a special emissary Major General N——— of the U.S. Marine Corps, who is noted for his courage, drive, and personality. While in Chungking, the general was invited to dinner by Tai Li with the usual playing of "finger-game" and consequent "bottoms up" [both games dealing with trying to guess correctly the total number of fingers held up simultaneously by two rivals] in fiery mao-tai spirit. The brave warrior accepted all the challenges, repeatedly lost despite his host's efforts to let him win, and soon got foolishly drunk. The party being strictly stag, he then wanted to know—half-jokingly—where were the sing-song girls everyone talked about? "In all the other places I've been in—Cairo, Tehran, Delhi, Calcutta—my hosts always furnished girls. But I've been in China four whole days and nights, and not one has been produced!"

Tai Li responded in much the same joking spirit, "In China we have a proverb: 'Women and wine don't mix!'"

But the general felt himself ticked off and riposted very unjokingly, "While we're on the subject of women, I might as well tell you that Madame Chiang is all washed up, and as far as we're concerned, she's shot her bolt. And it's common gossip amongst Chinamen in Washington that the Generalissimo has written her off too, in favor of an ex-actress." By calling the Chinese "Chinamen" and thus reducing them to the level of laundrymen he added so much injury to his insult that Tai Li snapped his fan with a crack like a pistol shot, which touched off the general into his final grand slam. "And you might as well know that OSS can easily do without Chiang's support since we now have a good working relationship with the Communists and no longer need him!" In vino veritas. But this kind of truth is a poisoned cup. Only two days later the general was recalled to Washington, where Roosevelt, to avoid the scandal of a court-martial, retired him into obscurity!

I must say I thought it was a pity that de Sibour was not permanent chief. And when given our statement of complaints, he expressed his sympathy and assured us he would present them fully to Heppner. But Gordon said later: "Where will that get us? He means well. Sympathy without relief is like mustard without beef."

Going the rounds, I found Faxon still operating as chief of MO. He reported that my teams were still doing well but that the Chinese American named Khan had been picked up by the Japanese when off on a mission in Swatow. "Here's a letter he left for you before leaving. We opened it thinking it would be strictly business, but it's just a little personal note referring to several letters he enclosed with it, such as to his parents, his girlfriend, and his American lawyer—'just in case anything happens' is the way he puts it. They're in my drawer here somewhere; I'll fish them out later. Would you care to have lunch with me at the Rotary Club?" Feeling too tired to think clearly, I said yes, so off we went.

The guest speaker was a missionary doctor who made a speech about "choice." There being several different Air Force personnel present, he started off about airmen making a choice concerning targets: "Could you bring yourselves to bomb civilians, including innocent women and children? What a sad dilemma for you airmen!" he lamented, although it was unlikely that a single airman present had ever given the matter a moment's thought when letting go his deadly load. The missionary then told us of the time he delivered a sadly deformed baby, already at death's door from the difficulty of delivery. "I seriously considered putting it out of its misery, but something beyond my free will made me save its life. Some twenty years later I went to a concert when a lady played on a harp so beautifully it made me cry; yes, I must admit I shed tears. Picture my amazement and joy when I discovered later that this lady was the deformed baby who had now grown to womanhood!"

When I read this story in the *Reader's Digest,* the woman played the piano. But "harp" was definitely an improvement.

Spending a day in and around OSS headquarters was rather like playing charades. There was, for instance, an MO team going north to conduct black propaganda under the cover of being a weather team, so they had not learned the drill but had full kits for meteorological analysis. But they also carried duffel bags packed with "black" leaflets, the cleverness of which they were happy to explain to anyone interested! A group of missionaries recruited to SI and going into the Shanghai district this side of the Japanese lines had decided to cover up by pretending to start a mission school. But although obviously convincing in this role, their experience in collecting intelligence came from one week's training in the Kunming Schools and Training program. I heard later that at the last minute they were saved—from ignominy or fame, who knows?—when General Wedemeyer proscribed their mission as "a travesty of Christianity." Apparently "Onward, Christian Soldiers" applies only when you are marching as to war.

The chief SI officer, Lieutenant Colonel Paul Helliwell (another lawyer), told Gordon and me that OSS had written off Indochina as being of no real importance. "The war there will be fought by MacArthur, combined with the U.S. Navy. Colonel de Sibour, being a Frenchman born, has always overrated its significance to us in China." Nevertheless, Helliwell asked a lot of questions, including, "How do you spell Vichyites?" and, in a written note to me when Gordon was talking to his assistant, "Is Gordon Jewish?"

Another OSS officer whose name I did not catch asked me about the "Mac" group still operating in the Canton area, under Faxon of course. "I'm going down that way myself, so I might as well get in touch with them. Not that one ever gets anything useful from our little yellow brothers."

But fair is fair: it is people you do not hear about who do the best job. The worst of having been a journalist is that the only "good" news is bad news. There were a lot of good men in OSS whose names I do not even mention because, as secret operators, they kept their operations secret.

Gordon asked me to dinner with a French civilian named Perrin, who had been active in the Free French underground in Annam, and Colonel Buchanan, head of the famous Force 136 operating in Burma, whom I'd met when I was in Detachment 101. Modest and sincere, Buchanan said nothing of his own remarkable exploits but listened to our chatter with bright attention. "A clever man learns to talk divertingly, but a wise man learns the art of listening." Perrin subsequently showed us his stack of gold plaques, each weighing an ounce and stamped Banque de l'Indochine, Or Pur. We fondled these pretty baubles as if they were works of art. When gold speaks, all men are silent.

Gordon now informed me that to get a clear directive he intended going to Chungking to see both Wedemeyer, the new U.S. chief of staff, and Colonel Grimsdale, head of the British Military Mission. "I'll then fly to Washington and give them the facts. I may be gone for several weeks, but it's the only way to get things straight. I hope things won't be too difficult while I'm gone." We little realized how difficult they would be!

From various sources I now learned that because of the constant Chinese retreats, there had been a big shake-up in Chinese political circles, and several big shots had been fired. In this way the powerful Soong family had put the screws on Chiang to get rid of all their opponents and to insist that Stilwell be sent home. The general had too often insisted that Nationalist troops were mostly reserved for use against the Communists, and this criticism had been taken up by students all over China, with massive demonstrations favoring the Communists and bloody reprisals by Tai Li's police. Because Mao was not ready for full-scale revolution, the Nationalists succeeded in gaining uneasy control. America, meanwhile, was split on the issue. The powerful China lobby, aided by reactionary voices such as *Time* magazine, screamed "treachery" about any support for the Communists, while State Department officials such as John Davies and John Service, who knew the facts, tried in vain to expose the truth, and as a consequence, their careers were ruined.

Following Gordon's visit, it was in fact John Davies whom Wedemeyer sent down to investigate the whole matter of GBT, and de Sibour instructed me to give him full information. Largely as a result of this admirable official's report, our group received a burst of support from OSS, and our work went smoothly for a while, during which my diary records only extracurricular activities.

I was given a lift back to the BAT house by Faxon, who drove through the pedestrian-thronged streets like a police car chasing bandits. Not satisfied with knocking down a Chinese soldier he then bawled out his victim for not looking where he was going. When I took the soldier's part Faxon exploded. "I've had more than enough of your damned impertinence! No wonder everyone dislikes you, you cause more goddam trouble than anyone else in the entire theater. "Lawrence of China"—God save us! That was all we needed from that idiot Little, it made you even more conceited and insufferable—if that were possible. I can tell you, Fenn, if you don't come down to earth p.d.q. you'll be on the next plane home!"

I invited to dinner John Vincent of the U.S. Office of War Information, "gold bars" Perrin, and another Frenchman named de Lesseps, grandson of the Suez Canal man and in many respects one of France's supermen. That particular evening being December 7, 1944, de Lesseps told me that by odd coincidence I had chosen for this little dinner party the exact fiftieth anniversary of his grandfather's death on December 7, 1894. So would we raise a glass to his memory?

Vincent, a personable intellectual with a dry sense of humor, told us about the Thanksgiving service he had attended, presided over by the Reverend Baxter, an American Episcopal clergyman. "The only prayer book available was one issued by the Church of England, which although much in line with his own, calls itself 'The Holy Catholic Church,' which by no means implies the Roman Catholic Church. But the mere word 'Catholic' is anathema to Episcopalians. So when he found himself inadvertently reading that phrase, he paused, coughed, and ad-libbed, 'That is to say, the universal church.' Then with much fingering of the gold chain around his neck and deft pats at his spit-curls he studied several sections with embarrassed frowns and much clearing of the throat before finding anything inoffensive. But when he was reading the prayers, 'the King and his relations' had to be hurriedly corrected to 'that is, the President and his relations,' while 'God bless the bishop' evoked 'that is to say, the bishop and all other clergymen.'

Meanwhile, a beggar outside in the street, finding a ready-made audience within earshot, was shouting, screaming and whimpering to solicit sympathy for his many aches and pains. So Baxter had found it necessary to shout down this competition with increasing vigor. They were both yelling at top decibels when the beggar was suddenly grabbed by a Chinese cop and stunned into silence, thus leaving Baxter bawling at the top of his voice, 'May the Lord God Most High have mercy upon us and hear our prayer; may His enemies be overthrown and their names blotted out for ever!' But by this time everyone was peering round to watch the struggle with the beggar!"

Joining us for coffee and a peppermint liqueur at the Commerce Hotel was Bill Powell, the U.P. correspondent, and a pilot friend who had just flown in from Sian. He said no supplies had been reaching them up there, not even ammunition. "For the past two months the Japs have been bombing us daily and we couldn't do a goddam thing except sit there with our fingers crossed!" While we drank one peppermint this pilot drank six and chain-smoked with the kind of suction that made his lips go white.

Meanwhile Powell told a story about himself and a friend taking two "fairly presentable" girls to the Hot Springs "sanatorium" (which is really a hotel). "When we asked for two double rooms, the manager asked, 'Do you intend sleeping with these girls?'

"'Please, what a suggestion!' I said, looking shocked. So my pal and I went into one room and the girls in another until after a bit they joined us.

"So we're sitting there drinking when the manager bursts in. 'No, this is not allowed!' he says.

"'What's not allowed?' I ask him, all innocence.

"'You can't have these girls in your room!'

"'Really? In that case, off we go.' And all four of us start moving off. As we hadn't yet paid, the manager is on the spot.

"'Do you mean you are leaving?'

"'Of course, we're leaving. You don't really think we came here for the air?'

"So the manager says quickly in his best missionary-school English, 'Listen, I compromise. You have quick fuck-fuck, then you can stay.'"

At a dance party given by the U.S. hospital staff to celebrate the arrival of four new nurses there was thus a total of eight amongst the forty or fifty male guests. When you got tired of waiting in line you could join in the game being organised by Colonel Ride, the former Hongkong University professor now heading the British Army Aid Group. Two teams competed in a memory game involving ever more complicated gestures. "War is hell," said Sherman; but it's the boredom that's the eighth circle.

Bernard had evacuated the BGT camp from Lungchow and temporarily established himself in Ching hsi farther north. When he asked for a million Chinese dollars (about U.S.$2,000), we could get this only in ten-dollar bills because the Chinese government resisted printing larger denominations that would reveal the appalling currency decline. This money filled two duffel bags, and we had no way of getting it to Bernard without a personal courier.

The one I had used previously, an out-of-work mechanic named Chan, was fond of a pipe, so at his request we met in an opium dive. We had no sooner gotten seated when in came three MPs, who ignored my pass from the provost marshall and hauled me off to their headquarters at the other end of town. Here the sergeant in charge grudgingly conceded that the pass did say "anywhere on official business" but wanted to know what the hell kind of business I had in a brothel. But he finally ordered the MP guys to drive me back. Although they swore black's blue that they never would, they finally gave in. So after a couple of pipes (which is my limit—and incidentally, since leaving China I have never felt prompted to smoke another pipeful), I made a deal with Chan, and two days later Bernard got his cash. In China I was twice cheated by fellow Americans but never by a Chinese.

At the Mongolian restaurant next evening, I had dinner with John Vincent, a new MO man named Dewey, and the Tass Agency correspondent Sepelnikoff, one of three I had known in various parts of China—all delightful companions. Dewey, a clever, eloquent, and amusing ex–chemical engineer, had been something of an old Russian hand, having actually stayed with the Litvinovs when Sidney and Beatrice Webb had also been there. So he entertained us with some very intriguing anecdotes. I heard he was subsequently killed when off on a mission, but I do not remember the details.

Gordon returned from Chungking with many a sigh of relief. "Compared to China's 'wartime capital' Kunming is a paradise of sanity. The Americans and the French vied with each other in giving me the runaround. I was reported to Wedemeyer as a British agent, to the French as an American agent, and to the British as a Chinese agent. Only the British disbelieved this nonsense. Texaco House was also a madhouse of overcrowding and domestic chaos. One American colonel staying there turned this turmoil into mayhem. Even when he was sober he was insufferable. And when he was drunk he was capable of seizing any verbal opponent and pitching him out of the house bodily. Between such outbursts he showed off his Masonic paraphernalia or his awards for winning bowling championships in Duluth, Minnesota, or by mouthing political platitudes, his grasp of the political scene. The new American ambassador is a millionaire lawyer from Oklahoma named Hurley. In Texaco House one day, after a few drinks, he demonstrated his parlor trick of making Indian war whoops. One Chinese woman present was so terrified that she ran out of the house screaming. As for his role as ambassador—he knows nothing about China and is never tired of trying to prove it!"

Later on I remarked to Bernard, "One couldn't call Laurie exactly pro-American!"

"But neither is he anti. When it comes to the AGAS crowd or State Department men like Davies, you might call him pro-American. Praise is due to those that earn it."

Or as Sidney Smith succinctly put it: "Among the smaller duties of life I hardly know any one more important than that of not praising where praise is not due."

8

REMINISCENCES AND
OTHER STORIES

I was instructed by de Sibour to call upon a Colonel Carlton of U.S. Army G-2 who wanted information connected with Indochina. I found the colonel showing Frank Shu (an old acquaintance of mine) how to operate an abacus. When the colonel finally gave me his attention, it appeared that his interest in Indochina was strictly limited to currency exchange. "Frank here is ready to make a deal on piastres against U.S. dollars. But as Uncle Sam is picking up the tab I'd like an official confirmation about the rate he's giving me." I told him the rate being offered was generous. Frank, after all, was something of a pal, whereas I'd never even met this Uncle Sam.

Faxon had also been asking to see me. I found him playing with his armory: a .38 Smith & Wesson, a .45 Colt automatic, a silenced .22, a .32 carbine, and a nonissue Beretta he had bought on the black market. I could not but wonder how many other tiresome old men were monopolizing weapons that were never put to use! While reassembling the Colt he had been cleaning, Faxon explained why this particular weapon had been adopted by the Army. "When we first took over the Philippines we found that a .38 bullet merely drilled a hole in those Negritos, and they kept right on coming and could easily kill you before they dropped dead themselves. But the .45 bullet carries such a punch that it knocks a man down as well as kills him." I said goodbye before he remembered what he wanted to see me about.

In the corridor I met an old friend I had not seen for years, Miss Eva Ho, staid daughter of Hong Kong millionaire Sir Robert Ho Tung. The Ho family being pro-British, Eva had escaped Japanese durance by fleeing to Free China, and now largely destitute, she was looking for a job. "But there doesn't seem to be anything here," she murmured bleakly. I had heard that a new SO officer, Major Leake, was looking for office staff, so I took her in to see him. Having noted her particulars, he said he would let her know.

As we were going out of the door, he took me aside and murmured, "Is she interested in sleeping?" Because Eva was neither young nor attractive, this illustrated the desperate boredom of Americans in China who never faced the enemy or cared about the war and pathetically missed their homeland with its plethora of fun, games, gormandizing, and sex. Or did Leake, perhaps wisely, believe that it is better to like what you can get than not get what you like?

Walking back to the BAT house, I stopped to watch the little man who runs the art shop, out in front making badger-hair brushes. His deft movements in assembling the little bunch of hair and gluing and binding it into the end of the bamboo tube were almost too quick for the eye to follow. And at the coffin makers next door, two workers in blue silk gowns were, with infinite patience and skill, cutting, assembling, and gluing together hundreds of fragments of wood into a coffin lid that would be indistinguishable from a solid slab cut from a tree.

That evening I was invited to dinner by Mr. Huw Jones, formerly of the Jardine Matheson Company in Shanghai. Wearing an old tweed jacket and baggy pants threadbare at the knees and puffing a stinking pipe with an excretion of spittle pops, he lectured his three guests on the necessity of keeping up pukka sahib standards in the Far East despite the hordes of GIs who were currently letting the side down. The foreign-style food his "number one boy" now served us was hardly edible, and the coffee was so bad that even he could not drink it. "Once you're away from the treaty ports, you can say goodbye to decent coffee, decent mess boys, or indeed to anything worth having!" Meanwhile, I had left my jeep in care of the driver and, with the evening looking rainy and the jeep being hoodless, had lent him my thick navy jacket. Upon leaving the party I found he had put it under the seat. As near as I could understand, his excuse was that he could not take advantage of the honorable lieutenant's generous offer because the rain might have damaged it.

In line with our improved relations following Davies' visit, OSS offered us as headquarters in Kunming their former radio station, which they had inherited from the Flying Tigers but now found much too small for their own use. I knew it well from the old days, so a day or two before Gordon left for the States, I drove him out to look it over. The site, about six miles out of town, was especially attractive, being on the bend of a stream amid the rice paddies and shaded by a group of towering hemlocks. Gordon decided to accept it, so he wired Bernard to come here with the rest of the group.

After organizing the reconstruction of the station to fit our own requirements, we then had to await Bernard's arrival. My diary reflects this fill-in period:

A prosperous Chinese friend of Faxon's, the owner of an engineering firm, invited us to his house at West Mountain, out along the Burma Road. I hadn't travelled this route since escaping from the Japanese in 1942. At that time the Burma Road had been littered with corpses of Chinese soldiers dying either from wounds or from the cholera then raging during that terrible exodus. Their bones were now amidst wrecked vehicles rusting in the valley-bottoms or sinking into the rice-paddies.

As usual with Chinese houses, Mr. Hsu's, although outwardly substantial, was inwardly monastic: a few hard chairs, teak chests and tables and a few scraps of charcoal burning in half a five-gallon gas drum. In the main room hung a scroll depicting rocks, trees, waterfall and mountain and inscribed with characters which Mr. Hsu happily translated: "Waterfall crashes down on rocks, and sprays out above carp safe in dark pool."

After being regaled with local brandy we were served real coffee and wheat cakes with strawberry jam—an unexpected and delicious treat! Later on we all drove to the nearby American Recreation Centre to see a movie called *Two Yanks Abroad*, written, produced and acted by escaped lunatics; quite well done, considering.

Next morning, in the BAT house, hearing a commotion downstairs I found a succession of crates, trunks, suitcases, sacks and dispatch boxes being off-loaded from a weapons carrier. Major Glass had returned from Indochina, having brought all this stuff every inch of the way. What else he had accomplished I never did learn, as it was Top Secret. But he proudly displayed his collection of weapons, which included a Wesley .45.

At dinner, Faxon flew into a temper with the "boy" about the plates being cold. The boy later confided to me with true compassion, "That poor old man should be home in bed being looked after." Nevertheless, Faxon was able to cap Glass's weapon assembly by his own acquisition of a "pocket" bazooka.

John Vincent of OWI [U.S. Office of War Information] stopped by to ask me about Lanchow in China's far north-west. It appeared that the Chinese government were now planning to vacate Chungking and set up headquarters there. So he had been ordered to establish an OWI office simultaneously. A BAT man present advised him to take along a few gross of Singer Sewing Machine needles because over the years thousands of machines had been sold in the area, but no one had sent any needle replacements. So if Vincent was on the ball he could make fifty bucks out of it! John, who had probably never sold anything in his life, except a used Cadillac or two, thanked him politely.

Ravenholt also called in and told me, amongst more serious news items, that one of his dispatches had been censored by the Chinese central government because he had mentioned that mules owned by the Communists looked well-fed.

Today in OSS headquarters Lieutenant Brody (no relation to Brodsky) was presented with the Legion of Merit in recognition of something he did in Italy. De Sibour had called for "a sizeable contingent of OSS personnel" to be lined up for this occasion. As Brody came out "front-and-centre," one of the guard dogs he was fond of followed behind and slowly deposited a shining mahogany turd which rather distracted the sizeable contingent of OSS personnel lined up for the occasion.

Ray Squires, back from Fuchow, said that the entire city had been taken by a small squad of Japanese soldiers merely out marauding. The Chinese troops, supposing this was the prelude to a full-scale attack, had promptly decamped so the Japanese looters found nothing to oppose them except a few Chinese soldiers mostly in the brothels.

Squires's second-in-command, a Methodist missionary recently elevated to the rank of captain, gave us a lecture on cooperation. "If we're ever to help the Chinese out of the woods we've got to hammer home the need for keeping their eye on the ball so then we can all pull together, sink or swim!" His euphoria about the amount of per diem he had drawn was truly touching: "Fifty-three days at $5.50 a day, that's close on three hundred dollars! So I felt justified in buying this carved ivory ball with seven smaller carved balls inside! But next time if I wait three months before drawing per diem I can send the money back to my folks as down payment on a new Olds!" Tolman [an OSS inventor of deception devices] was anxious to show him his new gimmick of Japanese prayer books with built-in explosive.

"All you have to do is get them circulated. Then as soon as they're opened—"

But the ex-missionary wouldn't buy it. "Following the example set by General Wedemeyer I draw the line at linking the Holy Scriptures with deceptive devices."

Over at the Commerce we ran into the Shanghai-educated Mr. Wong of the Young Men's Christian Association, who doesn't seem to share the high-mindedness of this Methodist missionary. He told us that when wanting to have a look at the Hot Springs Sanatorium he had been offered a ride by two GIs. "It was really most kind of them, especially since they had with them two Chinese ladies," said Mr. Wong in his carefully accurate if exotically-pronounced English. "At the sanatorium the manager refused to book the ladies in because he said they were prostitutes—common ones, at that. So one of the two GIs said, indicating me,

"'We're with this gentleman. Now I ask you, would he be the kind to associate with common prostitutes?'" Ha, ha, rather clever of them, eh?

"The manager then said, 'But the girls are so vulgarly dressed that people will certainly think they are common prostitutes and there will be complaints.' Well, in my own humble opinion the lobby was already teeming with prostitutes, although admittedly they were more elegantly dressed. So I suggested to the boys that if they were to buy a couple of the elegant flowered coats on sale in the lobby, this would not only enhance their lady friends' appearance but soften the manager's somewhat mercenary heart. So the boys went into the shop with the two ladies, who came out transformed and were booked in right away! After all, they had kindly given me a ride and one good turn deserves another, don't you agree?"

One of the fellows running the OSS Post Exchange who had been very obliging in supplying our group with extra odds and ends asked me if I would take him to a brothel to do some photographing. Although it was nice to have a reputation for seeing the sights, I wasn't entirely pleased at this particular endorsement. However I obliged and it was only after we had got started that I discovered he wanted flash pictures of sex in action. After one such shot, with the girl bursting into tears and the client leaping up in terror, I left the photographer to find his own way around.

A man named Goulart who has been working for the Chinese Industrial Co-operatives near the border to Tibet called to ask me for a job. A strangely elfin little man of Russian extraction, he was enormously vivacious, widely knowledgeable and, as I later learned, spoke six languages fluently, including Tibetan. He accompanied his speech with gestures reminiscent of a Balinese dancer. When expressing the mannerisms of girls belonging to a certain Tibetan tribe he not only imitated their movements but managed to stroke the girls from head to foot. When telling me of a prince of the Moos to whom he had offered suppositories as a treatment for piles he mimed the prince writhing with embarrassment when explaining that shoving suppositories up his royal arse would not be consistent with his dignity as a prince. Although I sent him along to OSS I felt they never would appreciate such histrionic talent.

Prior to attending a concert of phonograph records given by the American Red Cross, some of us at BAT house were invited for drinks by "Stemp" Smith, who for thirty years had run the Chinese postal service. Although speaking fluent Chinese and having been immersed in Chinese life for thirty years, no vestige of China was now allowed to intrude upon the decor of his residence, which included Czechoslovakian glassware, Italian majolica, Irish Beleek, and English seaside pottery inscribed "A present from Southsea."

Stimulated by homemade wine of curious taste but powerful effect, Faxon and Glass felt prompted to compete in telling stories. Here is Faxon's:

"When I was living in Peking a wealthy American asked my advice about buying high-quality jade. It so happened I knew of two magnificent pieces, Sung dynasty and priceless, which a dealer had bought from an impoverished Manchu family. After some lengthy bargaining the American bought them for forty thousand U.S. dollars, then quite a lot of money, although still less than they were worth. Several days later the dealer called to see me, chatted about the weather and other trivialities in a fashion that suggested he was building up to a complaint about the price he got. So I finally served him tea—the polite signal for 'time to leave,' at which he thrust into my hands a small package wrapped in Chinese newspaper, saying, 'Here's your commission, honorable sir,' and bowed himself out. Upon opening this curious package I discovered an assortment of U.S. currency in denominations from singles to hundreds, which when I totted up came to exactly four thousand dollars!"

The story Glass told showed the difference between Faxon's commercial realism and his own Seventh Day Adventist scruples.

"When I was living in Saigon, a friend I'll call Harry, who was stationed in Singapore, wrote me that he was sending his wife up to Saigon as a break from the heat and monotony which were rather getting her down. He enclosed a color transparency of an attractive young woman whose smile showed a slight gap between her two front teeth.

"When I met the boat she came on, the captain told me she had hanged herself the previous night. 'From the start of the voyage,' he told me, 'she seemed depressed and invariably drank too much. But unfortunately none of us realized she had any real problem.'

"As they couldn't, in the prevailing heat, send the body all the way back to Singapore, they asked me to identify the dead woman, if that were possible. When I raised the sheet covering the corpse I saw a face all twisted sideways and the color of mud—she could have been fifty! But the gaping mouth clearly showed that gap between the teeth.

"The captain then said he had checked through her papers and wished to suggest that I, as a friend of the family, should extract certain letters revealing that the deceased had been having an affair with D——— (mentioning a top newspaperman in Singapore) and was apparently heartbroken at having to leave him. But I felt that, really, I had no right to interfere, so these papers were sent back with the rest of her belongings."

This story, although almost de Maupassant in impact, did not, I fear, raise my opinion of Glass.

Perhaps to get us back onto a more cheerful note, a pilot whose name I didn't catch told a third story.

"Last month when I was shot down north of Canton I managed to walk through into Free China by following a river coming down from the Kweichow mountains. I was there in the middle of nowhere, not a soul in sight, nor even a hut, when along the bank comes an attractive white girl! Being tired and half-starved by this time I thought that when the girl spoke in English I must be in a delirium! But it turned out she really was the genuine article—an Australian girl married to a Hong Kong Chinese who now appeared out of the bush. It seems he had talked her into this way of escape when the Japs invaded Hong Kong. He further told her that in the Kweichow rivers there were gold deposits and they could easily survive by selling the siftings to the locals. So for the past four years they'd eked out a bare subsistence and even saved a portion of the gold dust to get them back to Hong Kong when the Japs moved out. They showed me a bag of gold dust weighing less than a pound and worth maybe three hundred bucks. Jesus, if I hadn't been so played out I'd have given her three hundred bucks to can this guy and mosey off with me!"

These three men were all of Anglo-Saxon stock. So their stories illustrated that the diversity of Americans is not always of racial origin.

The subsequent concert was not a marked success. Homemade wine goes well with storytelling but it's no help at a concert of scratchy phonograph records of Schubert and Tchaikovsky at their stickiest, plus the efforts of an unfortunate woman reading program notes against a background of chewed popcorn.

9

The Journey to Kunming

As the foregoing notes from my diary demonstrate, it is when nothing is happening that one has most time to record trivialities. At this point, fortunately, I was again immersed in action. Bernard had resisted bringing the group up to Kunming on several counts; for one thing, he was against our getting further involved with OSS; for another, there was no way to bring all our equipment, never mind that lovely gasoline, on this long and difficult journey. Finally, Gordon asked me to go down there and help him sort things out.

When I went to clear my trip with de Sibour, more out of courtesy than need, he said that because he was now going home I had better wait and clear it with Heppner. I told him we could not wait that long, nor, in view of my "open" orders, was it necessary. "You may be right," he conceded, "but don't blame me if Colonel Heppner makes a fuss." Our talk was now interrupted by the roar of exploding bombs. "No warning, either," growled de Sibour. But we had no sooner gone to the shelter (such as it was) than the all-clear went, which seemed peculiar. We learned later that a steamroller had been carelessly left on the runway and overlooked by Operations. A fighter plane coming in to land and loaded with antipersonnel bombs that the pilot had found no target for had hit the steamroller head on. So the bombs went off like firecrackers.

To help with my inadequate Chinese on this rescue mission, I took along one of my former agents, Tsung-wei, a refugee from Peking University. Fog had closed the airfield down south, so we caught the train that formerly ran all the way to Hanoi but was now cut at Kaiwan, halfway to the Indochina border.

The fog having lifted, I was able to arrange a flight for the following day. The French-style hotel being full, we got a shakedown in a tent. The neat and rather attractive town showed a mixture of French and Chinese architecture, shops full of Indochina imports, and a population interspersed with Annamite women wearing long black coats, white trousers, and the huge Tonkinese hats that look like lamp shades.

Taking a walk out of town, we came upon a pair of handsome commemorative pylons decorated with elephants and lions and bearing an inscription from Mencius, which Tsung-wei translated: "In overcoming problems, you must first decide what not to do. Only then can you take an action based on what you should do." While we stood taking this in we were astonished to hear, amid the wild desolation of these hills, a music like Javanese bells and gongs, which slowly increased in volume until we saw coming toward us along the rocky path a convoy of water buffalo, each with a deep bell at its throat and clusters of smaller bells around the yoke.

On our way to the airfield the next morning, Tsung-wei confessed that this would be the first time he had been up in a plane and that he had to steel himself! For my own part this was one flight where pleasure exceeded pain, despite the bitter cold when we reached altitude. The L-5 open cockpit revealed an ever-variegated pattern of red earth, golden stubble, lavender bean plants, and emerald rice, with huge slabs of violet rocks jutting out on the horizon like battleships wrecked in opaline seas. Despite the evidence of human toil, humanity itself was revealed only in sparsely dotted habitations, spider web paths, and rare stone bridges spanning the silver gleam of rivers.

Tsung-wei told me how his own flight had gone: "Frankly, I felt very queer watching the earth fall away from me. All one's life one sees it from a worm's point of view, and suddenly you're seeing it as a gull sees it, and I found that a peculiar sensation. I've always remembered what Confucius says: 'A kind man lives by the seaside, but a wise man lives on the mountain top where the view permits him to think broadly.' So I was hoping that while aloft I might get this sensation of thinking even more broadly. But I couldn't stop worrying about whether I'd get back to earth and ever think anything at all!"

It was still cold when we came down at Wanshan, high in the mountains. There to meet us (what surprising courtesy!) was the CO, Colonel Miller, a plump, urbane patrician, essentially West Point. To arrange horses for collecting some of Bernard's equipment, we were driven fifty miles southeast, where the Chinese general in command promptly served us tea and dishes of peanuts, which the colonel struggled vainly not to eat. During the large meal that followed, his favorite expression was, "Perhaps I will have just another tidbit," as he took another chunk either clumsily with his chop sticks or more successfully with the large porcelain spoon he carried with him for such emergencies.

Back at headquarters there was another large meal of mostly warmed-up rations. It did finish, however, with a substantial dish of "eight-precious-rice"— referring to the eight sweetmeats found in this particular Chinese pudding, but in this instance composed of candy bars, fruit slabs, chocolate, and other synthetic confections found in PX supplies, which the colonel exacted from his men in return for their getting a share of the pudding. As the contribution was supposed to be voluntary, nobody could complain.

Tsung-wei inevitably had to live in the Chinese section of the hostel with the domestics, drivers, interpreters, and office staff. All Chinese personnel shared this second-class status, with no exceptions except for very rare generals and top politicians having duties in this area. Tsung-wei assured me he did not mind; it was quite acceptable, although there were two small drawbacks: "The dormitory is supervised by one of Tai Li's agents, so everyone must watch his step. Any political deviation or suspected misdemeanor, and you're off to detention camp and sometimes even shot. But what really gets me down is the gambling, which sometimes goes on all night, mostly blackjack, a game which, as you may know, can get very noisy. They all gamble with U.S. currency, often with dollar stakes. When they run out of cash they think nothing of gambling away their watches, Parker pens, or anything imported they happen to own!"

After being visited by three Chinese generals, Miller vaunted his happy fraternization. "They appreciate my treating them as equals. Even when," he added long-sufferingly, "they talk utter rubbish. One must learn how their minds work. Stilwell never did, despite his long experience. That's why he was thrown out. And Wedemeyer isn't doing any better, always putting out press statements which steal the thunder from the Chinese P.R. section, such as last week about the Chinese army down on the Salween. He doesn't even get his facts right. The reason why they fight well there is not because they're better led. It's entirely a matter of utility. The fact is that when the Ledo Road is built right through to India the Chinese will make money from the new supply line. So Chiang ordered his generals to hold on and fight, or they'd be kicked out. Consequently these higher-ups ordered the field officers to fight or get shot. This severity went down the line to the fighting infantry, who really do get shot if they don't hold firm. But in the Kweilin battlefront it's been a very different story. The Japs there were allowed to advance simply because the G'issimo wants to break the power of Chennault and his Fourteenth Air Force, who've been getting entirely too arrogant." Although not given to handing out compliments, Miller commended my ability to make this present journey without a GI companion. (He considered

Tsung-wei merely a translator.) "I can seldom find reliable men to go off alone on long and arduous trips. They crack up mentally, then have to be rescued and sent into rest camps."

We were both invited to a feast by the commander of the Fifty-second Army. The table of twelve included five generals and four colonels. Miller knowing no Chinese and the Chinese no English, the latter consulted a language book published in 1922. "May I ask your name, sir? Which is the road to the station? Have you a room vacant? With a bathroom? A nice view? A well-aired bed? Kindly direct me to the WC." I later on remarked to Miller on their perseverance in trying to learn English, as against our neglect of Chinese.

"That's only because they're all hoping to go to America one day, whereas God knows we have no reason ever to stay on here."

After a two-hour struggle I got through on the telephone to Bernard, who said that with the horses we had sent he could get the team as far as Wanshan, but would I have two trucks waiting for him there? Fortunately, this offered no problem.

Miller asked me to join him in meals: a great honor, because he always ate alone, not fraternizing even with his field officers. I do not know whether this mark of favor was because I was an outsider, a "specialist," a Marine Corps officer, or merely a responsive listener. For a man who loved to talk, his self-imposed Coventry must have been a trial. I could of course respond with knowledgeable nods to much of his monologues, having run across a good many of the military personnel he had known, for example, Chennault.

"He thinks too much of himself. But one can't deny what he's accomplished. With a few old crates and a handful of pilots who flew for the money, he almost drove the Jap Zeros out of Chinese skies. But like most heroes he has his Achilles' heel. With Chennault it's women, as you probably know. One day some jealous member of his harem will stab him in the back, either politically or with that paper knife he imprudently keeps on his desk.

"I suppose you also knew Colonel X———, his second in command? He was a classmate of mine. That glamorous Russian girl he married was another in Chennault's stable, which was why the old man kept him in the group when he actually disliked him. X——— was always a schemer. In his first year at West Point he proposed to run a daily sweep on the number of shares sold each day on the New York Stock Exchange. When this came to the censorious attention of the CO, X——— quickly announced that he intended giving 10 percent to the camp benevolent fund. In ways like this he managed to establish himself as 'a man of ideas.' The same kind of finagling, plus his wife's exotic charms, carried him through his Flying Tiger days from beginning to end. Although I must say that here in China," Miller added loftily, "one hardly needs to be born unscrupulous to find oneself bitten by the grab bug. There's something about war-torn China that corrupts even the most honest American. I suppose it's partially due to the prevailing Chinese corruption due to war and revolution. But what really sets in the rot amongst our own people is this curse of per diem and nothing worthwhile to spend it on, coupled with this game of changing money and the constant scramble to get a better rate than anyone else. Only this morning a deputation of enlisted men asked me to consider dispensing with the third egg served at breakfast as a way to reduce mess expenses and then increase the per diem! Well, you know how minute Chinese eggs are, and they cost peanuts, but the men preferred to have this bit of extra cash to spend on—what? Prostitutes, PX rubbish, and imitation jade!"

The one army associate Miller praised unreservedly was General Donovan—"a considerable hero in World War I, having led the 'Fighting Sixty-ninth.' At one point in his career he could have scooped the nomination as Republican presidential candidate and probably have been elected president. But he preferred not to go into politics. The reason he's been able to gouge such enormous unspecified funds out of Congress for the OSS is that he's married to the richest girl in Buffalo and considered beyond temptation for personal graft. In American politics you must prove either that you're stinking rich before you entered the field or still dirt poor when you leave it." I was, of course, careful not to voice my opinion that the United States had been fortunate that Donovan only became head of OSS and not president.

Tsung-wei and I went walking among the sugarloaf hills technically known as "karst," from that region in Yugoslavia where this geological formation was first observed by Westerners. The basic rock, limestone, being both porous and soluble, constantly gets washed away. Where some harder rock forms a cap, erosion is prevented, and a towering crag builds up. Meanwhile, the disintegration of all the rest subsides to an overall plain so that each crag juts up monumentally, as we see depicted so often in Chinese paintings.

We walked for miles through this kind of landscape, totally deserted except for the occasional hovering hawk. Finally, the wilderness opened out into rice paddies. The crop now having been harvested, the tufted stalks were withering in the dried mud. In this wilderness we came across a grave marked with a beautifully carved horseshoe-shaped stone, with characters giving the name, high qualities, and age of a woman who had died four centuries earlier, in the heyday of the Ming Dynasty. Down below the grave a rivulet gurgled beneath a willow, from which a woman was lopping a few last branches. Giving me one look, she uttered a yelp of terror and ran for her life.

Reaching an isolated village we found ourselves attacked by six or eight dogs barking furiously. "Barking dogs don't bite," Tsung-wei assured me, but unfortunately the dogs did not know about this, and one almost had my leg before I shot it, which effectively frightened off the others. As the wounded animal still squirmed, I had to finish it off with a second shot, by which time several villagers appeared. I steeled myself for a difficult confrontation, but after a moment's silent contemplation of the corpse, they must have decided the execution was justified, so they lugged it off, no doubt to serve up for dinner.

In a shack serving Mohammedan-type food (not uncommon in this region thanks to ancient Mongol penetrators), we had a meal of steamed savory rolls. Lamenting that they had had to walk ten miles to get charcoal, Miao tribeswomen were offering the proprietor small baskets of the charcoal for a vast sum (almost equivalent to one U.S. dollar). "I use a basket a day for cooking alone," he told us gloomily. "All this inflation—when's it going to end?" Some of the more prosperous villagers were carrying pierced-pottery stoves of glowing charcoal. The men merely kept their hands warm with these small pots, but the women would periodically put theirs on the ground and sit over them with legs apart and skirts spread until an expression of beatitude would suffuse their shining faces.

During our meal Tsung-wei offered his own story about Chennault, having taken from his wallet a somewhat dog-eared photograph of the general dancing with a really beautiful Chinese girl. "She was a good friend of mine who married a wealthy engineer. A clause in the marriage contract permitted her to go out dancing, since her husband didn't dance. This really amounted to her having discreet affairs. But although she knew Chennault well, she wouldn't sleep with him, not only finding him sexually unattractive but disliking his shady deals with Nationalist officials. According to her he was piling up funds to run his own airline after the war." (This, of course, proved correct.) Tsung-wei also told me that this girl said Chinese men were often cold, indifferent, and too matter-of-fact; took a superior attitude toward women; and were sometimes even arrogant. American men went to the opposite extreme, affecting an overwhelming attitude of lust—usually feigned—to suggest they were virile, when quite often they were not; they were also too impetuous, impatient, uncontrolled, and, in the long run, just as unsatisfactory as the Chinese. She had liked best a certain Frenchman, "but that may have been a matter of chance!"

I asked him about his own attitude. (He was very good-looking and personable.) "I get along with girls pretty well, but I fear they find me typically Chinese, that is, on the cold side. They also resent my being interested in books, art, music, and nature, so they soon get fed up and drift away. Recently, one of my particular girlfriends, both beautiful and affectionate, finally gave me up as a bad job and married a banker. Since he's successful, generous, handsome, and cultivated, she was certainly lucky to get rid of me!" In Shanghai, after the war, when he introduced this couple, I found that he had reported them both rather accurately. I had already discovered that when the Chinese combine affluence with courtesy, modesty, charm, intelligence, and cultivated discernment, you may find yourself levitated into more rarefied air. In the West, civilization is the city-state; in China it is more likely to be the reciprocity of human beings.

Miller's camp was now getting ready for Christmas by stringing up decorations and adorning a tree, but the vaguely depressing atmosphere generated by Miller's lofty detachment dulled their efforts. The weather added to the gloom, with drizzling cold rain that seeped in everywhere. In the camp one tried to stay warm with extra clothing or even a blanket flung round oneself, but the populace out on the street hugged mere bits of rag to augment their thin cotton clothing and, to stoke up their metabolism, were often driven to beg for an extra bowl of rice. One woman, mere skin and bone but handsome still—an Asian version of Picasso's *Absinthe Drinkers*—held out her hand so pitifully that I instinctively pulled out my roll of bills, but finding only hundreds, went into a shop for change. By the time I came out she had already turned away, having no doubt despaired of getting anything. When I caught up and gave her the equivalent of ten U.S. cents she wept from sheer relief. I am rather addicted to saying that, because of their philosophic acceptance of hardship, the Chinese are perhaps the happiest people on earth, and then along comes someone like this woman to remind one that hunger, cold, and misery totally refute such conclusions.

Tsung-wei and I went back to the camp to sit resignedly over the usual scraps of charcoal glowing in a pan while he read and translated Chinese poems. Our room boy, Wong the Elder, peeped in to listen with sparkling eyes. Although he probably did not understand much of it he knew Tsung-wei was a scholar, someone to revere, and poems read from a printed page would have an additional aura of magic. Aged perhaps twenty-five and still a bachelor, Wong had informed us he could not afford to get married, but he was saving up for it and, if he could keep going, might manage it by the end of next year. He seemed always fit and efficient, so we asked why he would not keep going. He gave us an embarrassed look and told us roughly this: "It's the police spies—always on the watch. If you say a word out of turn they're on to you like knives. And if anything is lost or stolen, hold your breath! Someone's going to get it in the neck, guilty or not guilty. Only yesterday Fatty Chan was hauled off; we don't even know why nor what's happened to him." When our poetry session was over we discovered that Tsung-wei, having perched his legs on the pan, had burned not only his trouser leg, but the whole side of one shoe! That's real concentration!

Miller's G-2 captain took me along to meet the Chinese G-2 staff. Their hut had no door, and when I suggested that their pan of charcoal might be more effective if they kept out the gale, they told us they needed the door for a bed. I was reminded of my first visit to China, when a Chinese "expert," Colonel Evans Carlsen, had advised me, "Always carry a screwdriver. Then in Chinese inns you can take down the door to sleep on instead of lying on the damp earth floor." I thought at that time he was kidding.

On our way back from this visit we were accosted by Miller, who bawled out the captain for taking me off without his permission. Nor did this rebuke leave me unscathed: because Miller accorded me his own fraternization I should avoid palling up with his officers. It was perhaps because of this solecism that he now said that because he would send the trucks to pick up Bernard's outfit there was no need for me to wait around. Although not exactly a dismissal, this seemed like a polite discharge.

Having phoned Bernard to ensure this arrangement was okay, I got ready to leave. There being no L-5 available, Tsung-wei and I got a lift to Kaiyuan on a truck. Although the road was appalling, the GI driver kept his foot on the floorboards the whole 150 miles, meanwhile telling me with tears in his eyes of his happy home life in Oregon, where he had a mother (no father) and several siblings. Only nineteen years old when drafted, he had now been in the Army two long years and in China for most of it. "It's completely bitched my education," he lamented. I remarked that China, however, must have taught him quite a lot. "Oh, sure. It's taught me to swear, drink, lie, cheat, steal, screw, and never again get a job where some dumb bastard's going to push me around! No offense personally, lieutenant."

In the hotel in Kaiyuan we were lucky enough to get a kind of suite: living room, dressing annex, and a bedroom with springs on the beds instead of boards. But Tsung-wei was more impressed by finding in the back of a drawer a genuine Scripto propelling pencil—"and the lead almost unused!" When he offered it to me I generously informed him that "findings were keepings." But our night on the lovely soft beds was somewhat marred by air raids that had the hotel guests running in and out to the shelter for what seemed half the night.

On the train the next morning there was only one first-class seat available, which the crowded conditions might have prompted me to take. But a pack of cigarettes encouraged the conductor to tell me that the other first-class seats marked "reserved" would not be taken up until the halfway station. So with some juggling we got a pair together. We were later on enjoying a feast of ham sandwiches, onion omelet, and coffee, miraculously produced from the train's galley, when we arrived at this halfway station, and who should come strutting in but the fat ex–minister of war transport, General P. J. Wong, with his fat wife and fat son. Having been off for the weekend shooting geese, they came aboard loaded up with birds and guns. I quickly told Tsung-wei not to move and slipped the conductor another pack of cigarettes, whereupon he explained to the general that due to no fault of his own, there had been an overbooking, but he could still have two separate first-class seats and one in second. None of the trio accepted this alternative with any great show of gratitude, and Wong Junior almost missed the train by arguing on the platform before dashing off to his second-class seat, by which time it had been taken.

Arriving in Kunming shortly after dusk, we went straight to the BAT house, where Tsung-wei was welcome, too. I suppose even the devil does favors as possible bribes. At dinner we were seated with Faxon and Eva Ho, who now had a job with the Chinese Red Cross. She shortly complained that at our last meeting at OSS, I had introduced her to "a very undesirable person." "Really? He thought you very desirable," I bantered.

"There's no need to add insult to injury," she snapped—not unjustifiably. But I was in for a worse rebuke when Faxon told me sotto voce that he was shortly being replaced by a new MO chief. Thinking it of no consequence, I told him I already knew of this from Glass, at which he exploded into a raging attack against blabbers like Glass who betray confidences and busybodies like Fenn who pry into other people's affairs. Thus within an hour of my arrival, I was right back into the Kunming cement mixer.

10

A VISIT TO INDIA

Early the next morning, I went out to the Fourteenth "Ops" to arrange for a plane to collect Bernard's team from Kaiyuan. Luckily, there was a craft immediately available, and it was about to take off when Wedemeyer's chief of staff, General Dorne, sent an urgent message that he had left his mess kit (for a staff of ten) at Kaiyuan and needed it immediately, so there would not be room on this small crate for the GBT gang. By the time another plane was available, fog had closed in on Kaiyuan, and Bernard then had to wait two whole days to be collected. "*Mess* kit is right," said Frankie.

To urge forward the conversion of the radio station for our use, I called to see de Sibour before he left. He said I would have to see Colonel Bird, the new second-in-command and then said he wanted to give me some confidential advice. "You'll be well advised to transfer the GBT outfit to AGAS, yourself included." I was too surprised to think of any answer to this remarkable suggestion from the acting chief, and I have often wondered whether he made it because he liked us or because he disliked OSS. I rather concluded the latter.

Colonel Willis Bird, formerly a kingpin at Sears, Roebuck in Chicago and another pal of Donovan's, for reasons unknown dismissed my query about converting the radio station with a sharp reply: "We've got it in hand." Nor was he interested in discussing Indochina. "The Navy will take care of that theater. For our crowd the action lies up north. And the Chinese Commies are the boys to do the job. I'm bringing a thousand of their guerrillas into the OSS net."

"Won't Tai Li object?" I asked blandly.

"The hell with Tai Li. That guy is just an obstructionist, and if he doesn't watch out he'll get himself bumped off."

In the corridor I again ran into Faxon, who always seemed oddly mobile for his weight and age. Forgetting his dislike of busybodies who pry into people's affairs, he buttonholed me to dilate on a "highly secret mission" he was launching to Manchuria as a farewell demonstration of his skill. "The key to success here in China is to go around corners. The original scheme was for our team to fly to Sian and then go on overland. But we couldn't get a flight to Sian. Then someone told me that this fellow Hu, the Kunming station master, could always get us on a Sian flight. To anyone not knowing China, that might seem like balls, but to check it out I sent for Hu. It seems he brings in rum from Indochina to supply the U.S. Navy mess. So naturally they'd be glad to do him this small favor of providing a plane to Sian. So we got the team off without difficulty. In this job one has to leave no stone unturned." I refrained from asking him whether the Kunming station master could be trusted to keep this highly secret mission highly secret. Faxon had generously forgotten Mr. Busybody. There was no point in reminding him of Mr. Knowall.

At the finance office I found I had now accumulated a demoralizing sum in per diem. Spurning PX rubbish, prostitutes, and imitation jade, I wired off the money to my wife to buy herself a baby piano for her birthday. This may have been a gesture of subconscious guilt.

At a Christmas party in OSS headquarters, with White Label scotch for the officers and Schlitz beer for the men, 8 already pre-opted women staff were being eyed by 150 mostly sex-starved men. And Tolman was going the rounds with his customary gleeful gaze and a breast-pocket full of loaded time pencils, one of which went off when it fell on the floor, thus causing an air-raid alert. This false alarm was shortly followed by a genuine alert, which nobody took seriously until the lights went out. We heard bombs dropping here and there; then came a piercing scream. But it turned out to be only an attempted rape. Candles had just been lit when a terrible crash upstairs made us fear our end had come. But it was another false scare: a couple who had made it had fallen out of bed and had brought down a desk full of objects. A final treat was in store when a major who had just arrived from Detachment 101 started shooting out the candles. This Wild West show had the remaining girls screaming as if they had all been raped. As I made my way home through the blackness toward the BAT house, I could not help thinking what a success Christianity was, that after nearly two thousand years our Savior's birth was still celebrated with such unrestrained exuberance.

I had no sooner gotten into bed than a loud knocking summoned me back to the front door, and there stood Liangski and Bob Lee. It seemed that because their plane had arrived in the middle of the air raid they could not get transportation into town, so these two had walked the six miles to solicit my help. After much frantic searching, I managed to borrow a weapons carrier. Waiting at the field were several others of the team and a load of baggage enough for a regiment. A fuming Bernard said that half of this belonged to Madame Tong. "I constantly ordered her to leave it behind, and even pitched it all out twice, but somehow or other she smuggled it back. I've already told both her and Janet they can look for other jobs."

All my leads to accommodation having failed, we were rescued by Bob Lee's suggestion that the group bed down at his sister's place a few miles out of town. She took this startling proposal in her stride. By the time we got the gang settled, it was almost dawn. "One good mark for Bob Lee," I remarked to Bernard.

"As a matter of fact he's been very useful all the way with Chinese officials, managing to convince them I'm second in importance only to Chennault." Although sometimes acidly ironic, Bernard was inherently very good-natured.

Some five or six hours later, when I was trying to wake myself up at a somewhat late breakfast, a weeping Janet called to see me and, with suitably broken voice and tearful eyes, told me she and her mother had been fired. "Oh, Lieutenant Fenn, please help us! When will Mr. Gordon be back?"

A pretty girl weeping crocodile tears has one final resource. Fortunately, Janet did not seek it; neither did I.

Virtue is its own reward. Needing to find another cipher clerk, I was introduced by Tsung-wei to Susan Chang, a Soochow girl with a lovely oval face, superb skin, high cheekbones, and large dark eyes. Her physique below the neck I could not judge, because by way of a dress she was wearing what looked like a clean but well-worn sack. A refugee from Tsing-Hua University in Peking, she had no money to buy clothes and little enough even for food. Speaking English with painstaking correctitude, she said (or words to that effect) that it was generous of me to employ someone like herself with no qualifications or experience, and she could only hope I would be good enough to be patient with her shortcomings until she acquired the necessary skills. "Indeed, I am most gratified for this opportunity to do something for the war effort. So I place myself entirely in your hands." Chinese girls can say things like this quite genuinely.

Having hesitantly accepted an invitation to a meal, she climbed into the jeep, an act Tsung-wei later described as evidence of her "forthright bravery," because riding in a jeep with an American serviceman could put any Chinese girl into the demi-reputation class as a professional. At lunch our conversation was largely about English literature: Shakespeare, Swift, and Coleridge, as well as "moderns" such as Hardy. And I shortly perceived that like Hardy she was inclined to be a pessimist. Her face reflected this melancholy, but when she smiled you would wonder if it was the same person.

Gordon had been offered twenty thousand rupees (then about £2,000) by the British in Chungking for "operating services" to be collected in Calcutta. We had agreed that I should collect it while he was away in Washington, together with certain radio equipment for the camp. This visit would also help to cement our good relations with the British.

Although a trip to India was something of a holiday, the flight was always likely to be grim. On this occasion it was worse than grim. Going over the Hump we almost hit a peak and finally flew so high to get above the weather that I briefly went into a coma from cold and lack of oxygen. Luckily someone noticed, and I hurriedly whiffed at the tube. But there was nothing to be done about the cold or about the constant creaks and groans of the ancient crate we flew in. Then after we refueled in Assam, one of the wheels would not go up while we were taking off, so we had to turn back for a check.

Once safely in Delhi, it was all living-it-up time. Thanks to a friend of Bernard's, I managed to get a room at the Maidans Hotel, have a spirited lunch with O'Donovan of British Force-136, and enjoy tea with Preston Grover, a former colleague at the Associated Press; Al Ravenholt, now of the United Press; and Peggy Durdin of Time-Life. The liveliness of this trio lent the tea party a champagne sparkle.

On New Year's Eve, a company named Caltex gave a party at the Maidans. In addition to a generous supply of drink, there was one woman to every three men instead of every thirty. Among them was my old associate in MO-Washington, Dorothy L. We made a date for dinner for the following evening.

Checking in next morning at the OSS headquarters, I found another old acquaintance, Dave Hunter, formerly ground crew with the Flying Tigers and now, with the rank of major, operations chief for the OSS-Delhi headquarters. Planes ascend at an angle, but balloons go straight up. After we had exchanged the usual small talk, he informed me that a new OSS directive required all personnel to conduct counterespionage in addition to their regular duties. And after a brief stalling around, he threw at me point-blank: "It's time you told us the lowdown on Gordon and his outfit. What are they really up to with all this crap about 'independence' and playing up to the British as well as the French and Chinese?"

"I've said everything I know in my reports. Haven't you read them?"

"Certainly I have. I've also read reports that tell a different story."

"So you have to decide whom to believe. That's the trick, after all, don't you agree?" It was curious how different this Dave Hunter was from the Dave Hunter I had known in the American Volunteer Group. I guess he thought the same thing about me.

Dorothy L. and I had dinner at the Cecil, where the elegant dining room was adorned with snow-white linen, shining silverware, crystal goblets, and flowers, while the orchestra played "Pomp and Circumstance" and turbaned waiters glided in hushed reverence among the pukka sahibs and a scattering of female adornments. We were later joined by two old friends visiting from China: journalist "Eppie" Epstein and Elsie Fairfax-Cholmondeley, who had worked for the Chinese Industrial Co-operatives. Tall, blonde, gracious, and as elegantly Anglo-Saxon as the royal box at Ascot, Eppie had thrown all that over in favor of the hard life in China, where she had recently married left-wing Epstein, four inches shorter but outstandingly clever and well informed. He predicted that American support of the Communists in China would lift them halfway to controlling all of China. "When the war is over you Americans will immediately reverse this policy, but it will be too late to prevent a complete takeover." When in 1949 this prediction proved to be correct, the Epsteins were given jobs by Chou En-lai, but were later "disgraced" like so many intellectuals, whether Chinese or foreign, and not rehabilitated until Mao was dead.

I had dinner the next day with Major Gibson of the British G-2, who told me they had increased Gordon's rupees to thirty thousand. "He's well worth it— I only wish it were more. I suppose you chaps are bound to take him over? It seems a pity, because—in my opinion—his group gains so much from operating right across the board. But it's inevitable that America will run more and more of everything from now on. Even against the Soviet Union we shall have to take second place." At that time even the worst pessimist would not have predicted how far down the list Britain would go.

A large contingent of OSS top brass had now arrived in Delhi, including both Heppner and Herb Little, who with his usual Pollyanna glow was full of plans, good cheer, and compliments. "I've just been in Ceylon, where you made a big impression on your brief visit, and they'd like to have you down there permanently. But I want you to run the Chinese show for MO instead of this present work you're doing."

About a half hour later, I ran into Heppner, and he said, "Carry on with Gordon's group until we decide what to do about them." Or until Gordon decides what to do about OSS, I was thinking.

A cipher expert traveling with this contingent explained about the new "one-time" code pads. "Almost any code you can operate with agents can be broken within about fifteen hours when experts get to work on it. But these particular pads contain a different letter code for every message. At the other end of your radio hookup the operator has a duplicate pad. You start off with number 1, and having used that, you both destroy it and go on to the next. It would be too time consuming for the enemy to break it, since he would get only the contents of that one message and then have to start all over." We subsequently used these one-time pads whenever possible and had reason to think them highly foolproof.

I was invited to a cocktail party given by Prince Ferooza, who frequently offered lavish hospitality to British and American personnel (officers or top civilians only) in one of his palaces. If the British raj was splendiferous, it was, after all, only an attempt to keep up with the magnificence of Indian display. The decor of this particular palace was like a stage set for *Il Seraglio* devised by Hollywood. The food and drink were appropriately prodigal. But the lovely Indian women who sat around in exotic saris sipping champagne all belonged to either Ferooza or other rich Indians and were more untouchable than the Untouchables.

The party was in fact to celebrate the prince's birthday, and the American top brass were anxious to give a present appropriate to the prince's unceasing hospitality. Unfortunately, he already had everything anyone could think of. Then it was learned that he had run out of tennis balls to service his four courts, so a scramble had been organized to collect any not-too-threadbare specimens. In this way nine well-brushed balls were assembled and when packed three-square in a box looked neat if not elegant.

Meanwhile, Major Gibson had taken the problem all the way up to Mountbatten, who asked, "What does a year's supply amount to?"

"Three hundred dozen," suggested Gibson, after a few moments' thought.

"There are seven million Indians devoted to Ferooza," remarked Mountbatten. So three hundred dozen were flown out on the next RAF flight.

"Fortunately," remarked Gibson, when he told me this story, "tennis balls are still one thing our chaps make lots of."

Due to fly out from Delhi to Calcutta next morning, I was waiting for transport in the hotel lobby when a British colonel came up and introduced himself. "Thought you might like to join us at the bar for a drink." As it was only ten thirty in the morning, I almost declined but just in time noticed that he had two sweet-looking RAF girls in tow! Having followed him over, I felt more pepped up by just looking at them than by the double gin and lime he gave me. After a few preliminaries, the colonel, who, with some signals from the girls, had no doubt been sizing me up, said, "What about joining us for luncheon?" The temptation to miss the plane hit me like a blow. But at that very moment the taxi arrived and, as it were, spirited me away almost before I had time to thank the colonel and say goodbye to the sweet RAF girls whose own smiling goodbye revealed just enough disappointment to suggest all the joys our further acquaintance might have offered.

While checking in at OSS headquarters in Calcutta, almost the first person I came across was Dorothy L., who had arrived the day before. "I'm so glad you're here, too, because I want your advice about an MO plan I'm working on which requires cooperation with the British, which I know you're so good at," she said. At Schools and Training, all OSS personnel were taught how to use a two-edged dagger and actually furnished with a very pretty specimen when going out into the field. But I do not know of anyone who had occasion to use it, whereas verbal daggers were used all the time, and not necessarily on one's enemies.

I was to pick up the rupees from Colonel Gregory of the Special Operations Executive. He was out when I called, but his number two man, Major Miller, at once offered me the use of a small flat at the back of their office. What a haven! Two rooms and a balcony looked down on a garden bright with tropical flowers and palm trees, punctuated at the far end with a quaint Victorian summer house trimmed in red and blue. A terrier dog belonging to Gregory (who lived in the adjacent flat) came nuzzling at my feet. Until the day warmed up this animal wore a coat of pale blue suede edged with yellow braid.

While calling at OSS-Communications to arrange about the large transmitter we were getting for Kunming, I again ran into Dorothy. "When can we discuss those plans—will this afternoon suit you?" I sighed and agreed that it would.

Walking eastward to Calcutta's distinctly less-elite quarter, I tracked down the flat where John Vincent was briefly visiting his wife, who worked for the British Ministry of Information (equivalent of the U.S. Office of War Information) but not as well paid. The decrepit one-room flat was presently titivated with rugs John had brought down from Lanchow. His wife glowed like the rugs and had the same simple peasant quality, and their baby girl was what you might expect from such parents. While we were chatting I observed the Indian ayah lovingly wipe the baby's mouth with what looked like a floor cloth. Upon

Irene's frantic protests the ayah assured her there was no need to worry because she had been careful to wring out the cloth first.

India was then a slave state, and you were seldom allowed to forget it. Calling in at the Chinese Travel Service (run by the Chinese government) to inquire about flights to Kunming I was received by a Chinese already made haughty by the presence of an enslaved population so that he answered my questions with barely polite indifference while at the same time bargaining with an Indian peddling oranges and giving the fellow hell over a matter of two annas. In a shop where I had earlier bought hardware for the camp, I called back to collect the packages they had meanwhile been wrapping. The shopkeeper bowed obsequiously. "Yes, sahib, your packages, sahib, immediately, sahib!" And almost in the same breath he yelled over his shoulder, "Bearer!" When a shriveled, almost-naked creature sprang out of a hole in the wall, the shopkeeper barked at him in English, "The sahib's packages, quick, you fool!" pointing to my three small packages lying on the floor. The bearer lifted the packages and placed them carefully into the arms of his boss, who then ritually asked the sahib whether the sahib would like to carry them himself or whether the bearer should carry them.

One of Miller's Indian clerks disclosed that an Indian friend of his who worked at OSS headquarters had been asked to contact him and discreetly probe my reasons for being in Calcutta and particularly for staying at Gregory's hangout. "You can rely on Jawal to know nothing," Miller assured me.

A letter appeared in the *Calcutta Statesman* from a girl signing herself "Anglo-Indian" (a term that can mean "British but living in India" but in this instance meant of mixed parentage). She claimed to have been "betrayed" by an American soldier who had then promised, had indeed *pleaded,* to marry her, but his CO forbade the marriage and had him sent home. Now she was having this baby and had lost her job. So by the time the letter appeared, she would have drowned herself in the tanks (water reservoir). The American authorities insisted the letter was a fake and said the *Statesman* should never have printed it. It was subsequently traced to someone working for the British service magazine *Victory.* This caused explosions all along the line: because this man had been sacked, the staff went on strike, and publication ceased. Deprived readers then staged demonstrations, some anti-British, some anti-American, and some anti-Eurasian. Finally, there were anti-Indian demonstrations because a great many of the *Statesman* staff were Indian!

"There you have it," said Miller. "What with the overcrowding, mixed races, and social unrest there's always such a ferment bubbling in Calcutta that the least thing can cause a riot."

A wire came from Bernard asking if I could bring back a case of scotch. "Unprocurable," said Gregory, "except at fabulous prices! Two gallon-jars of Indian rum would offer a good deal more elevation at one twentieth of the price. What do you think?"

"Dear Harry's so fond of scotch—it's his only indulgence. So I'll take him one bottle." I had a job to find even that, at no matter what price.

The colonel himself drank Indian gin steadily from morning to night, interspersed with fastidious pinches of snuff, specks of which he flicked off his uniform with the index finger of one hand, usually to emphasize some point in one of his many stories, while with the other hand he stroked his necktie made from the kind of plaited cotton threads in variegated shades of khaki one got in wartime sewing kits. These stories, he insisted, were only prompted by the pleading of his blue-coated terrier. "He's just like a child," said Gregory, "in wanting me to tell him stories."

I suppose it was a trick he had taught the dog, but it did in fact place its head upon Gregory's feet and emit a brief whine, whereupon the colonel would reflect a moment before getting launched.

Once when I was out hunting tigers with a fellow officer and an Indian bearer, a large specimen suddenly popped his head out of the jungle before we had time to take aim. The bearer was petrified with fright, my companion leapt into a pond at the side of the path, and I myself fired at random. This luckily scared the beast off. But my pal now found himself caught up in the frightful thorns half submerged in the pond, couldn't extricate himself, and seemed to be imminently drowning.

"Guard the weapons!" I yelled to the bearer—an instinctive order in a wartime environment. And hurriedly stripping down, I clambered into the pond. But in my seminude condition the thorns were so lacerating I was soon horribly entangled. "Don't just stand there, you idiot," I yelled to the bearer. "Help to pull me out!" But the wretched fellow was taking no chances of being pulled in himself. "Sorry, sahib, can't help you, sahib. Officer-sahib order me to guard weapons, dare not disobey officer-sahib!"—pretending not to recognize the half-nude man in the pond! At last I managed to clamber out and subsequently hauled out my friend. But after twenty minutes' artificial respiration I realized he was dead beyond recall. Poor Gerald, a rugger blue [a top player in rugby football], too.

After the colonel had helped himself to another drink, the dog resettled on his feet and gave another little whine.

Oh, you want another story? Very well, just one more, then it's beddy-byes. Let's see now . . . In '35 or thereabouts I sailed out of Saigon on a ship loaded up in steerage with some sixty Chinese coolies who had slipped into Indochina without permits and were being shipped back to their homeland. At that time there was not only civil war in China but widespread famine plus a cholera epidemic. So all these Chinese were desperate to stay on in FIC [French Indochina].

After the ship sailed, one of them stripped down to his shorts, tied his money in a sash round his head, and jumped into the swirling river, which was actually teeming with crocodiles. We all held our breath as he was whirled away downstream. But he managed to breast the current and was soon scrambling up the bank. So very soon another Chinese tried the same thing. About halfway to the shore he looked like [he was] drowning but was picked up by a sampan. Meanwhile, we were sailing rapidly downstream, with the river getting wider and wider and the open sea not far off. The rest of the Chinese decided that what two men could do, they all might do, but soon it would be too late. So one by one they began jumping off into the river. Some of them couldn't swim a stroke and drowned after a few gurgles. Others disappeared from sight as if pulled down by crocs. The majority, however, were swept out to sea. Out of the whole sixty not ten reached shore!

Another drink and another whimper.

Now you're being naughty! But all right, since we've got company. Just a short one and that's definitely all. A friend and I went to a party in Saigon where two Annamite girls had—sh, sh—performed on each other—you wouldn't know about that. Afterwards I procured this toy they'd used called a phallus, made of leather and rubber, to keep as a souvenir. Some months later when I went home on leave, I had to pass through customs. And it wasn't until I had to open my bag that I remembered about the phallus. The customs man held it up like Miss Liberty's torch. "What's this then?" he asked me sharply. When I told him it was a kid's toy blackjack, he gave me a look and so did about twenty other travelers lined up with their bags! . . . Now that's definitely all; off you go!

—whereupon the terrier trotted back to his pad.

My last day in Calcutta was something of a nightmare. Wanting to buy a phonograph, I chased round for hours before finding anything suitable. There were, of course, no new ones, and the used ones were mostly battered wrecks. For our office girls I had promised to buy underwear, unprocurable in China. They all needed different sizes, types, and colors—what a circus! Then came the red tape in connection with my flight. Recently a concession had been given to the Chinese national airlines to operate this route instead of the U.S. Army doing it. For this chore one was forced to check in at three different locations. My baggage was, of course, considerably overweight, but although I paid for it, there was a big argument. Then at the last minute the British censor insisted on checking my papers. Because my notes were all in shorthand, he decided to keep the lot. Dear Miller, who, together with his wife, had given me unremitting help and hospitality during my stay, again came to my rescue. "Don't worry, I'll send it on by safe courier," he promised, which he faithfully did. There are some people who do you endless favors, and you never can understand why they bother.

Also on this plane, with a large new team of MO personnel, was Herb Little. Having at last despaired of China's T. E. Lawrence, he got in several digs about my trip to India, which everyone in OSS had been querying and nobody could explain. Although I told Little about the transmitter and other technical equipment, I said nothing about the thirty thousand rupees, nor did I mention that my visit to Delhi was mostly to chat up the British. When I had first met Little he was quite pro-British. But as the war developed he, like almost everyone else, grew more and more xenophobic until you would almost think it was the Allies we were fighting instead of the Axis.

We flew all night in appalling weather, with the plane periodically free falling to an ultimate check that thudded the fuselage into a shuddering groan. So almost every passenger arrived sick as a dog.

At OSS headquarters de Sibour gloomily informed me there had been another big fuss about my trip. After examining my "go anywhere" orders, he remarked, "These will have to be corrected." Luckily, he did not ask to retain them, which might have caused some small argument when I questioned his right.

The flying circus, formerly in India, had now arrived in Kunming, along with Wedemeyer, Donovan, and other top brass. The Kunming OSS hierarchy had the whole camp jumping through hoops to get everything just so. Nobody could get any transport because all the vehicles had to be left in the compound in order to make a show, but, as Bernard remarked, who was to be impressed by this lineup, and how, and why, would remain appropriately secret. Meanwhile, the yard was swept clean, the flags were put out, and no Chinese or low-grade American personnel were permitted to be hanging around. What they could not keep out was a team of water buffalo who came crowding in off the road and, failing to force the barrier, left the entranceway deep in shit. Everyone blamed the farmer, but Tan said Tai Li had really organized the demo.

Charles Fenn in 1942 (then a first lieutenant) after being awarded a Pistol Expert medal.

Fenn using indigenous transportation in China, 1942.

General Claire Chennault (center, looking away from camera) of the Flying Tigers (American Volunteer Group) with his pilots.

General Chennault briefs his pilots in the American Volunteer Group before operations, 1942.

Three of the Flying Tigers' (American Volunteer Group) "sharks" over China, 1942.

Burial ceremony for five American Volunteer Group personnel killed in action, 1943.

Fenn (sitting to the right) awaits transport in central China, 1943.

Checking the parachutes, central China, 1943.

General Chennault with Generalissimo Chiang Kai-shek and Madame Chiang, 1943.

American Volunteer Group pilots and ground crew in the hostel supplied by Chiang Kai-shek.

Fenn meets with an Indian officer in Delhi, 1943.

Fenn receives the Chinese Order of the Cloud on board an American Navy ship in 1945.

11

KUNMING

Feeling I had already trespassed too long on the hospitality of my friends, the enemy BAT, I was hoping to move into our new camp, but it still was not ready. So I fixed up a temporary berth with a friend of Tsung-wei's, a Mrs. Lieng, who was teaching in a local school. A cultivated middle-aged woman, she had inherited a small house in town from her husband, who had recently died of typhus (which had failed to kill me a year earlier). My room was bare and very cold, the lavatory consisted of two boards perched over a bucket (invariably full), and I had to wash at the pump, but because this resembled the accommodation I had often had during earlier days in China, it did not bother me much. And it offered the advantage of seclusion.

Bernard had meanwhile used the rupees to buy a small house in town, very suburban but comfortable, and had assembled furniture and some equipment. When everything was organized, he invited Tan, Liangski, and me to celebrate with dinner. "We've only got chairs for four," he explained when I asked about the others. Having loaded up the jeep with food, we took along the cook and one of the mess boys. On the way into town the cook told us of suckling pigs for sale at a farm along the route. When we drove in to buy one, two Chinese soldiers with ponies were buying eggs. Tan playfully suggested they let two of us ride the ponies while they went in the jeep. They accepted this swap with great glee. So having agreed to rendezvous at a teahouse in town, Tan and I galloped off.

Approaching Kunming through back streets, we were hailed by MPs in a jeep. "Hey, you guys, what the hell! This is off limits!"

"Chinese cavalry!" yelled Tan as we galloped around them, and we reached the teahouse before they could turn and catch up with us. The others were already waiting for us, so we quickly handed over the ponies and sat down in the open-ended teahouse. When the MPs came zooming up they were totally confounded to find there were actually two Chinese soldiers on the ponies.

With the celebration dinner we "bottomed up" a little too much mao-tai, that most fiery of Chinese spirits; Liangski soon went scarlet in the face and almost speechless; Tan told noisy stories; and Bernard, who had heard them all, took a consoling nip of scotch. I myself kept thinking that, chairs or no chairs, we should have brought our girls along and sat them on our laps.

Mac Wong, one of my former agents in Patpo, a personable, Westernized, missionary-educated Chinese who also claimed to be a U.S. citizen, invited me to dinner at Kunming's new "tennis club," which was mostly a nightclub. Mac brought along his latest girlfriend, who never stopped talking "Hongkong English" (English picked up by some of the Hong Kong Chinese population) about fun, money, success, and bright lights, which suitably matched both Mac's character and the atmosphere of the tennis club. A U.S. colonel at a nearby table was so drunk that he twice fell on the floor. At another table a Red Cross woman in her forties was being pawed by two lieutenants. Every so often she would absentmindedly remove their hands from various parts of her anatomy and murmur with a half-drunken smile, "Now, now, boys . . ." In contrast, there were, at various tables, at least a dozen U.S. officers and two or three civilian women who were behaving with bored perfection. Mac showed me some beautiful "jewel" jade (despised by connoisseurs) he had bought while in Macao and for which he wanted a beautiful price.

Mrs. Lieng had a party for someone's birthday. There were eight or ten Chinese sitting on hard square chairs in a line against the wall and smiling happily but not saying a word except "thank you" when handed another cake. But the party was suddenly transformed by the arrival of several celebrants from a local wedding who came bouncing in with mildly alcoholic gush, followed by the children fantastically dressed in Western-style sunsuits, which Mrs. Lieng told me was their "party dress" worn only on such special occasions. By the time this crowd had all used the bucket, the "lavatory" floor was awash, so I had no option but to use the courtyard. I was halfway through my performance before I realized that this area was overlooked by a teahouse where some of the patrons were curious to know how Western genitalia differed from the Eastern counterpart.

Calling in at the Red Cross for a coffee, I was served by Eva Ho, who, having apparently forgiven me, sat down for a chat. "Once did She hold the gorgeous east in fee; and was the safeguard of the west," as Wordsworth said, but now, it seemed, she was sharing a room with three others, and there was never any privacy. "They not only bring in men friends, but even kiss and hug, meanwhile calling me a crabbed old spoilsport," she reported.

We had talked for only five minutes when the boss of the hostel, a fading blonde hiding her wrinkled neck with costume jewelry, came up to ask, with withering politeness, "Miss Ho, will you kindly have a word with me when disengaged?" Poor Eva turned her head aside as if she had been slapped—a sharp Chinese movement of shame.

When at last we moved in, our new GBT camp proved a joy. On that first morning (and on most subsequent mornings), I sat out to have my simple breakfast in the rising sun. Silhouetted against the glowing ball, a string of Chinese soldiers on ponies made a long black frieze. On the riverbank lower down, women were hauling up buckets of water, cleaning vegetables, or slapping their washing on the stones. In the rice fields, blue-clad farmers were trudging off to their labors. Water buffalo made dark patches. As the sun came up, blue sky and greenish brown landscape faded off to a veil of yellow dust stirred up on the distant road by peasants going to market.

Electricity had been put in from our gasoline generator, and after the day's work I fixed up a reading lamp in my room and read Koestler's *Arrival and Departure,* lent me by Vincent. It told of a terrible world—full of horror and the desolation of the human spirit. A girl seduced explained why she accepted an outrage not physically enforced: "You keep on protesting; then comes a moment of weakness, and you think, 'Why struggle any longer, what does it matter?' So in that moment, out of weakness, you give in. And while the man ruts and sweats and gasps for breath, you lie there inert, remembering the ethereal embrace you had imagined at puberty . . ." How often the sexual act for some poor women must be like that!

Little confided that Heppner wanted to send me home. "Coughlin told him that you always cause trouble. No one doubts your ability, Charles, but it can't be denied you do get people mad. But I reminded Colonel Heppner of all you had accomplished, and he finally agreed you could stay on and do a great new job I have in mind for you—running our new MO training school in Kunming!" I was briefly shaken. Might I really be thus entrapped? But as things turned out, that was the last I heard of this menace.

Meanwhile, de Sibour (still kept on hooks!) told me that he had now straightened everything out. I was to go on working with the group and help to bring them into the OSS orbit; this was being arranged with Gordon in

Washington. Although I was skeptical of this information, we were indeed given most of the equipment we asked for, albeit grudgingly. AGAS help in setting up the complicated radio transmitters was, on the other hand, given quite cheerfully. To replace Janet Tong as cipher clerk, Tsung-wei found us another of his earnest but attractive girlfriends, Miss Lillian Chen, who had features like the Chinese goddess of mercy and a gaze of nunlike innocence. She had formerly worked in a Catholic mission, although she was now a devoted Communist. When Tsung-wei teased her about the former, she retorted, "There are many good things in Christianity!"

"Better not let them hear you utter such blasphemies at Party headquarters!" said Tsung-wei, as if seriously.

At the entrance to our compound we built a little guardhouse where two Chinese soldiers were detailed off for guard duty, one taking turns as sentry while the other slept, shopped, cooked, or cleaned up. They lived in their box in all kinds of weather and never seemed to go anywhere except to the lavatory or to buy their simple wants, yet I never passed them without getting a smile. It struck me they might be glad to earn a few PX trifles in return for helping us pump water from the stream into an overhead tank for our cold showers. Indeed, the guards seemed glad to help, and for about a week all went well. Then their efforts slackened and at last petered out. The sergeant on patrol subsequently informed me, not without embarrassment, "The difficulty is that their rice ration is based on 'no hard work.' So when they do this pumping, their energy gives out. If you'd like to supply them with some extra bowls of rice, I'm sure there'd be no problems." He was right. Like those boatmen on the sampan, all you had to do was to put the necessary fuel into the tank.

The weather continued perfect: warm sun all day and cool, starlit nights. And each morning I had breakfast on the riverbank. On most days we would receive intelligence from agents, some by radio, some by messenger, and send, code, decode, and circulate it to all our outlets. In the evening, around our charcoal braziers, we wrote reports and sent off further inquiries, answers, and instructions. Everything was ticking over nicely when a frantic message from André, then back in Hanoi, told us he was being harassed by the French authorities because he had been reported to be working for the Americans! Even the Free French were now anti-American because we Americans would not recognize French rights to Indochina, whereas the British had done so. Churchill and de Gaulle had made this arrangement to recognize each other's colonies on a reciprocal basis, but Roosevelt, disliking colonialism, had naturally opposed it.

As a result, all our agents now found it difficult to get information and even more difficult to keep up radio schedules.

Despite this handicap, André now managed to rescue two pilots and to keep us advised of his progress in getting them to the border, where AGAS agreed to send a plane to pick them up. While I was arranging this with their CO, Colonel Wichtrich, he suggested, rather cautiously, that I might like to team up with them. "If you can clear it with OSS and General Wedemeyer, please put my name down," I told the colonel. I thought from the start that I could happily work with him. The *hsu* I had experienced with Gordon is what I now felt with Wichtrich.

Susan Chang had arrived in the camp with two woven bamboo cases: a larger, rather heavy one, and a small one no bigger than an attaché case. I later on learned that this small one held her clothes, and the larger one contained nothing but books. The first two days she was with us she walked around in a daze, hardly saying a word, and I feared we should have to get rid of her. Then suddenly came a transformation: she woke up, got on with her work, learned rapidly to encode, speeded up her typing, and began to talk.

We arranged for Mac Sin to go to the OSS parachute school so that he could be dropped into a key point inside Indochina. Tan, always a joker, told him that for the first week the trainees had to jump without chutes to get toughened up, and the smallest would have to jump first to get the effect of what height the others could safely jump from. Mac was taken aback but "determined to be brave." When he learned that it was a joke, his puckish face broke into a sweet smile of relief. He never took exception to our leg-pulling, feeling confident we all "loved" him. But Susan was dismayed by it all: first by the terrible prospect of jumping, then even more that it was only a cruel joke.

To placate the French establishment in Indochina, Bernard and I decided it might help if I went down to the border and met some of their officers. I might at the same time help André get the two pilots across the border. To keep in touch with the camp I took along Lao, one of our radio operators. But as we were about to fly off on the first leg of this journey, our enemy, fog, closed in down south. "It might be days before it clears," the pilot told me gloomily. "The whole of last Christmas we were trapped down in that dump—can you imagine! Kunming promised to try and drop in some Christmas goodies if it cleared even briefly, which it did on Christmas Eve, three cheers! And we all yelled like crazy when down from the skies came six or eight bundles! But we noticed they seemed kind of long, and when we tore them open they were Chinese carrying poles—destined for the coolies working on the strip!"

In this plane we were due to fly in, a Fourteenth Air Force team was also going down with a cargo of fragmentation bombs already loaded alongside our seats, each of them marked heavily in red, "WARNING! Do not knock, jar, kick or tread upon!" Three times we were ordered aboard for a takeoff, and each time both the bomb team and the pilots played games up and down the aisle with total disregard to these warnings. While I was in Kweilin, one of these bombs had exploded when the two Chinese carriers had slipped, killing one and half killing the other. So I told these bomb-happy Fourteenth Air Force children that I would rather die in bed. "Calm down, lieutenant," said the sergeant. "We have been transporting these loads for months. Them notices are a load of horse shit!" Job's comfort indeed!

While we were still waiting, Tan came to tell us that André had already gotten the pilots across. "And get a load of this! One of them had been totally brainwashed by some pro-German French nurse who had given him medical treatment en route. Amongst all the crap she told him was a story that the Germans are working on a secret weapon that's at least a hundred times more powerful than their present rockets and makes it absolutely certain they will win the war overnight! When André asked her where she got this peculiar information, she said, 'Through occult means!' Had she been pro-American instead of pro-German, she might have got it right."

On the third morning, when we were again alerted for a takeoff and about to board, a P-51, coming in to land, careered off the runway, plowed into a truck full of Chinese soldiers, turned a somersault, and landed upside down in a second truckful. Unbelievably, the pilot crawled out alive from his demolished plane and stood there swaying, but did not fall. It turned out he was, in fact, only superficially cut and bruised. The rest of the scene was ghastly beyond description, with bodies littered as on a battlefield, the blood still welling out, splashed across the grass in shining streaks. Fifteen soldiers perished in this disaster, with an equal number crippled for life. I thought the pilot would have been better off dead than have to go on living with this memory. But he only said, "It's the luck of the game," and went off deploring his broken tooth.

Flying high above the fog, we had the usual bitterly cold trip and then dropped through the blanket with a series of lurches that ripped one's stomach out. Then nose-diving into the valley, we felt the plane warming up, and as we came into the clear, the mountains were so close that the plane slid over the edge as if on skis. A few minutes later we stepped out into semitropical humidity. The fragmentation bombs having been off-loaded with further catch-ball antics, the plane was reloaded with Chinese sick or wounded from somewhere down the line, including six or eight cholera victims. "Before we get them off-loaded," groaned the pilot, "they'll paint the deck brown with shit. If the doc had been there, he'd have fixed it so they'd all die peacefully, with a quick hygienic burial, instead of dragging it out."

The airfield "hostel" was only a collection of tents and shacks, with a taller hut as a control tower. The CO, Major Clites, said he could give me a weapons carrier as far as Tengyuan, but the track would need horses from there on, and they were hard to get. Luckily, my friend Frank Shu had moved down here for his smuggling operations and gave me a letter to the magistrate in Tengyuan that he said would do the trick. As Faxon had so rightly said, you have to know the right people.

This way-out forward post had sunk into the squalor of the cave, and we snatched our rations sitting around on old crates amid piles of litter thrown all around since the camp was started. Clites was sharing a shack with the camp doctor who was then away, so I was offered his bed for the night. The shack was a junk shop of clothing, equipment, medicines, rations, and litter scattered pell-mell. Several boxes of rations had been opened merely to use ingredients such as coffee powder and chocolate bars, and it was no doubt in search of the remaining contents that once the lights were out rats came marching in four abreast. There being no window, the door was left open, and in the moonbeams slanting through I could watch them performing maneuvers up and across the door lintel. I was thinking of chasing them out and shutting the door when Clites came in and, having left the door open, started setting traps. Several rats were caught in an instant, the traps going off like pistol shots, and all the other rats hurtled off into the night. When Clites sat down in the doorway, I thought he was enjoying the moonlight, but he had a more practical objective. When the rats again began climbing up the door jamb, Clites would grab them and dash them to the floor. From time to time he would gather up a stunned rat by its tail and wham it dead against the floorboards. Sleep finally rescued me from this bizarre diversion.

I woke up the next morning convinced it had all been a nightmare. Clites was sleeping peacefully in his bunk, and there was no sign of rats either in traps or on the floor. But then I saw, out there in the morning sunshine, a Chinese boy busily skinning the corpses. It seemed that Clites was having a coat made from these rat skins and had already collected 240 of the 300 it would require. As he told me later: "I'll have the only genuine ratskin coat in all Minnesota!"

Despite the prevailing chaos, the cook served up generous portions of bacon and eggs—what ambrosia! In the Navy Intelligence hut I learned that André had also brought to the border three Frenchmen: an army captain, an engineer, and the former governor of Cambodia, who had been imprisoned for three years on charges of pro-Gaullism. I also learned that the Civilian Conservation Corps was the second-string contact for horses.

The road to Tengyuan was so comparatively good that the truck got us there in an hour. Because it stopped outside the CCC camp, I checked with them first about horses, but the major in charge said the magistrate was the man to see. "And I just had a note from him about two pilots." He handed me a slip of Chinese rice paper on which was carefully inscribed with a brush, "Two frymen you ask about have now come across river from Indoor-China."

After arranging for the horses and escort guards, magistrate Tong invited me to dinner and a subsequent movie, organized by one of the town's wealthier inhabitants. The movie was shown in an old temple, with the usual life-sized gods crumbling inside against the walls. The projector, hand operated, went clicking away like a mechanical lawn mower, often so slowly that when the operator grew tired or absentminded the eyes began to register the individual frames. The first item was a preview of next week's feature film, dated 1915, starring Bertha Ford. The current feature film had just started when there came an air raid alarm. Although half the audience panicked and went to the exit, the film went clicking on regardless. This Chinese epic, silent of course, bore captions in both Chinese and English. One of the latter read: "I wish to meet you in the breech—[bridge?]—come this night." It was the story of a married woman in love with a young admirer who was an expert swordsman. Arriving one night at the lady's house when her husband was away (although quite by chance), he was given shelter. When she visited him in his room and carefully closed the door behind her, the snoozing GIs in the audience perked up hopefully and even whistled when the young woman addressed him passionately. But alas for the vanity of the human hopes and joys! The caption read: "I wish you to give me a display of your military arts!"

12

MISERY IN THE MOUNTAINS

The soldiers and horses having been promised for five in the morning, I was up at four to get the loading organized. But it was after six before the horses arrived—five instead of six, with a half-dozen coolies to replace the missing horse. The track was a mere mountain path, with boulders periodically falling down from the heights above and often blocking the route entirely. Although I mostly rode, it was often easier to walk because of the constant dismounting. The coolies carrying eighty-pound loads tripped along hour after hour with only brief pauses to eat their cold rice rations.

Although the weather seemed wintry enough, wild cherry trees were already thick with blossom, and the shrubbery tinkled with birdsong. Amid the rocky wilderness a few scattered inhabitants had hand gouged some beautifully terraced rice paddies. From time to time we would wind round sugarloaf peaks towering up out of the mist in poetic glory. More rarely we would meet a string of peasants carrying enormous loads of wood, charcoal, vegetables, ducks, and chickens—the birds strung alive by their legs or packed in baskets, with their heads poking out in wild-eyed terror. One group carried pigs, securely strung up to prevent their struggling and consequently losing weight in transit.

When we stopped to eat at a shack, the occupant blew up a fire out of twigs and made hot water for our tea. From a woman carrying oranges to market from a distant point down south, I bought several dozen and shared them around. To go with our cold rice we had only bits of tough chicken, but appetite made the dish tasty. Arriving at Sunshi in late afternoon, we put up in a farmer's shack, got a charcoal fire going, and cooked rice and eggs. By distributing a cigarette to each of the soldiers and coolies, I earned a lot of cheap gratitude. Crouching over our small fire, soldiers chatted happily as they eked out the last half inch, but the coolies smoked theirs avidly before sinking into total exhaustion, with nothing to protect them from the cold night beyond the rags they wore all day. While crawling into my sleeping bag (more precious than rubies), I could hear the horses in the adjoining room snorting, farting, pissing, and dropping offerings of redolent dung. After sleeping soundly, the sharp chill of predawn made me also want to urinate. "Oh, to be a horse!" I thought, hearing the rain now pattering down outside. But there was nothing for it but to brave the black wetness.

When getting up at dawn I found the coolies had disappeared. Soft-hearted Lao then revealed that on the previous evening they had insisted on being paid for their day's work, and he did not have the heart to refuse. "Why the hell not!" I yelled. "You might have guessed that with this cold and wet they'd probably slope off!" Poor wretches, why would they not! That was the curse of coolie labor: you accepted using it and shut your eyes to the suffering, but you could not shut out the guilt.

It took us more than an hour to round up another team, all this in icy rain. We had also had a change of horses, and I now had a bad-tempered beast that kicked and snapped every time I dismounted, which, thanks to crags and pitfalls, was often enough. But I really should have been grateful he was so sure-footed on these treacherously muddy slopes that might easily have tumbled the pair of us down a thousand-foot slope. The rain penetrated everything: raincoat, uniform, shoes, and cap. The coolies glistened in their soaked blue rags like seals emerging from the depths.

At a community of huts where we stopped to get hot water, an old woman selling tea, peanut oil, and pickled roots also had—incredibly!—sugared popcorn. Lao bought a huge bagful and shared it round with that glee that suffused his saturnine features whenever he could offer small services. I made up some soup from my so-called mountain rations and eked it out with cold rice and popcorn.

Meanwhile, two travelers had arrived, one going north and the other south. The first, a merchant from Indochina, wore a tattered grass cape, an old trilby hat, and a pair of steel spectacles halfway down his nose. These, however, were his least remarkable accoutrements, because his merchandise consisted of an enormous load of "footballs" tied in clusters at each end of his carrying pole. They totally obscured him when he had come toward us, so he had looked like a creature from outer space. It seemed that he had invested half his fortune in these footballs (mere inflated spheres of thick rubber), the other half going to maintain himself while making this five-hundred-mile journey on foot to a Chinese town where footballs (used mostly in basketball) commanded a profitable price. Although handicapped by this appallingly awkward burden, he had crossed several mountain ranges, negotiated a swift, deep river as well as several smaller ones, and, finally, eluded armed guards on both sides of the border. "By making this trip twice a year," he told us, "I manage to live quite comfortably." When Lao translated this, I laughed, but I should have cried.

The traveler heading south was a girl. Wearing a long green corduroy coat and a Chinese soldier's cap, she looked almost as bizarre as the football merchant. Puckish rather than pretty, she radiated a certain charm with her bright smile and eager flow of talk. It seemed that Lao knew her already, which was perhaps why she suddenly appeared.

We were now going over a mountain pass that the Chinese had torn into gaping holes, now full of ice-coated mud, to stop the Japanese from using it. So we had to haul ourselves along with ropes, while the horses made perilous detours along the mountainside. The stunted foliage was now draped with ice pearls, and the rare trees were weighted with icicles. Then, after two hours of this misery, we were suddenly over the pass and going down into Tienpso, with bright-green mimosa trees already showing a haze of yellow bloom and occasional palm trees reminding us of the unbelievable fact that this area was actually as far south as Cuba.

The chief of police received us royally, with hot tea, hot towels, a good meal, and a place to sleep. When Lao discovered that, despite my pan of burning charcoal, I was still cold, he warmed up a brick in the oven to put in my sleeping bag. He was, indeed, always fussing over my welfare, which would have been even more pleasant if I had not felt guilty at being thus coddled.

Our next day's journey took us to Chung Hsi, where Jo-Jo had moved from Lungchow. He was now living in one room, with an outside door that would not close and let in every breeze. The furniture consisted of four stools, a table, a board bed, and the back seat of a car, with the springs breaking out all over. The Chinese can enjoy comfort or dispense with it as we put on and off a coat.

Invited by some other officials who dealt with refugees to a session of poker (which Jo-Jo had now taught them), I found them living in the same bleak decor. Shortage of furnishings may have been unavoidable, but there seemed no reason why the open windows could not have been repapered! In addition to the actual game, Jo-Jo had also taught his friends the English ejaculations he had picked up from us: "Hold on to your hats!" "Stultifying!" "Piss-poor pair!" and "Graveyard face!" These expressions thrown into their Chinese sounded oddly comical.

The final trek to the border on the following day required me to be up at five-thirty, so I went early to bed. Again the prevailing cold awoke me with a need to urinate. At the inn where I was staying, this function required a journey to the backyard, through a door that had to be unlocked, and across an area slimed with pig shit, after which one might in the darkness easily fall into the cesspit at the other end. I therefore decided to hold out until the dawn's first glimmer. This was a terrible mistake. I started urinating in my sleep, and before I could stop, everything was soaked, including my underclothes, which I had kept on for warmth. Because I had no spares, there was nothing for it but to wring them out, get a fire going, and dry them a little before putting them on again. But they were, of course, still quite damp when I miserably got going.

On this final stretch I was joined by Simon Yu, whose fluent French, keen mind, and considerable knowledge was supplemented by the additional advantage of his walking speed: my final journey across the border and back had to be accomplished before the Japanese got on to us. The route through mountainous jungle was so eroded by recent rains that we had to dismount and scramble along sidetracks barely kept open by infrequent travelers and matted with overhead growth coming so low for riding that we had to drag the horses along behind us. In fourteen hours we covered thirty-five miles of this grim terrain. What with cold, fatigue, and the misery of my urine-wet underwear, I could barely finish the final stretch without collapsing into sobs. Yet the coolies kept up the same pace carrying eighty-pound loads!

Darkness had fallen by the time we arrived at the hut of Fung, our border agent inside Indochina. While we sat there shivering, the two sticks of charcoal he got glowing seemed determined never to boil the water for our tea. The French group arrived before even the first bubbles appeared. There were two captains and a lieutenant from the local army post and a lieutenant and two sergeants who wanted the protection of our group on their journey into China.

Opening up our mountain rations, we gave them what hospitality we could. Although formal and polite, they were obviously suspicious of our intentions. We talked and talked in French, which seemed to get increasingly rapid and more technical; following the exhaustion of the journey, I was eventually operating in a dream world that was made even more chimerical by the minute pithwick lamps, which was all the light we had. Nor could I forget that these Frenchmen might be all pro-Vichy and potential allies of the Japanese, whose troops were off there in the blackness and might burst in any time.

However, my purpose was to win them over, if that were possible, so I listened sympathetically to all their complaints, discussed problems, conceded grievances, promised we would try to do better, and finally distributed bribes in the form of PX supplies, gadgets, and a carton of mountain rations, all of which they accepted rather like children who have been warned not to take sweets from strangers but cannot resist the temptation. And when I gave them the portable radio sets, they were stunned into incredulous silence until one of them cried, "*Sans blagues, c'est le comble* [No joking, that's tops]!" and the atmosphere grew distinctly warmer. It was midnight before they left: a four-hour session after our fourteen-hour day. Despite my urinous sleeping bag I fell asleep at once; only when I woke at dawn did I remember to start worrying again about the Japanese. But luck was on our side, or perhaps the three Frenchmen we were escorting formed a kind of assurance we would not be ambushed. On this homeward journey it was not danger that bothered me so much as the grinding pain of keeping going. Toward the end of each day, only the thought of that wonderful moment when I would climb into my warm sleeping bag and pass into oblivion kept me going.

As we approached Chung Hsi, the French consul, Tiercy, came riding toward us, elegant in a tweed jacket, whipcord breeches, and bright print muffler. That particular day having been less exhausting, I accepted his invitation to a meal. He was living in a little Chinese house built amid a garden of plum trees, which were already bright with blossom and decorated in honor of the Chinese new year with miniature pagodas, pavilions, bridges, priests, nuns, and dragons—to mention only the oddments I could identify. While we were eating, a stream of old men well clad in padded gowns, fur caps, and earmuffs, carrying teapots and cups and smoking long-stemmed pipes, came shuffling by to study this display, drink a cup of tea, break off a fragment of blossom, and depart with satisfied bows and smiles. Poor Tiercy was so starved of sophisticated Western conversation that he drank in my remarks on books, painting, music, and politics with a flattering attention quite unrelated to their trivial worth. But he was quick to let me know of all that China had taught him. "Although I don't intend to settle here for life, I think I'll never get China out of my system. Indeed, there are times when I feel quite captivated. And recently I've felt that the Chinese and the French have so much in common, especially in regard to art, women, food, festivities, and formal politeness. Don't think me chauvinistic, but I feel we're both essentially civilized."

"And both irreligious, too intellectual, and essentially rebellious!" I added with a smile.

"I suppose you're right," he conceded, also with a smile.

The nice girl in the corduroy coat reappeared, and I noticed that Lao disappeared that evening.

Among the wires that came in from Kunming was one asking us to see whether Jo-Jo could find us Chinese or Annamite agents to go inside Indochina with radio sets. "I might find some Chinese," Jo-Jo told us, "but even if there were Annamites who could operate radios, we shouldn't want to use them. We formerly tried it on our own behalf and even supplied them with arms. But when we agreed to recognize France as a power again, with de Gaulle as leader, we also agreed not to support the Annamites. So we've stuck to it." In this instance, Chinese scruples exceeded our own.

When we started out the next morning, the corduroy-coat girl introduced herself as Miss Chao. "I am on my way to Kunming to join my sister, and I wonder whether, for safety's sake, I might accompany your group as far as Tengyuan?" Mostly to please Lao, I agreed that she might. I was also able to repay his kind attentions by medicating and bandaging his leg when he gashed it falling from his horse. The three Frenchmen were still in their beds. Because Jo-Jo had told me he was sure they were Vichyites, I was glad to seize this chance to leave without this sour-faced trio.

The rain finally ceased, and the temperature grew almost warm. Apart from my aching limbs, traveling now became almost pleasant, and the countryside took on a charm that rain and mist had formerly obscured. Rocks that had seemed only gray and hazardous now revealed delicate pinks and blues, with a veil on the shady side of variegated lichen. Through the gushing rivulets I caught the flash of kingfishers, bee-eaters, and the rarer orioles. While we ate our lunch snack, a red-tailed rock thrush was so bold that it took the crumbs from my hand, while a scattering of magpie robins, fearful to be thus venturesome, chattered in envious rage.

In Sunshi the farmer's shack was now full of chickens. He led us to an abandoned schoolhouse scarcely larger than his own small hut. The windows had long since lost their paper coverings, and a colony of swifts had nested in the rafters. The dirt floor was plastered with their droppings and littered with torn exercise papers. Peeling scrolls on the walls bore characters for such sayings as "The Kuomintang Is Our Salvation!" "Drive the Wicked Japanese Out!" and "Clean Bodies Make Clean Minds!" And the usual oleograph of Sun Yat-sen still bore its wreath of withered flowers.

Two little girls perhaps six years old ran in selling glutinous rice wrapped in banana leaves. They were both shivering with cold but had to be coaxed into drinking some warm powdered milk, apparently fearful we might then fail to buy the rice. Nevertheless, when the sale was made, the bigger one was careful to count and examine the bills we handed over and even flipped one aside when it bore a design she could not recognize. In China, as I had long since noticed, every child is grown up almost from birth.

At dawn it was again drizzling rain. Lao was missing, but I could not blame Miss Chao because she was already waiting, armed with a basket of oranges that she insisted on sharing around. It then appeared that Lao had gone to buy something and would catch up with us. Some thirty minutes later when he came trotting up, he was happily sporting a new leather cap with earflaps, a pair of pigskin gloves, and a French .38 revolver complete with bandoleer.

On this final stretch I felt my knees could never last the day. But short of expiring in a ditch, there was nothing for it but to stay on the horse until I half-fell, half-slid off and walked a short distance as a way to change one pain for a worse one and thus have the relief of getting back on the horse.

At Tengyuan a truck had already been arranged to collect us: oh brave new world! We drove at a fast clip to Posi, where I had the great good fortune to find a pilot friend who was flying off in an hour. He took not only Lao and myself but two others of the group plus Miss Chao, who could hardly believe her good luck. But she might have felt differently when airborne; this being her first flight, the poor girl soon turned as green as her coat.

A signal having gone forward, Tan was there at the field to greet us. Among lesser news he informed me that while I had been away there had been two pilot rescue operations. Four days ago a pilot named Shaw had been rescued by some Annamites and safely brought all the way to Kunming by a man named Ho and his younger companion. "He refused a pile of cash and wanted to meet General Chennault—'just for the honor,' he said—but probably for political ends since the French say he's an active Communist. So, of course, Chennault refused to meet him."

The other rescue was a pilot named Settler and his copilot, Knight. They had been shot down over French Indochina and, thanks to André, had been rescued by the French and brought safely to Kunming. Because Settler was too ill to talk, Knight told us the story:

> Making a final pass we came down to seventy-five feet. The ack-ack was coming unpleasantly close, with the bursts following us down despite our speed of 270. Suddenly seeing the plane was on fire, we opened the rear hatch to get clear of the flames. Just as I was hoisting myself out, the

plane took a violent swing, and the ground below came rushing up like a vast green mound. That was the last thing I remembered until waking up in the muddy water of a rice paddy. My hands were all skinned off and my eyes so swollen that I was practically blind, and feeling the blood streaming down my face, I thought I really was: a ghastly moment! Then the vision of one eye began to clear, and I could see my watch said ten o'clock. In a kind of delirium this very oddly took my thoughts to memories of home so that when I suddenly saw the Japanese control tower, I thought, "What the hell is that doing here?"

Finally both vision and thoughts began to clear, and I suddenly saw the whole shebang—our plane in flames, big crowds converging in all round, and a Japanese truck hurtling towards me on the road. So I swiftly turned to bury my chute, but to my amazement some natives were already doing this! Then I remembered I must clear my pockets; and when I started pulling things out a native grabbed my silk map and buried it in the soft mud with a single movement. Then one of the natives who seemed like the boss gestured towards the pearl-handled knife I carried in my belt. I thought he wanted to bury it, too, and since I had my pistol I let him take it. But he just admired it, like a kid with a new toy, meanwhile bowing his thanks—at such a time, can you imagine! But already the others were hurrying me off, and they hid me in a nearby hut. About fifteen minutes later several Frenchmen appeared. They offered the natives a wad of money, but they wouldn't accept it and finally went off bowing to me— Jesus, what a circus if it hadn't been a nightmare!

After being screened by these Frenchmen as to who I was and what all else, I was taken to a hospital, where sometime later a three-pip general named Aymé came to see me. Later on I could hear several other visitors outside the door, and the only one who came in was a civilian named Meyer, who came every day and apparently fixed up my escape. But this must have been done through the connivance of the higher-ups since we left without hindrance, and no alarm was raised until three hours later. Then this man André, whom I'd already noticed outside the door, took over from Meyer, and I learned later that he'd directed the whole deal.

André led me down towards the sea, and we walked a good long stretch along a rocky shore before turning inland and being picked up by a car. Once when crossing on a ferry I got out of the car for a smoke and suddenly saw with a jolt like I'd hit a brick wall that a truckful of Japanese troops was parked out in front! But then later on I grew used to seeing the Japs, sometimes even sitting inside cafés with them alongside and once in a department store André took me into. Somewhere en route we picked up Settler, who had been smuggled to that point by a different route. Most of the time he was totally dazed. And when he did come partly out of it, he was like a sick child, with pathetic complaints as if he were appealing to his mother.

He was of course still too dazed to give any coherent story, so it was useless to interrogate him, and both men were promptly shipped home. The explanation of the Japanese noninterference was that it had been agreed that when a prisoner fell into French hands, they were allowed jurisdiction, although not of course to connive in this fashion at a rescue! And subsequently, the news of this escape added one more affront to the list of grievances that, only a few weeks later, would bring nemeses down on the heads of all Free French in Indochina and a muzzle down over our own.

I tried to get the story on the other rescue but could not track Ho down, although it was rumored he was still around. I was further disappointed to learn that Shaw had already been flown home.

13

THE WINGS OF GENIUS

Our relations with OSS now went steadily downhill. They started declining when the new personnel officer (another Major Little but no relation) took umbrage because I did not go in to report.

Then came a fight with OSS Transport because Bernard, a good judge of motor vehicles, complained about the poor quality of the motorcycle they supplied us with. Another row came when the PX cut down our rations. The only department that stayed really friendly was SI, whose people were grateful for all the intelligence we were giving them.

Then a new row came with Transport over tires. Our agents down in French Indochina had reported having several old trucks they could get operating if they only had new tires. So we requisitioned for thirty, which the Fourteenth agreed to drop in. But Major Driver, the aptly named OSS Transport chief, exploded. "You can't really believe we'd be crazy enough to supply tires to Frenchmen!" But when de Sibour, still awaiting a replacement as CO and always inclined to be helpful, okayed the requisition, Legion of Merit Brody at the delivery office hit the ceiling.

"Thirty tires to goddam Frenchmen! D'ya think my name's Dopey?"

Tan, who was helping me push through this deal, now did his own exploding. "What the hell's the matter with you? Can't you read? Didn't you ever go to school, or maybe you're just dumb—a clot, is it?" When our hero heard himself addressed in this fashion by a Chinese half his size, he screamed with such rage that the dogs began barking for miles all around. But we got the tires.

In order to get some British B-2 radio sets, which both Gordon and Bernard rated better than the U.S. model supplied by OSS, we decided to send an emissary to India. This trip was awarded to Simon, for whom we got British travel orders and an RAF flight. When I drove him to the airfield, I found that de

Sibour, returning home at last, was traveling on the same plane, with Adjutant Krauss seeing him off. Immediately concluding I was off on another spree, Krauss saw the chance he had long been waiting for to pounce on me. "I warn you, Lieutenant, if you get on this plane, it will be a court-martial case!" When I politely informed him that the traveler was actually Mr. Yu, he recovered from the shock by hurling a counterattack. "And where, may I ask, are his orders?" What can the best player do when you hold all the aces? First Simon showed his British orders. Then, not too hurriedly, he showed his French passport duly visaed for India. Such moments as this are sweeter than honey.

Susan asked if she might have the day off and, when I agreed, asked if I would have lunch with her in town, an invitation I could graciously accept, having business there with OSS. Instead of her usual sack, she wore her other attire, a knitted woolen jacket over a cotton frock quaintly Victorian. Only after we were seated in the Yunnanese restaurant did she reveal that the outing was to celebrate her birthday. "In our family my sister and I followed the tradition set by my father of doing something to please parents on this particular day, while at the same time giving ourselves a particularly precious memory. So that's why I took the great liberty of asking you to come." Although this sounds like dialogue from Jane Austen, the obvious sincerity of the speaker precluded skepticism.

At OSS I had been called to a meeting with Little (the new one), Faxon, and a recently arrived Chinese American named Kwok. Faxon opened up proceedings with a complaint about two men I had introduced through Graham Peck: Alec Ma, a graduate from Tokyo University, who spoke fluent Japanese, and Dick Meng, formerly of the Chinese Industrial Co-operatives, both of whom were technically and linguistically skilled. Although grudgingly conceding the quality of these men, Faxon said they were both "goddam Communists." I pointed out that, considering he intended sending them into the Communist area, they had better be Communists, or they would either be sent back or shot.

"I don't care about them being Chinese Communists," snorted Faxon, "but these damn fellows are more like Russian Communists, advocating world revolution and so forth!"

"Frankly, Major," put in Kwok, "all Chinese Commies are liable to spout that kind of propaganda."

"Yes, yes, but nobody listens to them, whereas these two fellows spout such crap in English right there in our classroom!"

Little then brought up the problem of Mac Wong, who was being investigated by X-2 on various charges: first, his U.S. citizenship, which had gotten him several privileges, was now in question; second, he had consorted with the Japanese while in Macao; third, it could have been through his indiscretions (if not worse) that Lieutenant Kan had been picked up by the Japanese; fourth, he had never properly accounted for the OSS funds allotted to him; and fifth, he was selling jade to the GIs at exorbitant prices. "Wong is another of your introductions," Little told me. "So what have you to say about these charges?" (Prisoner at the bar, what have you to say . . .)

"It's true I introduced him. But X-2 subsequently cleared him for acceptance. I agree he's a smoothie. Indeed, I told Major Faxon that fact at the time. May I also mention that I've contributed more than a dozen agents in the past six months who have done good work. Mac Wong was a mistake, but in my opinion he should have been written off long ago."

"Are you implying—!" began Faxon angrily.

But Little, always the softly-softly lawyer, quickly interrupted. "Please, let's not argue about it! Lieutenant Fenn has admitted he was wrong. Let's get on to Schools and Training . . ."

So it was another ten minutes before I could escape. Proceeding to Communications, I handed back to Brody two AR-2 radio sets we had found to be defective. This, of course, sent him into another rage. "You're a right stooge for those GBT sonsabitches! I thought Bernard headed the list for goddam arrogance, but that Tan sonofabitch beats everything!" Despite this barrage we got the two replacement sets. "You are welcome to hate me," said Napoleon, "provided you give me the horses."

A crowd had gathered round the bulletin board, where a brief statement announced that Colonel de Sibour was relieved of his temporary command and that this post was being taken over by Captain Krauss. "Well, for Chrissake!" I heard one GI mutter. "It's like appointing the janitor of the Automat to run the Waldorf-Astoria!"

On my way to the jeep, I was addressed by an attractive, smartly dressed Chinese girl. "Don't you remember me, Mr. Fenn? Yu-ren, from Kweilin." I certainly had to do a double take. When she had been working there with Smith, she had seemed a badly dressed creature whom nobody would give a second glance at. But when I congratulated her on having made the grade, she confessed rather sadly that she would rather be back in Kweilin. "Under Major Smith, we were a rather happy family. In this place it's dog eat dog."

A Navy plane came down near Pleiku, central Indochina, with eleven crew on board. We worked out a scheme to drop supplies, but no weapons, which might have gotten them shot. When Bernard and I went to clear this scheme with Krauss, he said, "First, I'll have to check with Wedemeyer."

I could see Bernard tighten up. "But that delay will bitch the plan, since they'll have to move on fast, or we'll lose track of them!"

"There's no need for you to get excited," said Krauss haughtily. "You might as well know that we're already working on this rescue job ourselves."

When we got outside, Bernard blew out a breath, "They'll do nothing about it until it's too late!" He proved to be right.

Along the corridor I was buttonholed by Kwok, who wanted to continue the Schools and Training waffling of our previous meeting. But Helliwell, appearing at the end of the corridor, called him over sharply and hardly bothered to lower his voice while hissing, "Never discuss your plans with that fellow!"

The soya beans that the peasants had planted around the camp had grown into a carpet of iridescent blue-green, adorned here and there with streaks of yellowweed, possibly mustard, that the peasants fought in vain to eradicate—much to our visual satisfaction. In the prevailing fine weather, the air was so calm that the stream showed no ripple, and smoke from the guard's cigarette (made from substitute leaves wrapped in scraps of toilet paper) rose in a thin blue-gray streak to the very top of the trees. Then, without warning, a violent storm blew up, flattened the fields into a sheet of silver-gray, blew up from the road a blanket of dust, and took off part of our roof. A group of army conscripts being marched toward town took advantage of the storm to break away and race across the rice fields toward the distant hills. But they had no hope of reaching this haven. Before they were even halfway, a truck came zooming down a side road to cut them off. I watched them darting this way and that like hunted hares, with the guards closing in and finally jabbing with their rifles. Soon enough they were all herded back into the truck and carted away. These conscripts, mostly mere boys, had been dragged off from their homes, then bullied and starved, so if they did not die from a Japanese bullet, they were all too likely to die from hunger, ill-treatment, and disease.

Still gloomy from this sad spectacle, I was further cast down by hearing about one of my Flying Tiger friends, now in the Fourteenth Air Force, Captain Pietsker, who had crashed somewhere in east China. Coming out of his daze, he had found his gunner jammed in the wreckage and screaming with pain. They were off in a mountainous wilderness with no one to help. Pietsker had no morphine. And all his efforts to ease the gunner's agony were useless. His agonized screams finally drove Pietsker into the desperate remedy of firing two shots into the gunner's temple. When ultimately rescued he had to admit this sad deed and consequently face a court-martial. Although it was touch and go, he was finally acquitted. This story left me brooding. In the trauma of war, death is everywhere, but you hardly ever think about it until suddenly it impinges with a visual impact you simply cannot erase from your memory.

On that same morning of March 10, 1945, came a wire from our agent in Mengkai; its mere six words shook me from sad cogitation into something real to worry about: "Japanese seized all posts throughout Indochina." This laconic statement had us puzzled as well as concerned. But it was not until the whole day had gone by without a single message from any of our stations that we became seriously alarmed. The following day the BBC in London carried our own brief report (relayed by Delhi and the only news of the coup received anywhere) as "an unconfirmed rumor." The French Military Mission reported that all their own contacts had also gone dead, and they had no information as to how and why.

A second wire now came from Mengkai that the French had resisted here and there but had suffered bad casualties and were pleading for help. Bernard and I quickly worked a plan for dropping in all available parachutists and supplies the moment we could establish where the French were holding out. But our Mengkai agent, already on the run, could send us nothing more than the tale of his own difficulties. So not only could we send no help, but even our air attacks had to cease, because we had neither weather reports nor any check on Japanese movements. Both Wedemeyer and the U.S. Navy sent us urgent pleas to get a new intelligence net operating—with natives if necessary! The question was—what natives? Nobody knew any they thought could be trusted.

It was at this point I remembered that a month earlier a pilot named Shaw had been brought out from Indochina by an Annamite named Ho who would not accept any reward but had asked to meet General Chennault. This request had been refused on the grounds that no top-ranking American officer should have contact with Annamites for fear of annoying the French. War correspondent Ravenholt had gotten a story out of Ho but had not been allowed to send it. It said that Ho was still around and that he went to the Office of War Information to read *Time* magazine and any other news literature they happened to have. This combination of Ho's interest in American news plus his having rescued an American pilot seemed to indicate a bias in our favor. So I asked John Vincent to try to fix a meeting. He subsequently sent a message that he had fixed an appointment at the nearby Dragon's Gate for eleven o'clock the following morning.

Ho turned up right on time with a younger man named Pham. (Subsequently, this man, Pham Van-Dong, became prime minister of Vietnam.) Ho wore a whitish cotton suit, Pham a button-to-the-neck jacket; they both wore sandals. Ho spoke French, Russian, English, Siamese, some German, and two Chinese dialects, but because Pham spoke only French, we used that language. Ravenholt had called Ho "old," and although he was younger than I had expected, we did subsequently call him "Old Man Ho" because we were all much younger. As I learned later, Ho was over fifty, but his face was unlined, and his wisp of beard and thinning hair were only barely touched with gray. His alert, eager look was enhanced by the brightest eyes I ever saw. I have heard much the same comment from people who have met either Lenin or Picasso, and it is said that such eyes are an indication of genius, intelligence, determination, and purpose. But it wasn't just Ho's eyes that got me hooked. As had happened with Gordon and Colonel Wichtrich earlier, I like to think that Ho and I had *hsu* from the start.

When Ho told me about his "Vietminh" or League for Independence, I realized he was the Ho I had heard about from Jo-Jo, who had said the group was "Communist." "Is that label correct?" I asked him.

"Some of our members are Communists, and some aren't. The Chinese and French call all of us Communist who don't fit into their 'pattern.'"

"Are you against the French?"

"Certainly not. But unfortunately they are against us." A nice distinction!

"Would you like to work with the Americans?"

Not surprisingly, he looked puzzled. "What kind of work?"

We discussed his taking into Indochina a radio set and generator and collecting intelligence as well as rescuing more pilots.

"I suppose we could do all that. But you'd need to send a radio operator— we have no one trained in that. A generator would be too noisy and therefore dangerous with the Japanese around. Why not use the battery-operated sets the Chinese use?"

"They're too weak for the distance. Besides, the batteries soon give out. The hand generators we use don't make much noise. And if you use them by a waterfall, for instance, that covers up the noise."

"Anyway, we could try."

"And what would you want in return for helping us?" This, alas, might be the snag! Support against the French? Arms and ammunition? To meet Chennault? This might now be possible.

"American recognition for our league."

"We'd have to play that carefully not to cross the French. De Gaulle is getting very difficult."

"Medicine and arms."

"Why arms? You aren't fighting the Japanese."

"We certainly should be if we help you! When they find out, we'd need to protect ourselves. In any case, we want to fight the Japanese. At present it's they who run our country, so we want to get them out. To do this we are more than willing to work with you. We would be willing to work with the Chinese and even with the French if they'd let us," he added. An ambitious program!

"How big is your league?" I had thought in terms of hundreds. Was it really more than that?

"Several hundred at our base. But many thousands scattered over Annam." I thought he was boasting; dissidents always do. But if he had even a few dozen it would be a start. So we made a date to meet in two days' time: I wanted to find out more about him and get clearance for taking him on. But I had already decided that he was our man. Baudelaire felt the wings of insanity touch his mind, but that morning I felt the wings of genius touch mine.

14

QUIET CONVERSATIONS

During the next two days, I learned from my French contacts that Ho was a long-standing rebel, anti-French, of course, and strictly Communist. The Chinese did not much like him, either. From their point of view, the only good Communist was a dead Communist. This might have tallied with the U.S attitude if the exigencies of war had not pushed the Soviet Union into our lap and temporarily canceled our anti-Communist hang-up. So when I gave the facts to Colonel Richard Heppner, who had finally taken up his post as CO, he told me to use Ho if I thought he would do the job.

To devise a simple number code that might be learned, along with Morse, by Ho's disciples, I obtained a copy of "Basic English" (put out by the British Ministry of Information for teaching foreigners simple English). I was working on this when a message came from OSS X-2 (Counterintelligence) that Lincoln Kan (my former agent who had been picked up by the Japanese) had now escaped and had established radio contact with OSS; so could I think of a way to check his authenticity? When I suggested asking him to identify "Fearless," he immediately did so. By asking other questions I also helped X-2 to establish that he was genuinely free and not under Japanese duress, and he subsequently gave OSS some useful information. In the meantime, because Service of Supply (U.S. Air Force) had installed a refrigeration unit, AGAS sent us a container of ice cream. What a treat—a gala evening indeed because in our poker session that evening Helen had a royal flush, and Susan subsequently got four queens!

After the others had gone off to bed, Susan was in an unusually communicative mood:

Helen long ago realized she wasn't as pretty as Janet and would need to make up for it by always being pleasant. As she's naturally good-natured, this hasn't been difficult. I expect you noticed how Janet used men to get things done even when being thoroughly unpleasant to them. It's true that some men exploit women, but some are plain masochists in the way they let women exploit them! One marked difference between Chinese women and American women is that the former trust men more, and the older they get the more they trust them, whereas with American women, the older men are the less they trust them. But because of the difference between American men and Chinese men, both groups of women are approximately right.

I seem to be talking a lot tonight—it must be all the excitement! My father always taught me to listen and not to speak, to assess and not to declare, to prefer and not to choose. There are two subjects we never discussed at home: one was food, and the other money; they were both taboo. Another thing my father always impressed on me was that it was not the nature of a person's work that was important but the way he did it. Whatever job a person had he should treat it seriously and do it to the best of his ability. In this respect, Helen is one girl in a hundred. Despite not being pretty, she deserves to get a first-rate husband. But I sometimes wonder if that's possible in present-day China! We're both of us fed up with the way Chinese young men go on. When they can't get their own way—I don't mean sexually, but in small things—they first of all sulk, then they threaten, and finally they declare for suicide. When all this doesn't work, they are quite capable of really committing suicide on your doorstep, merely to disgrace you!

I listened with concealed amazement. Only a month or two earlier, this girl had seldom spoken English outside a classroom!

Bernard and Tan both agreed that the best way to utilize Ho would be for Tan and Mac Sin to go with him. Annam being full of Chinese, they could easily assimilate. When at our next meeting I put this suggestion to Ho, he asked if I could not come myself.

"I'd be very glad to come, but I'll probably have to stay here and organize. How do you propose to go back in?"

"If you could fly us to the border, we'd then walk in. To elude the Japanese it would mean walking at night, which slows things down, so it would take us about two weeks to get to our base. It's a pity you can't come, not only from my personal preference but because an American would be most welcome."

"Mr. Tan is actually American, so your people can regard him as such. And since he's spent several years in Annam, he has more understanding of everything there than I do, including the racial and political complexities. You couldn't hope to have a better man to work with."

"I'm looking forward to meeting him."

"I'll arrange that. I've already arranged about medicines and a few things like radios, cameras, and weather equipment, which Mac Sin will train your men to use. I fear we must leave out arms for the present. Perhaps later on we can drop some in."

"And what about meeting Chennault?"

"Why are you so keen about that?"

"He's the Westerner we most admire. So I'd like to tell him so myself."

Although this sounded harmless, I suspected Ho's real objective was to win Chennault's sympathy for his political aspirations. That, of course, was why his first request for a meeting had been refused. But things were different now. We were no longer dealing with an insignificant peasant in a faded cotton jacket. The jacket was the same, but the peasant inside might be the key to all our future Indochina operations.

Fortunately, I knew Chennault well from having covered the Tigers' exploits as a war correspondent. So out of channels I went to see him personally (another transgression that the OSS sniffer dogs got wind of) and explained the importance of playing along with this old man who had not only rescued one of the general's pilots but also might well rescue more if we gained his future cooperation. This approach did the trick, and a date was fixed for a meeting at the end of the week. There were two limitations: no favors must be asked and no politics discussed.

Armed with this verbal agreement, I went looking for Ho in the candle shop where he and Pham had a room. The downstairs bristled with tapers—red, white, and orange. The candle maker paused in his operation of adorning candles with red and gold filigree to inform me that Ho and Pham had gone off on some unexpected business. Would I kindly come back in two days' time?

Held up on business, I filled in on pleasure by calling to see Kasy S.

You just missed seeing Carton de Wiart. He's my idea of a real English gentleman, in fact you might say the very epitome of knight-errant—as it says in the books. What a contrast to Colonel J———, the military attaché. Do you know him? Last week after we had danced together twice, he offered me a pad in Florida if I'd sleep with him! Can you imagine! And the next day he told me he asked General Chennault, "Who does that girl Kasy belong to?" So the general said, "Why not ask her?" And J———

said, "I'll do that; she's certainly a nice piece of arse!" Can you imagine! But that's not the end of the story. The next time I turned him down, he went from a mere pad in Florida to an actual proposal of marriage—that is, as soon as he got his divorce—ha, ha! And all the time acting like I was some kind of musical instrument he was tuning up on. So I finally said, "I've simply got to get out to Hostel Six. May I borrow your jeep?" He pulled off his hands as if he'd been stung. "Honey, you know I can't lend you my jeep. That's U.S. Army property, strictly off-limits!" "Then fade, scram, beat it, get going!" I guess he took the hint, 'cause I haven't seen him since!

When climbing into my jeep, I was hailed by a girl in a rickshaw. This turned out to be Miss Chao of the green corduroy coat: would I care to take a drink of tea in the inn where she was staying? So she transferred herself to the jeep, and off we went. The "inn" proved to be a matshed, with cubicles around a center court, and her room had a board bed on trestles, a washstand, and a chair, which she offered me with bowing courtesy. The room boy brought in tea on a tray made of a biscuit tin. With the aid of my dictionary, we managed to exchange a few bits of talk, during which I learned that GIs were always coming here to look for girls and that was why the room boy was hovering around in case she needed protection. In the open wickerwork case she had carried on the journey lay some odds and ends of clothing. The corduroy coat was hanging on the door. On the wall hung a flyblown calendar dated three years earlier.

Back at the camp the cook was in a heated argument with a woman selling charcoal at a price 50 percent higher than last week. Because of recent cold weather, all the GI hostels had been stocking up, and the price of wood and charcoal had risen tenfold. As a result, more and more farmers had become woodcutters, with disastrous results. Cutting down trees except in the so-called wildernesses was forbidden, but there was no rule against lopping off branches. This maltreatment had been first confined to lower branches, but finally the all-too-few trees within a twenty-mile radius of Kunming had been denuded to the topmost tuft. Demand was now driving the woodcutters to even more drastic measures. Each morning would reveal that the severed bole of a tree had been chopped down during the night and rapidly disposed of before the culprits could be traced. No one dared touch our trees for fear of getting shot. But each morning with the first glimpse of light, a string of women would come stumping goatlike on their bound feet along the path bordering our stream, bent down beneath illicit loads of wood from all around. One or two at the rear also carried babies whose bare buttocks glistened in the rising sun like taillights.

Later on I had a visit from Betty M., whose arrival from India close on the heels of Heppner proved not without significance. She had come ostensibly to solicit my help with a clandestine newspaper that purported to be published by guerrillas in the Canton area. But after I had made a few suggestions, she came out with another request: would I mind driving her to the GI hospital a mile or so farther west? "I managed to hitch a ride this far, but there's not much traffic from here on." When I obliged, she asked me to wait a few minutes while she delivered a package. She shortly reappeared with someone wearing the standard hospital garb of blue-and-white bathrobe, and who should this be but Heppner! He was very polite, and we had a cozy chat, after which I drove Betty to a designated point on the road and said good-bye. I could not quite work out what lay behind this exchange. Was Heppner making a special effort to be friendly, or did the pair of them want me to know of their special relationship?

Back in the camp, I found Lao almost hysterical over some letter he had received. He had already missed two meals and was now refusing a third. He told me he had had bad news from his family. But Tsung-wei told me the real reason for his breakdown was unrequited love for Lily Chao.

"Let's hope he won't commit suicide on her doorstep," I remarked. "Good radio operators are hard to replace."

Mac Sin paid a visit from the parachute school. Someone had given him a magnificent slouch hat, Aussie-style, which transformed him into a diminutive top-heavy cowboy. He told us proudly that in a class of fifty from all parts of the world, he was the only Chinese. "And they think I'm the cutest little guy they ever saw and treat me wonderfully! Oh, they are grand to me, really grand!" To understand his nature, one has to visualize a very clever adult who has somehow retained the open, good-natured delight of a child. "I've been trained to use all the weapons, including the Tommy gun. They teach us how to fire it in short bursts, the shorter the better. Not to save ammunition, mind you, but to be sure you have plenty left—that is the art of it!" he exulted. And: "The mortar shells cost sixty-five U.S. dollars apiece, but we shoot them off like peas, like peas!" he gurgled ecstatically.

"That's how America will win the war," commented Tsung-wei, "shooting everything off like peas." Tsung-wei had also gone to Schools and Training, where he had as his room companion a Chinese American named Wong, destined for SI. "He talks endlessly about the rate of exchange, per diem, what's new in PX, and the price of peanut candy. Whenever he thinks I'm not looking, he opens his carefully locked suitcase, pulls out something small, which he stares at lovingly, then puts back and relocks in his case. He sometimes does that several times a day and never catches on that I know his secret treasure is a U.S. one-hundred-dollar bill!"

The personnel officer had told Tsung-wei, "I'm putting you and Wong together because you'll have lots in common, both being Chinese." And here is another example of the gulf between Chinese Americans and indigenous Chinese: Bob Lee had pleaded to be sent on a different assignment elsewhere because Tan did everything possible to make his life miserable. Yet Tan is basically very good-natured!

Upon driving to the airfield to collect Simon Yu arriving back from India, I found everything in chaos. A transport plane coming in too low had caught its wingtip on the roof of a house in the village at the far end of the field. In the ensuing crash, the plane had caught fire and exploded. All five of the crew were killed instantly, along with thirty-five villagers, with more than one hundred injured, many perhaps fatally. Rescue teams were now digging out bodies from the mounds of rubble. A few exhausted MPs were trying to hold back howling relatives. Clinging to one of the bodies being dragged out was a small child wailing like a bagpipe. After this infant had been torn away, the corpse was lumped, along with several others, into the hospital truck. Of the plane itself, only the tail was visible, sticking up from the rubble like a battered derrick. Already a team of engineers was getting a purchase to drag it away. Everything had to be cleared away fast to avoid any demoralizing effect.

Simon had had to wait three days in India to get on a plane to Kunming, because they were all full of Frenchmen coming to join the FMM in Chungking. "Nobody knows what they are going to do there, least of all the Frenchmen, who are mostly businessmen the war has stranded across two continents. According to Major Hunter, Washington had thought it would be a nice gesture to the French to assemble them all in Calcutta, then ship them across the Hump for use in Indochina. 'Because after all,' said Hunter, 'that's a French show down there'—as if he were talking about a movie. The OSS HQ in Calcutta is another grand spectacular; they've now got as many women in the cast as men, and they're proving they can do the job with equal incompetence." In addition to our equipment, Simon had brought back some rosebushes and banana seedlings to decorate the camp, making me feel ashamed that I never remembered things like that.

Late that evening I found Susan still at work in the office typing up the report of developments to date with Ho Chi Minh. "Finish that tomorrow," I told her. "You look quite worn out."

She gave me a long solemn look and finally confessed, "I'm not worn out, I'm just so depressed I feel like going off and killing myself."

"How?" I asked, not feeling inclined to take this seriously.

"How? Well, I suppose I'd hang myself." And after a pause, "That's what one of the students did in Yenching when she got depressed over bad examination reports. Hung herself with a piece of silk cord."

"And what's depressing you?"

"It's two months since I heard from my father."

"Great heavens! Does that also rate suicide?"

"When you're feeling low, even small things can push you over the edge. But really, my father's a big thing. In fact, he's everything to me since my mother died. I was only eleven at the time, so from then on all my love centered on him. And he was infinitely loving to me, always kind, never gave me a harsh word, never once raised his voice in anger. Nor did he ever expect anything from me, no demands, no criticism, only the example he set, to follow if and when I pleased. And of course I always tried hard to do so. Then when I got older, and young men told me they loved me, I found that their kind of love was merely demanding and even bullying. Twice when I was sought in marriage, I asked myself how I could possibly marry someone who shouted at me when I didn't do just what he wanted! That's why I'm so grateful that you're kind and don't shout at me."

"But I'm often bad-tempered."

"Not often and never with me. Although I've been stupid in learning this work, you've never been angry with me. Oh, Mr. Fenn, isn't there something, anything, I can do to repay your kindness?" I suppose it never occurred to her that such a question, put with such emphasis, might be misinterpreted!

On my next visit to the candle shop I took along Tan. As I had hoped, Tan and Ho hit it off. Keen minds, intuition, enthusiasm, and directness developed into a friendship that lasted all through their months of subsequent contact down south. After fixing Ho's appointment with Chennault, we agreed on the details of our future operation. As previously suggested, Ho would be flown down with equipment in one L-5, while Tan and Mac Sin would fly in another. They would land at Ching Hsi, almost on the border, and then walk in to Ho's base. He would organize an intelligence network of couriers until Mac Sin could train further operators and establish further radio contacts. If things developed according to plan, we should later on drop in an American officer and arms. Meanwhile, Pham would stay on in Kunming to liaise with me. As we were winding up this meeting, I heard a shout from our guard who was minding the jeep. Through the shop opening we then saw two MPs climb into the seat and drive off despite my shouts.

There had in fact recently been a regulation against leaving jeeps in the street because these vehicles could be started simply by turning a switch and were thus easily stolen. But a minder was considered an adequate safeguard. Any sort of protest, however, was wasted when you were dealing with the U.S. Military Police. It took me two hours to get the vehicle back, and then we found that two silencer .22s that had been in the glove compartment had been stolen. We were never able to retrieve them.

During a quiet half hour, Tan told me some of his own background:

I was born in Boston of Cantonese parents who were already much Westernized. My father was a doctor, quite successful, and most of his patients were non-Chinese. We were indeed very cosmopolitan, hardly ever went to Chinatown, and if we did, mixed only with the upper-class Chinese who were also partly Westernized. So my sister and I had no idea what China was like or how the indigenous Chinese behaved. We both went to good American schools and knew only American ways and American standards of hygiene and cleanliness. But I soon began to sense that there was always a barrier, always a feeling that we were discriminated against by the whites. My father must have felt it, too, because in 1931, when America was hit by the Depression, he decided to take the family to China.

He'd always been very active on behalf of the Kuomintang Party, and over the years he'd sent them thousands of dollars for party funds. So when we traveled round in America we were always received with great respect by the Chinese hierarchy. Since my father knew all the top people in Canton, we expected to get the same treatment there. But it was soon obvious that they now considered us merely a nuisance—wanting jobs and favors and contributing nothing! So the big shots who had formerly written letters full of politeness and flattery would now send out their secretaries to give us the brush-off.

Indeed, the first day of my arrival, I had a taste of what lay ahead. I was walking along the street beneath the SUN department store, where the top floors were used as hotel rooms. Feeling something hit me lightly on the head, I automatically reached up to brush it off, and my fingers came away covered with green snot. I guess you'll see how it was, Charles, that this little incident typified what I went through in discovering not only the filth of China but the disdain, the contempt, the arrogance with which the indigenous Chinese treated us "overseas" Chinese who were neither true Westerners nor true Chinese. I had to start learning not only the Chinese language but Chinese ways. It was a hard and endless task.

After six months in Canton, we moved to Shanghai, where my father said the people were much more friendly, but they weren't, and now we had to struggle with Shanghai dialect! So after a year we moved to Nanking, no help with language since there we had to learn Mandarin, but my father said the people were less commercially minded. By this time he'd spent almost all his savings trying to bribe so-called friends into giving him a job or helping him to start a practice. He finally landed a small job in the Kuomintang office in Nanking. With the little money he had left, he bought a small house, and we were just settled in it when the Japs took Nanking, and we all had to run for it, and I mean literally. That same night on the road, we were attacked by robbers and fleeced of all our few possessions. So we got to Hankow totally destitute, and I had to find a job fast to keep us going.

There were only two employers—the political end of the Kuomintang Party or the army end. I chose the latter and got a job laying mines in the Yangste. The engineers on this work were Germans, quite good fellows, and I got along with them fine. There were also some Fukienese engineers who'd been trained in England, but they weren't as skillful as the Germans, nor were they as trustworthy vis-à-vis the Japs. So they were seldom told about the final hookup and timing of the mines.

The river ran two kilometers wide and about a hundred feet deep, with deeper pockets causing dangerous swirls and currents, so laying the mines was always dangerous. After considerable experimenting it was found that 970 kilos of TNT gave the necessary blast at the surface of the water. The explosive was formed into a beehive and then reinforced with concrete. When detonated it would throw up a solid chunk of water with all the different shades of the river still in layers, so it looked like a chunk of layer cake!

One day when I was tying cables to connect the charge, some Jap planes came strafing. The operation boat ran for shelter without waiting to pick us up. A line of barges had been strung across the river to hold the cables, and attached to this were a few sampans for getting about, each no bigger than a canoe. But my crew and I crowded into the nearest one, covered ourselves as best we could with our jackets for camouflage, and cut ourselves adrift. The Jap planes meanwhile proceeded to strafe up and down the river with repeated passes. One of the boys started paddling to get us into the bank. This was fatal. A plane that must have seen the movement peeled off and shot us up. One man caught a burst of machine-gun bullets, and another one had his belly totally scooped out by a bomb fragment. I and the two others were totally unhurt, but you can imagine how we felt! One was so paralyzed with shock we had to carry him ashore.

Mine laying stopped for two whole weeks while we tried to repair the chaos. During this time there were no raids. But as soon as we started laying new mines, the Japs came raiding again. This showed they must be getting tipped off by radio spies. Everyone suspected the Fukienese. The night of this first new raid the man in charge of their group had shown up on the south bank, although they were then only working on the right bank, and even though the October weather was warm, he was wearing a black coat, which made him almost invisible. Therefore, when the planes came over, the Chinese immediately started shouting, "Traitor, traitor!" and grabbed hold of this Fukienese.

Two peasants then testified against him. One of them, a woman, said she had been sleeping in the open to guard her harvest of peanuts, and as she awoke she saw the Fukienese standing there flashing a light. He retorted that he'd been looking for a plan of the mines that he'd dropped and in evidence presented a piece of rough paper with some scrawls on it. I pointed out that the moonlight was so bright that you wouldn't need a light to see this paper lying on the ground. But thanks to bribery, the Fukienese was finally released.

And soon afterwards I myself was arrested on the charge of spying trumped up by these Fukienese. I was allowed to see a German friend, but not alone, so I couldn't give him any useful tip-off. But he knew I had a girlfriend, Pearl, in the generalissimo's office. So I asked him to bring me something to read, like a book called Sea Pearl in my room. (I should mention that English was our common language.) He caught on immediately and lit off to Hangkow to contact her. But his quick departure made the Fukienese suspicious, and they sent two men in hot pursuit. By following the dikes instead of the road, my German friend outpaced them and with Pearl's help finally got through to the g'issimo, who ordered my release.

But even then I wasn't out of the soup. While I had been in jail, the adjacent fields had been laid with mines against a possible Jap flanking movement. Not knowing this, I started walking across a mined field before anyone shouted a warning. So there I was in the middle of this field, daren't go forward, and scared to turn back in case I missed my exact outward path! So every step I took was like playing Russian roulette. Although I finally made it, that was the payoff, and I decided to quit that work for good.

After a good long stretch out of work, the only job I could get was with a bogus American company set up in Indochina by a Chinese group who used me as a front to conceal their smuggling activities. The Americans, not yet being in the war, were still allowed to operate in Indochina. So I was used as an American to sign checks, tie in with the American consulate, and so forth. This went along pretty well for a time. But soon the Japs got wise and suddenly pounced so that I had to make a fast getaway in a cutter, taking all the papers relating to the transactions and a sheaf of returned checks all signed by myself. I also had a sealed envelope containing an intelligence report that a friend had asked me to take to Hong Kong. All this I stuffed behind the drawers of a small wardrobe trunk I put on board the cutter.

I hadn't got far when a Jap police boat came tearing up alongside and forced me back. When they systematically searched the boat and found some mildly compromising documents, I quickly showed real alarm, so they thought they had the full score. When they came to searching my trunk, they only emptied the drawers and compartments and never looked in the recesses. What a break! The papers they found weren't considered fully incriminating, and the American consul got me released on temporary bail. So then I promptly disappeared in the back streets of Hanoi and kept on the move for months until the Japs gave up trying to track me down.

"So life these days is comparatively dull," Tan concluded as an air raid warning sounded, and we watched the other diners scurry to the shelter.

15

TOWN LIFE

At a further meeting in the candle shop, I spent several hours teaching Ho about SI, SO, MO, X-2, and particularly about weather reports, which were, indeed, almost the top of the list, because without them our planes could not fly. Nor were weather reports confined to "sunshine or rain, clouds or clear skies, windy or calm"; they required a whole mass of detailed observations. Luckily, my pupil learned fast!

When we relaxed with a cup of green tea, Ho asked me if he might have six new Colt .45 automatics in their original wrapping. "No problem," I told him, relieved to be asked for nothing more. And that is what he was promised.

As a return gift, he gave me one of the Annamite lighting devices. In a small tube carved from buffalo horn, with one end left closed, a "pencil" of hardwood was made to fit like a piston. On one end of this "pencil" you attached with a dab of spit a fragment of a certain type of pith that ignited easily. Then with a further dab of spit to lubricate this "pencil," you inserted the tip into the open end of the cylinder and stuck it sharply right in. The intense compression on the pith caused sufficient heat to ignite it, so when you quickly extracted it and blew on the smoldering fragment, it burst into flame. Such was Vietnam in 1945!

When I happened to ask Ho when he had learned English, he explained that in his early youth he had wanted to meet French revolutionists in Paris pledged to help Indochina get free from French rule. So he had obtained a job in the galley of a French packet boat sailing to France. From Paris he had also gone to London and Liverpool and subsequently even sailed to America, where the ship tied up in Hoboken. "One day I got the ferry to Manhattan and the subway to Chinatown. That was a revelation! What struck me most was to find all those Chinese equal citizens with the Whites—at least in the eyes of the law! Although I found out later they were still second-class citizens, it was such an improvement on what we had in Indochina that my admiration for American ways, already stimulated by books on the subject, became permanently fixed from then on!"

The following morning, shortly before we were scheduled to collect Ho for the meeting with Chennault, Krauss (now back to being mere adjutant) telephoned that he urgently wanted to see me. So I raced to town and into OSS headquarters. To my barely concealed fury, all Krauss wanted was to bawl me out about the MPs picking up the jeep! "We got a bad mark for that, and I'm half a mind to ground you for two weeks! As for those two missing guns—what were they doing in the jeep? Do you usually leave weapons lying loose in an unlocked vehicle? And what have you done about getting them back?" By not arguing I shortly escaped and arrived at the candle shop more or less on time. Ho came pattering out almost before I had switched off the engine, dressed as usual in his threadbare cotton suit. But in honor of this special occasion, he had replaced a missing button on his jacket.

Bernard joined me outside Chennault's offices, and we were shortly taken through to the inner sanctum, where Doreen brought forward two chairs while the general himself presented one for Ho personally, after which he went back behind his desk which was the size of a double bed. We must have seemed a curious quintet: Chennault in a smart tropical-worsted USAAF uniform complete with Sam Browne and two rows of medals; Bernard in a khaki shirt and pants; me in my gabardine bush jacket and Marine Corps cap; "Old Man Ho" in his cotton tunic and sandals; and Doreen in her khaki jacket and skirt made by Saks Fifth Avenue, which had been flown out express. A Eurasian girl served the coffee, but I did not notice what she wore.

Chennault led off by telling Ho how grateful he was about the rescued pilot. Essentially the Southern gentleman, the general invariably treated Asians with the courtesy that Southerners are noted for. On this occasion he turned on all his charm because he hoped that in this sandaled peasant lay our best chance of redeveloping a radio net.

"I'm always glad to help the Americans," said Ho.

"That's great—because now we'd like your help against the Japanese. I think Lieutenant Fenn has already told you how. Is there anything you'd like to ask about?"

"No, thank you, General. But there's one small favor I should like to ask . . ." I drew a deep breath. But it was too late to try to intervene. Ho had already come forward. "May I have your photograph?" I almost gasped with relief.

"With pleasure!" Chennault pressed the bell, and in due course Doreen produced a sheaf of eight-by-ten glossies from which Ho was invited to take his pick. After tendering his grateful thanks, Ho then asked the general if he would do him the honor of signing it, whereupon Chennault took up his Parker Golden Arrow pen and wrote across the bottom in a clear, bold script, "Yours sincerely, Claire L. Chennault." So after warm goodbyes, we trooped out into Kunming's sparkling air and drove away.

Without radio contacts to Indochina, our life at the camp became rather limited to leisure activities or unexpected entertainment, such as when Bob Lee used a match to investigate "an empty can," thereby blowing up the residual gasoline with a whoof that removed his eyebrows and part of his hair.

Bernard, who liked dancing, went to a dance party at OSS and later reported, "Two cases of rum and one of whiskey were consumed by eighty men and thirteen women dressed up like whores at a wedding. Betty M., being queen of the ball, wore a dress shrunk on her so tight you could read her pulse. General Chivas went the rounds adding to his collection of empty cigarette packs, boasting he now has seventy-three, all different. And Colonel Smith wanted to know whether you've received your star." "Twinkle, twinkle, little star, How I wonder where you are."

By way of an outing for the staff, we drove them out into the mountains to visit a temple. Getting conflicting directions from woodcutters, charcoal coolies, and tungsten miners, we got hopelessly lost in the barren mountains until a little old woman driving a pig set us right. The landscape suddenly became green clad and almost tropical, and there amid a grove of towering eucalyptus was a red and gold temple, inside which a dozen monks were busily redecorating the eight hundred life-size gods, horribly grotesque, yet distressingly lifelike, around the walls. Other monks were playing fantasias on gongs while a third group tapped their heads on the floor in measured unison. On an altar decorated with an enormous gold Buddha and two bodhisattvas, clusters of incense tapers sent up long curls of smoke to a ceiling festooned with streamers. Then through the midst of this Hollywood spectacle came six or eight neophytes bearing buckets of night soil, which, after suitable bows to the monks, they carried off through the doorway.

On the way home we passed a village holding a market fair. Hundreds of peasants with mules and donkeys piled high with goods were milling around as if in a ballet. Most of the men wore the usual blue shirt and trousers, but some of the women wore costumes of pink or green with gold and silver brooches adorning their hair. At the bottom of the social scale were those in rags so far gone they seemed draped in withered seaweed.

When I got back to camp, an excited Liangski said he had renewed contact with our former Mengkai agent, who had now crossed the border into China near the coast and wanted to know if we could arrange to pick him up by submarine! However, this suggestion, then ludicrous, later gave Gordon the idea for a practical scheme.

After working seven days a week since she arrived, Susan asked if she might have three days' leave. "I'd like to stay with my friend Miss Wong at the university," she said. She had mentioned this friend before and had revealed that several male students had called their friendship "unnatural." "That was because I didn't respond to their own overtures. I've read *The Well of Loneliness,* so I know enough about lesbianism to be convinced I'm entirely heterosexual." A few weeks earlier this girl had never before talked to foreigners nor scarcely spoken English outside a classroom. Even her Chinese environment had been sheltered, conventional, and limited. Yet already she could discuss such esoteric subjects.

Early on the morning of Ho's departure, Bernard and I drove him to the airport, along with his small plaited case, packet of pistols, and a couple of packages done up in rice paper. As previously discussed, Pham was to stay on for a while to liaise with me. Mac Sin would fly with Ho, and Tan would fly in a second L-5 with a generator, transmitter, and various small arms he insisted on taking.

When shaking hands to say goodbye, Ho murmured (his voice was always soft), "You have faithfully done everything you promised. You will find that I shall do the same—or even more. Try to visit us if you can. Our life down there is, of course, primitive compared with here. But we have a saying that 'a warm welcome makes a soft bed!'"

Their immediate destination was Ching Hsi, a small town on the border some three hundred miles southeast, where we still had an airstrip not yet in Japanese hands. We shortly had a wire from Tan that they had all arrived safely and were now collecting a team together for portage and protection in the two-hundred-mile walk (through Japanese-held territory) to the village of Thai Nguyen, northeast of Hanoi, where Ho had his base. This meant walking at night for two weeks. Mac Sin might have jumped in, but we could not risk breaking Tan's leg, never mind what Ho might have suffered! Indeed, for a man over fifty and already somewhat frail, a jump into a wilderness of jungle might well have been fatal.

Meanwhile, to keep in close touch with Pham, Bernard, always considerate, suggested I bed down in town and thus save the journey back and forth. So I applied for a room at the Commerce, Kunming's only hotel where one might secure a small degree of "Western" comfort. Although rooms cost the then-high price of ten U.S. dollars a night, they were nevertheless hard to come by, so manageress Mrs. Brown suggested I might buy a Mandarin coat for twenty U.S. dollars. When I declined, she then proposed I buy four places for the special Easter Sunday breakfast at only three dollars each. Having agreed, and been given a room, I was then subjected to a lecture on how to behave. "We hope you won't be bringing in any noisy company or having drinking parties. And of course no bad women, that's absolutely out." Looking duly shocked at such a deplorable concept, I paid a week's rent in advance plus the $12 bribe for the special Easter Sunday breakfast and hurried off before being further swindled.

Due to the Japanese coup, our work went slack until the Fourteenth Air Force and AGAS, both cut off by lack of intelligence (especially weather) from operations in Indochina, decided to increase their attacks on the Japanese in south China and needed more intelligence. I therefore enlisted a dozen recruits to be trained for this coverage. The increase in our personnel called for a big expansion in supplies and equipment, which OSS was loathe to give, even though it received from Washington all the funds and matériel it asked for and, of course, copies of all the additional intelligence we collected for the Fourteenth and AGAS. Sometimes we would spend hours cajoling first this VIP, then another, and working through the various delivery sections to get what was needed. OSS always varied between cooperation, which was apparently urged by someone higher up (perhaps in Washington, where Gordon was still bargaining), and hindrance, which was created by the hostility of department chiefs either wanting to control us or resenting our being first with operations they wanted to do themselves.

These new ventures imposed burdens on our office staff, who also had to organize larger domestic arrangements. So by way of a small treat, Bernard and I took them to dinner at the Commerce, where John and Irene Vincent and Graham Peck joined us. The girls, having touched up their complexions with cosmetics I had brought from India, were lustfully eyed by the eight or ten service personnel sitting in reluctantly male segregation. Graham Peck, celebrating the publication of another book, got two-thirds drunk instead of only half and told stories even more risqué than usual, which the girls listened to with either real or well-simulated noncomprehension. Irene, considerably traveled, was still so full of wide-eyed naïveté that she told about a girl living in the house where she and John were staying who taught GIs how to paint on plates. "She has at least a dozen pupils, and they come only one at a time because it takes a lot of concentration to paint on plates."

Susan told me later:

I'm glad you have John Vincent as a friend since he is one of the nicest men I've ever met. Yet it's curious you're such friends because he's a pessimist, and you're an optimist, nearly always cheerful; indeed, you radiate liveliness! It sometimes takes me out of my own depressions. Feeling blue has always been my weakness. I suppose it's because of my childhood. As I've told you before, I was only eleven years old when my mother died, and it left a terrible hole. Then my grandmother on my father's side persuaded him that since he had no male heir he should immediately take a second wife. And my aunt, too—she was my mother's sister—kept urging him to get someone soon. "These halls will not sound so empty when the second wife comes!"

Before this, I had loved this aunt dearly. Now I almost hated her. And yet the house was indeed so empty! I did have an older sister, but she was off at school, and since my aunt lived elsewhere, I was left to look after the house. In those days we were quite well off and had lots of servants, who now sat around at their ease and when I appeared did nothing but stand up and look sulky! In order to win their respect I tried hard to be grown-up and dignified. You can imagine how hopeless this was for a child of eleven, especially since my father was so easygoing.

In this big house where we then lived, the days seemed endless. Often my father would stay in his room all day, and I wouldn't see a soul except the difficult servants. They would ask me sullenly, "What are your orders for meals today?" and I would try desperately to think of something. Then when my sister came home for the holidays, my father said to her— jokingly, of course, but it went to my heart!—"I hope you can suggest some new things to eat. Susan's idea is always eggs!" Although he meant it kindly it was too near the bitter truth not to wound me terribly.

When at last my father decided to take a second wife, I wept even more bitterly than when my mother died. And for at least a month after this newcomer arrived, I would have to struggle against tears the whole day, until I could go off to bed and cry myself to sleep. I suppose this left a permanent wound, and that's why I get so gloomy.

"Evil is wrought by want of thought, as well as want of heart."* I could not help feeling that Susan's "kind" father had dismally failed his motherless child!"

In OSS headquarters, a new girl, Lily B., a languorous lily indeed, who certainly looked as though she had toiled not, neither had she spun, was running a clandestine news sheet to circulate in Shanghai. At Betty M.'s suggestion she called to ask me whether I could find a translator who also knew that area. "Someone well educated, see," she explained in a drawling Southern accent, "because the publication is aimed at top-level readers." Top-level readers in Kunming, where 99 percent of the population were destitute—but I promised to bear it in mind. Because it was lunchtime, we were then on our way out. Near the parking space we were joined by a major I did not know, who cut in to ask Lily to a dance that evening.

She looked him up and down. "Can you get a jeep?"

"I guess not, honey. Not for a dance. They're getting kind of hot on that."

"Then it's no deal. I hate dancing in my walking shoes."

"Couldn't you carry your dance shoes?"

"But I'd still have that long walk to the hostel. No thanks!"

After he had made a dejected retreat, Lily lamented, "You'd think, being a major, he could get a jeep!" And she gave my own vehicle, then me, appraising looks. I felt briefly tempted to respond. But there was something slightly predatory about her request. Although men think it is part of nature's great plan for them to exploit women, for women to exploit men is strictly for the birds!

That afternoon, Mr. Kenneth Hinks, a former director of the J. Walter Thompson Advertising Agency and now kingpin on the OSS planning staff, called to see me. After courteous preliminaries, he proposed: "How would it be if we brought the GBT group strictly within the OSS orbit and made you the CO?"

"That's a generous offer. But Mr. Gordon would never agree to it."

"I rather think he's already decided to opt out. And the work has to go on."

"But what about Bernard and Tan, not to mention all the others? If they should all opt out, the group would vanish."

"Then we should have to replace them. Would that be so difficult?"

"It wouldn't be difficult, it would be impossible."

He began to lose his cool. "The fact is, Lieutenant, General Wedemeyer [with a slight emphasis on these two ranks] insists that all civilian groups come under military control."

* Thomas Hood, "The Lady's Dream.

"Yes, Mr. Hinks, but does he insist that they come under OSS control?" (I remember that when I worked for one of the largest textile companies in America, their financial success hinged on the astuteness of the advertising department, who consequently were the tops. Small wonder that this former director of the J. Walter Thompson Advertising Agency, although fundamentally an amiable man (as was indeed essential in the advertising world), did not take my irony too happily.

"It so happens, Lieutenant, OSS are in the best position to take over!"

How right he was! "Let Rome in Tiber melt, and the wide arch of the rang'd empire fall! Here is my space. Kingdoms are clay."* But OSS (subsequently CIA) survived all the ravages of time and tribulations to become the most powerful, long-lasting political organization of the twentieth century.

The following morning came a host of small problems: the shower went dry; the generator gave out; the cook complained that our new recruits were invading his kitchen for midmorning snacks; and then came a message from Dick and Alec, the prestigious but exacting recruits introduced by Graham Peck, asking for field jackets, fountain pens, wristwatches, and PX dainties. Here in China, even Communists suffered from the gimme-gimme disease.

But a worse jolt came when the guard on duty fell prostrate outside his hut, coughing up blood. While I examined his prone form, someone woke up his off-duty companion, who stated flatly, "He's finished, poor fellow!"—as though he were talking about a sick dog. And when I drove the inert form to the hospital, the lieutenant on duty gave us a surprised look.

But he subsequently rendered some treatment to his little yellow brother and even added a kindly afterthought: "If that doesn't work, we'll try something else." (It did not work, and he died before they tried "something else.")

By midmorning, therefore, I was already feeling stretched. When John Vincent called in to give me the news of Roosevelt's death, I stared at him in blank incomprehension and at last exclaimed, "Roosevelt dead?"—as if he must be lying. Out there in China we had hardly heard that he was sick and simply could not believe he would ever be dead. I suppose nobody not alive at that time could understand the shock of that death to those of us who lived in America during the Depression and into the war years. Radio broadcasting was still a recent craze, and Roosevelt was the first president fully to exploit it, not only in language suitable to a president's eminence but in a voice that projected an "all men are brothers" conviction. Nor were women left out in that good-looking

* William Shakespeare, *The Tragedy of Anthony and Cleopatra*.

masculine image of Roosevelt that appeared in *Movietone News*. No other two words had the magical charm of Roosevelt's opening: "Ma friends!" That he rescued America from the Depression was more appearance than reality, because only the war really set the wheels whirring again. But Roosevelt got credit not only for that but also for his initial defiance of the Axis even before Pearl Harbor. His subsequent inspiration not only to the American people but to most of a war-shattered world surpassed that of all other great leaders of the period, even Churchill, whose charisma was less international.

This eulogy, of course, ignores the reverse side of the coin: Roosevelt was hated, maligned, and thwarted by that element of the population resenting change, particularly when it affected their status or pocketbooks. This hatred went even deeper than that. Some people resent any change. Even when you do them good, they think you are up to no good.

Another factor swaying ultimate judgment that any man is "great" is the state of contemporary events. The three presidents usually considered the greatest— Washington, Lincoln, and Roosevelt—all had to face the challenge of momentous wars. These wars were what gave them the chance to achieve their ultimate stardom.

I drove into town to give Pham some of Tan's latest reports of progress in French Indochina. After leaving the candle maker's, I was again hailed by Miss Lily Chao, who asked me along to her new abode, a small room behind a tailor's shop. Over tea and peanuts brought in by the tailor's assistant, a boy of perhaps twelve years of age wearing an old battle dress and battered bowler hat, Lily revealed that she had already obtained a job with the Fourth War Area group as a "spy" to uncover Japanese agents. "So if you don't mind, I'll lock the door as they sometimes spy on me because nobody trusts anybody else!" And after she had done so, "I've already tracked down one suspect who's been helping the Japanese in black market gasoline deals."

As near as I could gather with constant use of a dictionary, this gas had been stolen from the Fourteenth Air Force by a Chinese gang. Although this job inevitably tied her up with the Kuomintang, she explained that she was really sympathetic to the Communists, because they were the true patriots. "Almost everyone in the central government is out for what he can get. You can never run a country on cynicism and selfishness because that won't win the hearts of the people as Mao has done everywhere!" In this instance she was, of course, right. Mao did indeed win the hearts of most of the people. But unlike Ho, he failed to live up to his early devotion to their welfare and instead let himself get trapped into futile and even harmful initiatives, such as the Great Leap Forward to transform industry; the Cultural Revolution, whereby his Red Guards destroyed culture and even scholastic training; and the Little Red Book, which promoted the cult of Saint Mao. Finally came his carnival, the "Gang of Four," led by his wife (and subsequent widow), Chiang Ch'ing. Mao's devotees blamed her, but it was Mao who condoned the operation and thus inspired those devotees initially to promote it.

There now came a knock on the door. "Don't take any notice," Lily admonished. But the knocking continued, louder and louder. Then came shouting and thumping: no doubt the tailor had told the caller that Lily was home. Suddenly, I recognized the visitor's voice. When she opened the door, in burst Lao, his face purple with frustration—or was it jealous rage? When he registered that this rival, whom the tailor had probably described as a plain GI, was actually his CO, the need to show respect took precedence over his jealous doubts, and he managed at last to get himself under control. So, with an air of avuncular goodwill, I said goodbye and left.

After dinner at the Commerce, I had a final happy hour in my room playing phonograph records of Mozart, Haydn, and Scarlatti on the secondhand shop's battered machine I had laboriously tracked down in Calcutta. At ten o'clock came the blare of loudspeakers in the street announcing the curfew: "Attention, attention, all U.S. personnel! Ten p.m., ten p.m., everyone out of Kunming! You have been warned! You have been warned!"—a proscription aimed at keeping the men from whoring. One curious aspect of the war in China was that although U.S. personnel were not involved in military combat, they were unceasingly involved in the conflict between those chasing tail and those dedicated to stopping them from getting it.

For a special job in the Lingshan area (south China), Susan introduced a student named Hsu who was a native of that district. I warned him that the post we needed him for was very isolated and that he might be by himself for weeks on end. "I shouldn't mind that in the least," he assured me. "You see, I have a violin I can play happily the whole day long! That is," he added hastily, catching a look from Susan, "except of course when I'm engaged in my duties!"

Lillian Wu, always the earnest Communist, engaged me in a complicated political lecture in the manner of a well-intentioned missionary who cannot bear the thought of a good friend going to hell through sheer ignorance. Meanwhile, her beautiful features registered an expression of St. Joan of Arc hearing the Voices. While pretending to listen to her exordium on the virtues of Marxist-

Leninism, I could not but wonder what lay beneath the two-piece ensemble made with exquisite stitchery and total disregard of fit from discarded GI parachute cloth.

Ken Hinks came to tell me that he was not, after all, quite ready to promote me to CO of an OSS-controlled GBT and dished out a lot of excuses, although I knew that the Kunming hierarchy had meanwhile warned him not to get mixed up with troublesome Fenn. Meanwhile, Gordon wired us that he would be delayed several more weeks and would probably make a deal either with the British or with AGAS—certainly not with OSS.

When appointing a supervisor for the women's quarters at OSS, Krauss chose a certain Captain Wise, nicknamed Preacher Wise because he read the service on Sunday. With this halo hanging over him, the captain's moral conduct had to be above suspicion. Wise cleverly overcame this handicap by becoming engaged to one of the OSS's primmest women, with whom he could then go everywhere, including in and out of the women's quarters, because, after all, he was the supervisor and she was his fiancée! As Bernard remarked, "That's putting OSS training to really practical use!"

Further to develop my Chinese, I invited Lily Chao to the Commerce, where my room was a slight improvement on her own hen coop. Later on, while we had dinner in the dining room, the Iron Duchess (Mrs. Brown) muttered snide comments, not voicing doubts about moral behavior but about Lily's table manners (which indeed were hardly adapted to the current Western-style service in the Commerce dining room) while also giving up-and-down looks at her attire. Of Lily's two dresses, one seemed to have been made, like Susan's, from an old sack, the other from a well-worn calico curtain. Possessing no handbag, she carried her few scraps of paper money in a handkerchief that, as one might expect, daily grew dirtier, having to be washed and dried as seldom as possible because there was no available substitute. When she discovered that I was adding a few bills to her small store, she was full of surprised gratitude. "Oh, Elder Brother [she always addressed me by the respectful title of "Elder Brother" and asked me to call her by the diminutive "Smallest Sister"], how generous! Nobody ever gave me anything before that I didn't have to work for! Lao not only never gives me anything but actually borrows money from me, which he never pays back. I'd like you to know that there's nothing between us but friendship. I don't care for him at all in that way. He complains about my 'coldness' and is always pestering to know about us! So I tell him you're married and devoted to your wife—which is probably true, but you don't need to tell me; it isn't my business."

I must explain that we always conversed in Chinese, and because my Chinese was still very limited, I had to guess quite a lot—sometimes, no doubt, very inadequately.

When she mentioned a friend, Miss Chung, who wanted to meet me, I asked Vincent if he would like to make a foursome, Irene having gone back to India. Miss Chung, although not unattractive, was very short and rather plump. She fell for handsome Vincent and after dinner suggested strolling in the park, with an eventual sit-down on a bench, where she probably hoped he might even kiss her as in Western movies. But we were no sooner seated than a couple of Chinese MPs strode up and told us to get moving. I tried to suggest (big deal) this was hardly the way to address people who were enjoying the park, which was there for public use. This attempt at a courteous protest immediately calmed them down. (Although my vocabulary was poor, I had a rather good ear for the tone and rhythm of Mandarin Chinese.) "It's only for your own sake we want you to move," they equivocated. "After nine o'clock there are robbers in the park, and we can't guarantee your safety." This of course was flimflam. They, like our own MPs, were obeying that curious compulsion engendered in childhood, whereby elder brother says to elder sister, "Let's see what little Willie is doing and make him stop it!"

So after formal salutes and handshaking, we went off to the Canton Café for an ersatz coffee. A waiter impersonating a girl in the traditional style of Chinese opera was entertaining two or three tables of Chinese and one of GIs, to all of whom in turn he was making gestures of mock love. The GIs seemed unsure whether to be amused, uneasy, or annoyed. Not being able to decide, they got noisily drunk on Indochina rum. Anticipating a scene, we called for the bill and left. At the door the manager discreetly suggested we could have rooms if we wanted. Lily, with suitable indignation, said no thanks. Outside, she said she hoped we would understand why they could not take advantage of the offer. And when we said good night (perhaps with a tinge of regret?), Miss Chung remarked that she would never have believed foreigners could be so well behaved.

16

OF CUSTOMS AND CONNIVANCES

The eleven Navy pilots who had come down near Pleiku were still on our conscience. To make contact we needed to drop in a radio operator and someone who could speak Annamese. It was through an unexpected source that I worked out a scheme. Lily Chao had an operator friend, Humphrey Ho, who was willing to be dropped in if we would also send an Annamite as interpreter. Although it was a long shot, I thought we might try it. Pham introduced me to an Annamite volunteer named Tuei.

So we sent this pair to the parachute school. I did, of course, feel dubious about including an Annamite who was potentially anti-French to rescue eleven Frenchmen and even more dubious when I learned that Tuei's father had been executed by the French! But Pham assured me I could absolutely rely on Tuei's obeying orders as given, without a thought about whom he was helping. If Pham, representing Ho Chi Minh, told Tuei to kill Frenchmen he would kill them, but if he was now told to save them he would save them, or certainly try. That was how things worked in the Vietminh.

Pham also insisted that Tuei would not want to be paid anything beyond expenses. But because we had to bribe Humphrey with generous pay to do this very dangerous job, I thought it would be unfair, not to say demoralizing, to pay Tuei any less, especially given that Humphrey, not knowing a word of the language, would be entirely dependent on Tuei's goodwill. "It's long odds," Bernard remarked.

"But at least we'll have tried," I countered.

Bernard gave me a wry smile. And I couldn't help remembering he was the best poker player because he knew the exact odds of all the combinations!

It always seems surprising that in this world of teeming humanity, our paths with certain individuals cross and recross in the most unlikely manner. This has never happened to me more oddly than one morning when Wichtrich asked me if I would take into the GBT a certain AGAS officer he had not found a niche for. "He's a great guy, as I'm sure you'll agree, and speaks fluent French, so that would be useful in negotiating with the French!" I didn't mention I spoke enough French myself to get along. "Moreover," continued Wichtrich, "he's also a Marine Corps lieutenant, so you two will have lots in common."

Because I was not all that keen to have Marine Corps companionship, this sales talk suggested a certain shuffling off. But Wichtrich was too good a friend to disoblige, so I told him okay.

Now it happened that sixteen years earlier, when I was working on the HMS *Aquitania* as chief steward in the tourist class, a young man traveling first class came to ask a favor. "There's a girlfriend of mine traveling tourist, and as they won't allow her in first class, could you arrange a dinner party here for the two of us plus a couple of other friends?" Nothing could have been easier, and the morning after the dinner he came back to thank me very courteously with a ten dollar tip. It was not because of this that I subsequently remembered him so well but because he was one of the handsomest, gayest, and indeed most charming young men I had ever met. Also, as I later learned in newspapers and magazines, where his picture often appeared, sometimes with a smashing girlfriend, this Mr. Winston Churchill Guest was also a famous polo player and very rich socialite. When one is twenty-two years old and still a greenhorn, one cannot but be impressed by such a combination.

When Wichtrich called his new man in, I found myself shaking hands with a Marine Corps lieutenant whose somewhat bloated face and paunchy figure I would not have known from Adam if he had not been introduced as Winston Guest. I do not doubt he found me equally divorced from the unlined, bright-eyed helot of 1929. But when I reminded him of our former encounter, he politely pretended to remember me quite well.

Guest, indeed, exhaled good nature. He suggested that, as an introductory get-together, I be his guest for dinner. "And I hear you have some girls working for you, so you might care to bring a couple along?" I felt reluctant to include our own girls in a personal relationship, but to be obliging I invited Lily and Miss Chung. This, as I should have known, proved to be a poor choice. The girls spoke no English, and Guest, of course, spoke no Chinese. His very bulk intimidated

Miss Chung, who hardly reached his shoulder. Guest was always good company, and he had bought, at a fabulous price, a bottle of genuine Hennessey, which greased the works for himself but did little to help the girls, because they only sipped it out of politeness. Guest drank half the bottle, with mounting enthusiasm and conviviality despite all these handicaps. When he got amorous with Miss Chung, it was with the good-hearted approach of an extrovert. She was not exactly on a par with those American belles in the polo photographs! But both girls were dismayed at his fondling Miss Chung in a restaurant. Guest pretended not to notice the girls' noisy guzzling of soup, regurgitation, and spitting out of bones all over the table. Even by Chinese standards Lily and Miss Chung could not be described as dainty eaters, life not having blessed them with that cachet. Guest's own background precluded snobbery, but no Westerner attending his first meal in China with members of the Chinese proletariat could escape being somewhat disconcerted.

When Guest suggested going to the Commerce for coffee and liqueurs, Lily begged off and later confided to me, "I'm so sorry, Elder Brother, but Mr. Guest was too bad mannered for us to have any more of his company." Each of us carried his own special thermometer to register the social temperature.

Radio messages from Tan informed us that Ho, having crossed the border into Indochina and having set up a small, secluded base, had then sent back a team of twenty men to escort Tan and Mac Sin with their equipment through the Japanese lines and the numerous bandits infesting those jungles. For further protection, the group had also disguised themselves as border smugglers, hiding their arms and equipment in the rough baskets used locally for merchandise.

We later received reports that after a difficult and dangerous journey, they at last reached Ho's main base, a mere hut in the entrance of a cave beside a waterfall (the subsequently famous site of Bac Po, currently visited by crowds of devoted pilgrims). In this area Ho had a few dozen followers, but claimed to have several hundred nearby. Tan mentioned that in Ching Hsi, Jo-Jo had warned him that Ho was a Communist and dangerously anti-French. When I sent OSS this report, I was asked to investigate Ho's background in detail. Pham helped me assemble the following:

Ho Chi Minh was born near Vinh, a coastal town 200 miles south of
Hanoi. This area had become a center for revolutionists, since the rough
terrain offered good shelter. So from an early age Ho became rebellious to
French domination, even though his father was a small government official. Ho's education included a spell at a technical school which trained,

amongst other workers, various types of seamen. It was thanks to this he subsequently got a job as kitchen porter in French ships sailing to Africa, Europe and America. Always looking for contacts to help his countrymen get free from the French, he finally realized this goal could be achieved only through organized groups. So he settled in Paris and became immersed in left-wing political groups, which ultimately brought him to the notice of the French Sureté, although they didn't actually arrest him.

In 1923, the successful revolution in Russia encouraged his socialist friends, already impressed by his vigorous grasp of revolutionary principles, to send Ho to Moscow as a representative to the Fifth International Congress, a famous milestone in socialist development. Also impressed by Ho's potential, the Soviets trained him in the technique of communist-revolution, which has nothing to do with throwing bombs or spouting on street corners, but with organizing, enlisting effective support, and preparing for armed resistance, and ultimately sent him to Canton, then a major center of revolutionary activity under Chiang Kai-shek, at that early period still an opportunist revolutionary. Very shortly, Chiang double-crossed his Communist partners, incarcerating some, executing others. Ho escaped only by a hair's breadth, eventually getting back to Moscow. [At that period, this was a difficult journey and merely one of several prodigious treks that Ho made in the next twenty years.] His later mission took him to Brussels, Siam, Yenan, and Kunming where in 1940 he founded the Vietminh and met Vo Ngugen Giap, later to become General-in-Chief of the North Vietminh army which overcame the French and helped defeat the combined American and South Vietnam forces.

In 1942 Ho received reports that Chiang Kai-shek, ever more encircled by the invading Japanese, was now ready to make a deal with the Vietnamese in return for their help. But when Ho went to China to exploit this possibility, either the information was false or Chiang reneged on his tentative promise: Ho was arrested and harshly imprisoned for a year until 4th War-Area Chang Fa-kwei (left-orientated) helped to get him released.

Ho then returned to Vietnam for the first time since going off to sea twenty-five years earlier, and actively promoted Vietminh enclaves. His recent trip to Kunming was in connection with the rescue of the pilot, Shaw.

Despite this confirmation that Ho was indeed a Communist, Wedemeyer instructed us to go on using him and indeed to expand all our operations both in Indochina and the border areas. We therefore enlisted more agents for training in radio, maps, weather, and general intelligence. I often went to bed dazed from talking, explaining, and listening to problems, many of them personal and even emotional. It is a myth that the Chinese are serene and withdrawn. Indeed, it was because Confucius considered them too emotional that he preached the virtues of impassivity, which subsequently became doctrinaire, until at least the Communist takeover.

The indefatigable Betty M. cornered me with a new scheme for MO work in all the main Indochina cities; would I kindly introduce her to this Annamite named Pham who was still around someplace? When I obliged she tried to wean him away from GBT to work directly with OSS. But Pham, of course, was not interested.

We had been hoping to get one of the kerosene refrigerators that were recently made available to VIPs in OSS. When my requisitions were turned down, I became acquainted with the man delivering this equipment and asked him what he would want to deliver a refrigerator without a delivery note. "How about a couple of 'thirty-eights' for myself and my buddy?" These Smith & Wesson .38 revolvers, issued to the Navy and Marine Corps officers but not to the Army, had a certain cachet through being romantic "six-shooters," so they were always popular.

"Bring the refrigerator, and the guns are yours," I told him. He delivered it that same afternoon. "The stupid man argues, the foolish man pleads, the honest man sighs, the weak man weeps, the clever man bargains, but the successful man connives."

When the weather got cool, Lily had nothing to wear that had any warmth, so I gave her an old GI blanket, out of which she made a lining for her corduroy coat. My Chinese had sufficiently improved so that with the aid of a dictionary I was able to understand the following stories:

> Yesterday Miss Chung and I were having coffee in the Cantonese restaurant when two GIs came in already half drunk and ordered a bottle of Yunnan wine. Then one of them came over and filled Miss Chung's cup with wine, even though it was still half full of coffee, and ordered her to drink it. When she refused he got abusive and tried to kiss her into the bargain. Of course, he didn't know that she taught athletics in a factory she worked in, so she gave him such a clip that his cheek turned scarlet.

When his pal hurried over, I gave him a clout with a chair, and he actually drew his gun! But meanwhile the boss of the restaurant had brought in some American MPs, and while they were all arguing, Miss Chung and I walked out. Did you hear about the accident on the Kweiyang road? Two trucks crashed head on, and twenty-three people were killed and another thirty-five injured. A friend of mine was amongst the latter, and while I was visiting her in hospital the head nurse asked me to tell her that her young sister was amongst those killed. So what else could I do except tell her? And the poor girl fainted dead away!

On my way to the jeep, an AGAS officer I did not know handed me a small packet. "It seems you left this in the safe in Colombo last year, and they're tired of seeing it around." It proved to be some jewelry I had bought for my wife in Kandy and forgotten about (let me plead the weight of problems, not indifference!), although it was beautiful stuff: a gold and opal necklace and a gold bracelet woven in the form of a snake with ruby eyes. Eyeing these treasures I felt a wave of fond memory for that beautiful Kandy with its mountains, tropical exuberance, and Temple of the Tooth mirrored in the lake. (I will add here that fifty-three years later, when I went back to have a look, everything was much the same except that the Temple of the Tooth, almost empty on my earlier visits, was now invaded by several thousand visitors, most of whom were Buddhist Sri Lankans, but included some foreign tourists, six of whom were accidentally shot and killed a day or two later by Tamil insurgents staging a coup.)

Tuei, now training in the parachute school, wrote me a note in curious French that he was determined to serve me to the best of his ability. But would I please include among his equipment some really fast poison pills in case he got caught by the Japanese? When I solicited a couple from Dr. Lomas, he gave me a small packet of powder simply marked "Poison! In case of accident, drink quantities of magnesia, soda, Epsom salts." I was tempted to keep it for personal emergency. One never knew!

Heppner sent for me and wanted details of our operations with Ho. After some discussion he said, "Since you yourself organized this hookup, why not bring the whole setup into OSS—to which, I must remind you, you are still officially assigned?"

I gave him all the reasons against, which I had already given Hinks. He stalled the way Hinks did and when we parted gave me a look partly puzzled, partly annoyed. There was always this wall between Heppner and me. This was partly my fault in wanting to do things my way and partly his in wanting to direct operations—as he was, of course, entitled to do! But operations in OSS, not being strictly military, required cooperation, leeway, concessions, and insight. Sometimes, of course, this could prove a weakness: dimwits in responsible positions, recalcitrants needing control, and idlers exploiting the chance to do nothing. Operations like this needed either military discipline or (preferably) trust. In OSS they substituted efficiency with what got them into the organization: prestige, pull, high connections, and sales talk.

The same thing happened (to my more distant observation) in AGAS. But Wichtrich was (to my somewhat closer observation) an exception, and his staff on the whole seemed more approachable, responsive, and genuine. The "born leader" is no doubt the "leader born." And that requires character, brains, drive, and Ho's determination. I think Heppner had all of those, but there was one essential he lacked (in my opinion): a personality that sent out a signal somewhat akin to Confucian *hsu*, but one that evoked enthusiasm, trust, and response. That's what Wichtrich had, and that put me in his camp. (Many years later, Betty M., who had married Heppner [since dead], wrote me: "Dick once told me he had two crosses to bear, both named Fenn: one was Missionary Fenn, always clamoring for handguns to bribe his flocks, and the other [was] Lieutenant Fenn, always so sorry that he always knew best!" Funny, I never remember being sorry!)

Mrs. Brown asked me to write a letter for her in French addressed to the French Military Mission inviting the ladies employed there to a party in honor of the American task force that had just arrived from the Burma front. Although I obliged her, I could not help visualizing the spluttering rage of the Frenchmen at being asked to contribute their girls to a party given in honor of *ces sâles bêtes, les Americains* (that dirty lot, the Americans)!

Susan offered me her assessment of Chinese-American relations:

The Americans have come to China unwillingly. Even if they happen to be volunteers in the Army and anxious to do something useful for the war effort, they are still reluctant to come to China and be deprived of everything they are used to at home. Having arrived, they find places like Kunming full of lazy, pleasure-loving Chinese who in turn are automatically despising the Americans as ill-mannered barbarians. Most of these Chinese take no interest in the war except as a way to make money. It's true some of them, mostly Communists, are trying to fight the Japanese, but most are only pretending. But when accused of this, they retort that the Americans won't even pretend. "They come to China supposedly to fight the Japanese," our people complain, "but they are careful to stay where it's safe and meanwhile criticize the Chinese for running away as soon as the Japanese appear." All this may be true or false, according to the way you look at it, but it means that both sides are constantly misunderstanding each other and steadily disliking each other more and more.

Although this analysis exaggerates, it comes near enough to the truth and emphasizes how essential it is to teach those engaged in war overseas the realities of life among the inhabitants. How ironic that nearly all these ground forces in China were taught a mass of detail about weapons, tactics, maps, the enemy, and how to survive, when for the majority, none of this was ever applicable, but almost nothing was discussed about how to get along with and even win the cooperation of the people among whom they had to live.

Whenever I took our trainees off to the hills for firing practice (more as a substitute for any other entertainment than practical use), the curiosity of farmers and Chinese soldiers prompted them to come and watch, with imminent chances of their getting shot by stray bullets or ricochets. Although I shouted at them or drove them away, they only thought I was being aggressive, so they always came back when they estimated I had cooled down. The women were more sensible. At the noise of the first shot, they ran like hares and then stayed well out of sight.

The cook bought two fine geese that lorded it around the compound and gave the camp a fine farmyard appearance as well as extra sentinels. When they hatched goslings, these young ones followed us around everywhere, beseeching food, while their parents squawked indignant protests. When a jeep injured one of the parents and squashed two goslings, I regretfully ordered the cook to get rid of them. The wounded bird turned up on the dinner table, and the cook sold the other goose and surviving goslings. How empty the compound then seemed!

Outside the kitchen door hung a dove in a cage. Whenever I passed, it turned its head to watch me with what seemed ineffable sadness. "How would you like to be shut up in a cage?" I protested to the cook's plump wife. She stared at me for a moment in bewilderment and then burst into a roar of laughter. "Must be mighty big cage!" was roughly her comment.

Surprised by Simon's bananas and roses, Susan prompted me to make our living quarters more attractive with plaited grass mats, cushions, and Chinese scrolls. Considering my desire for visual gratification, it was curious how little effort I made to procure them. Perhaps I did not want to include anything that suggested permanence. Although one snatched a few pleasures when possible, one was always longing for that wonderful day when the exile would end.

Hearing a shot fired inside our latrines, I found one of the AGAS men who had had business in the camp now poised over the "drop" and waving a revolver. To discourage rats we had thrown down lime, which made the excrement inedible even for rats. Thus deprived of their bread and butter, the rats had learned how to grab the desired morsels before they dropped into the lime. So the AGAS man had been ready with his pistol. "Missed the sonovabitch!" he lamented. So that rat lived to seize another turd.

A second shooting scene that day was rather more serious. An appalling crash inside the cipher room sent me running to investigate. I found Helen sitting back at her desk with her mouth agape. A bullet had come through the wall from outside, passed two inches above her head, and then gone clean through the opposite wall! Had it been the taller Susan sitting there, she might well have been drilled. We later found the spent bullet, a steel-jacketed .30-caliber rifle bullet, outside in the courtyard. It had no doubt been fired by a GI out hunting in the rice fields—the only kind of shooting our boys ever did in China.

One evening when I arrived at the Commerce, I found Lily asleep on the bed. The room boy told me that when Miss Chao had arrived a little earlier, he had let her in—he trusted that was in order? I assured him it was and ordered a pot of tea. While I sat there sipping, Lily slowly opened her eyes, obviously unable to fathom her curious locale. Then suddenly registering, she jumped up with a start exclaiming, "Oh, I hope you didn't mind! It's so lovely to come to this refuge!" Refuge—that was how I felt about it myself. Camp life had become an endless buzz of activity and problems. The one thing I had previously enjoyed was waking up with the sun and having breakfast on the riverbank. But this idyll had been shattered by the mob of new recruits clamoring for their own meal. And the servants had begun to get difficult, not so much because of the extra work but because these newcomers took advantage of the unlimited food, PX goodies, and sugar ad lib! One morning when they complained that there were no eggs, I asked the number one boy why not.

"Sir, eggs have gone up to sixty dollars apiece!"

"So what—it's not your money!"

"No, sir, but why waste money buying eggs for such riffraff? Let them eat what they always get—rice gruel and salt!"

On arrival for the Chinese lesson, Lily mentioned that a friend of hers, Miss Lok, had had a rather bad accident. "There was a fire at this place where she's staying. The girls had wanted to clean their dresses, so the boy brought them a can of gasoline. When one of them threw away her cigarette stub, it fell in the opened can, which exploded and set the room on fire in a flash. Miss Lok was the last one to get out, but she thought she was perfectly all right until the other girls started screaming at the sight of her. So then she saw in the mirror that her hair was burned off clean to the scalp! And as if that wasn't bad enough, her boyfriend now refuses to kiss her!"

"But you told me once that Chinese boys and girls don't kiss!"

"Oh, they do when they're sleeping together," said Lily brightly.

Later, in the Commerce dining room I met an amiable French civilian who had been among those flown in from Calcutta. When we happened to discuss Malraux's *La Condition Humaine* (*Man's Fate* in the English edition), I made a no-doubt clumsy speech in French to the effect that Malraux had no real under-standing of China, and the political background he presented had no relation to the reality of Chinese politics of that time. The Frenchman heard me out with a polite smile and replied in perfect English, "I quite agree, it's all balls." At this point two U.S. Army officers sitting at another table, and no doubt hearing my French, came over to ask, in terrible French, where the French consulate was. When I told them in English, they said, "Gee, you speak good English!" And having studied my bush jacket (which bore no insignia) and my Marine Corps cap badge, they asked, "Are you with the French Marines?"

An OSS man who had just arrived and with whom I had shared a room in Schools and Training, Washington, told me confidentially that my reports about GBT-OSS relations had been raising a lot of eyebrows among the hierarchy back home. "I guess you make everything too goddam clear. They hate anyone to be critical, especially anyone in charge of a significant project, in case Donovan happens to see it personally, which he did in the case of one of your reports about Ho, and said they'd screwed up in not getting him lined up themselves." Oh hell, no wonder they had put the screws on me to bring our outfit into Central! Considering my obstinate refusal to play ball, I could not help feeling that Heppner had been very long-suffering.

After reading my copy of Lawrence's *Sons and Lovers,* Susan told me with some embarrassment that she had not been able to refrain from pencil marking certain passages that particularly struck her. I found they mostly had to do with the love between Paul and Miriam, especially with the girl's inability to face up to the reality of sex and how she had brooded over the effect this might have on Paul, perhaps leaving him full of frustration and even of anger. Although I myself was never "full of anger," I was often enough full of frustration—not, indeed, on account of Susan (delightful though she was) but because no sex was ever available except by buying it, which I almost never did. Chinese women, except the bought ones, were almost inviolable, and not only were "foreign" women very scarce but also there was never any privacy! Furthermore, to cap all, a sexual relationship was then a much more serious matter, partly because birth control was so primitive and partly because moral standards (or perhaps one should say, moral taboos) were much more severe at that time. The Japanese were more realistic in meeting this problem by providing large retinues of women for their armies. The French also installed camps of prostitutes ("native" of course). How odd that in wartime, certain nations, including the USA, can so easily resort to what is usually considered the worst of all crimes, i.e., wholesale murder, but cannot condone the much smaller offense of fornication! One must concede, however, the more realistic concern of the authorities that this offense is condemned less as a sin than for the often resultant disease.

Lily used her handkerchief to carry money in, and Susan used hers as a table napkin. (Tissues were not yet in general use.) I did not remember seeing any Chinese use a handkerchief as a nose wiper. They considered that wrapping up snot and spit and putting it in one's pocket or handbag was unhygienic at best and disgusting at worst. Sun Yat-sen told a story of the time when he was traveling up the Yangtze on a boat captained by an Englishman. The captain came into the lounge one day when a Chinese passenger happened to clear his throat and spit on the carpet. The disgusted captain, having used his handkerchief to wipe up the spit, then threw it into a wastebasket. The Chinese vainly tried to hide his own disgust at this gratuitous squander mania!

Susan confided that Helen distressed her at times with her endlessly cheerful gossip and total oblivion of Susan's disgust. Subsequently, Helen confided to me that she found Susan's habit of staying up half the night reading very distressing. "If I suggest that she turn out the light and go to sleep, she can hardly suppress her frustration! And you know how good-tempered she usually is!" Because Susan so often looked tired out, I decided to raise this point with her. She admitted being inconsiderate but emphasized that the night was the only time she could call her own. "So I treasure every minute I can stay awake!"

On the first of May some of our personnel asked to listen to Soviet broadcasts celebrating the big day. When I asked Liang jokingly if he intended reporting all these Communists to Tai Li, he replied, "Since about half the population of China is potentially Communist, I can't think Tai Li will need to know the names of these particular rebels!"

When Humphrey Ho called in from the parachute school to finalize our plans, he asked whether I thought that despite not knowing the language he had "a reasonable chance" of getting back safely. So we went over his cover story in repeated detail, including his procedure if he got separated from Tuei, until we were both goggle-eyed from tiredness. I had no sooner gone to bed than a knock on the door announced Humphrey again. "No more, for Chrissake!" I yelled. But he only wanted aspirin for one of the other boys who had a headache. The next morning before he went off, he confided that his sister had spinal meningitis and had small hope of survival. It was mostly to pay hospital bills that he had taken on this mission.

Another visitor was Charles Kwei, one of my agent-friends I had handed over to Faxton. He had just completed a mission in the Shanghai area with two OSS civilian personnel. "They were very friendly and good-natured, and at first we got along fine. But soon I could hardly bear their drunkenness and chasing women half the night. Then the day after, they'd laze in bed and do no work. Not once the whole mission did we make contact with headquarters. After setting up our base of operations in Chi-ning, they stayed only a week because it was 'a dump.' We organized two other bases for similar brief periods. But most of the time we were moving around because the boys wanted 'a change of scene,' which really meant a change of girls. The total of four months' time and two million Chinese dollars netted zero accomplishment."

I had a final talk with Pham before his intended departure to join Ho, going first on the train to Kaiyuan, then walking about three hundred miles, a lot of it through Japanese-held territory. "Not that I care about that," he had told me, "being young and healthy. It was a different story with Mr. Ho. Your flying him as far as Ching Hsi was literally a lifesaver. His health has never been good since that horrible year in the Chinese prison. Even the walk from Ching Hsi—fifteen nights—almost finished him off."

17

MORE QUIET
CONVERSATIONS

A courier brought letters, maps, documents, Japanese leaflets, and other MO material from Tan, plus a brief note from Ho, written in careful English, although with a Chinese brush. Tan's letter reported among other things the Japanese coup of March 9:

> In Hanoi all prominent French military personnel and government officials were invited to a banquet. Then suddenly, after being fed, they found themselves escorted to prison! Most other Frenchmen were simultaneously arrested in a swift house-to-house round up. Those willing to submit to total Japanese rule were turned free, wearing an arm band with OK on it. . . .
> Mac and I are living on corn-mush. Could a courier bring some powdered milk, coffee, and ration fruit-bars, or anything else not weighing too much?

The courier reported that Ho had now alerted all his group to be on the lookout for downed pilots. And would we be sure that before setting out on their missions they wore native clothes beneath their uniforms? They should then take off the uniforms fast, as well as their shoes, and bury them. In their native clothes they should have a thousand piastres distributed here and there to pay for food and other expenses en route. The sign to and from the Vietminh would be to raise the left foot and scratch the ankle. From now on it would not be safe to contact any French because those pro-Allies people had nearly all been put behind bars or had fled into China.

Ho's brief letter thanked us for our help, reported his safe arrival, and asked for news of Pham. "Excuse me that I do not write more just now, rather tired after long journey. My best regards to You and Mr. Bernard."

When I took Tan's material into the MO section, I was received by Jim Withrow, a lawyer-partner of Donovan's and a pal of people such as Litvinov and the Webbs. While handing round marrons glacés, he told us stories about his recent mission in Burma utilizing Japanese prisoners for MO work. "We were amazingly successful in extracting information thanks to a special interrogation method I worked out." He then went on about it for twenty minutes. But I knew from my own experience in Burma that when Japanese soldiers allowed themselves to be captured alive instead of committing suicide or at least biting off their tongues, they considered themselves disgraced beyond all salvation and would talk freely, not having been told to keep their mouths shut because that would have conceded the disgraceful possibility of their staying alive or not biting off their tongues!

Japanese advances into China had become so serious that all transport planes were detailed off for emergency use. Consequently, two GBT teams thankfully dispatched to the airfield several days earlier came back to the camp and drove us up the wall again with their noise, disorderliness, and "gimme" clamors. Sugar vanished as soon as it was put into the bowls. Coffee, tea, and milk disappeared with almost equal speed. The final indignity was when some of them "borrowed" a jeep and shortly came walking back to camp, reporting it had broken down. I warned them that if they did not have it back within an hour, I would fine each of them ten U.S. dollars. After a horrified gasp they scurried off and ultimately pushed it back two whole miles! I trust that taught them.

Tuei rang up to tell me that he and Humphrey had also been held up and then asked whether he could have some cigarettes. I had no sooner agreed to that when Humphrey came on the line to ask for a fountain pen. "Gimmegimme" is a disease like syphilis: after being spread by "civilization," it becomes even more virulent among the natives.

I received a document from Marine Corps headquarters announcing I had been promoted to the rank of captain. To celebrate I took our original staff to dinner at the Commerce and bought everyone a ticket in a raffle Mrs. Brown had organized for a box of liqueur chocolates imported from Indochina. This was won to loud applause by Liangski, who seemed to get more joy in handing them around than from eating any himself.

John Vincent gave me his analysis of our girls:

Helen's expression is always aware, lively, and eager. Her eyes are moist, which makes them shine, thus adding to her liveliness. Although she isn't attractive physically, one always enjoys her vivacity. Lilian has the face and

expression of a child, the eyes of a madonna, and the smile of a buddha.
Susan has the face of a Sung princess and the smile of a Mona Lisa. I often find myself watching her. You don't often see a girl like that!

We were sitting outside while the sun went down in the usual red glow behind the hills, making a black silhouette of the two-storied temple decorating the village far away. The last of the peasants were trudging in from their long day in the fields, cheerfully gossiping despite their weariness. A string of high-spirited asses frisked past, heads perked up, flanks as neat and plump as deer in parks: no sad donkeys like those you see in Spain or Italy. In the middle of this bucolic idyll, Liang rushed over from the radio shack to tell us breathlessly that he had picked up a broadcast: "Germany has collapsed, and the Russians are already in Berlin!"

We were briefly startled into silence. "So all we have to do now is finish this one," I finally remarked.

"It's going to be a long haul," said Vincent. "We're further away from finishing than we were at the beginning." In China that's how it seemed and really was until the very end.

I was awakened at four the next morning by a phone message that the Fourteenth was now ready to fly off the GBT team. Even at a hurried breakfast they emptied the sugar bowls and asked for PX dainties! Our transport man, Yip, was sick, and his substitute had vanished, so I had to drive them to the airfield myself, but it was a small price to pay for getting rid of them.

On the way back I called in at the customs house to clear some packages they had told us to collect. This was another time when I thought I must be dreaming. Not only were there five men sleeping on the small floor, but hanging on the wall in dazzling array were five tiger skins! It seemed that five Frenchmen who had arrived from Indochina had nowhere to sleep except here on the floor, and because each had bought a tiger skin, there was no room except on the wall.

On arrival back in camp I found Liangski, who had a heart of gold, busily grabbing the baby sparrows from their nests around the eaves and flinging them into a box. "We'll feed them up on various tidbits," he explained, "and in about a week they'll be ready to eat!" It was useless to protest; he would not believe I was serious in caring what happened to birds.

Pham having left, I now had no excuse to keep my haven at the Commerce, but the rent was paid for one more week. Lily had not shown up for several days. Then I had a note that she was confined to bed with jaundice: the result, no doubt, of poor diet. Assembling some bread and butter, milk powder, and sulfadiazine, I called to see her. A Chinese "doctor" had administered a pot of "blood restorer," consisting of chicken entrails and other nauseous ingredients, which the poor girl was sipping at with grimaces. Should I or should I not throw it out? How could I be sure it would not do her good? When the proprietor's wife looked in and saw Lily eating the bread and butter, she remarked, "I'm so pleased Lily has a polite foreign friend. Chinese men are never so thoughtful."

"Mrs. Mak has been very kind," Lily told me later. "I feel so sorry for her, because her husband is a very bad type, always sleeping with prostitutes. She told me confidentially he has a lump on his penis as big as a walnut." This piece of news required not only some searching in the dictionary but a few eloquent gestures.

Americans arriving in China for the first time were handed a leaflet that included the following: "The Chinese are a proud and sensitive people who must never be treated as anything less than equals." I have previously alluded to this leaflet (the rest of which dealt mostly with more practical matters, such as the penalties for consorting with whores). The admonition about how to treat the Chinese was not only absurdly inadequate but also came for the first time three years after the initial arrival of American forces in China and a mere few months before we left! Even to call the Chinese "a proud and sensitive people" shows a total ignorance of reality. The Chinese are never "proud"—they are (or were at that period) self-confident in the innate superiority that comes from four thousand years of continuous history. Their written language, unparalleled in its combination of ingenuity, artistry, and expressiveness, has existed for similar millenniums. Not surprisingly, the Chinese word for China, Chung-Kuo, means "Middle Kingdom" or "Centerpiece of the world."

It is, of course, true that this innate superiority has been frequently shaken, never more so than during the "Opium War" in 1840 when the British fleet invaded China to inflict opium on the obstinate barbarians. Some gilt has thus been worn off the superior Chinese image, but the solid body of innate superiority always remains and indeed was still intact at the time we are dealing with. Whether or not it has remained in Communist China, I cannot say, not having been there. As for the leaflet calling the Chinese "sensitive," this was also nonsense; they were merely indignant, which is very different!

In offering this assessment I do not mean to ignore the existence of an uneducated and ignorant Chinese peasantry constituting the bulk of the population, who had neither contact nor knowledge of this wonderful Chinese heritage. Nor do I wish to overlook the behavior of upper-echelon Chinese emigrants who promptly shed their Chinese heritage of culture and tradition in favor of money grubbing strictly in line with the once-despised but nonenvied Westerners.

This leaflet did not prompt OSS into taking down the notice prominently displayed in their entrance hall: "Chinese personnel are not allowed in the sitting room." Dick and Alec came to see me specially about this. Fuming, they asked what action they should take. "That's easy to answer. You can either put up with it or resign."

"I don't see why we should do either!" protested Alec.

"Okay, then, waste your time arguing. But please don't waste any more of mine." So they went off, still fuming. Sometimes higher education is a curse.

Another courier arrived from Tan, bringing letters and more MO material: Japanese newspapers, leaflets, notebooks, and some pills the Japanese were distributing to the Annamites as "medicine." There were also many Annamite documents I could not classify. When I sent this stuff to OSS, Betty M. sent back a request for "Japanese postal wrappings" and names of more Japanese officers to whom they could send letter bombs. "Our Chinese spies," wrote Betty, "say this ploy has had quite some success in blowing off hands of Jap officers." (Cardinal Newman, who wrote, among other lovely hymns, "Lead, kindly Light, amid the encircling gloom," also wrote: "There is such a thing as legitimate warfare: war has its laws; there are things which may be fairly done, and things which may not be done." Did *anyone ever believe* that—not, of course, that blowing off hands with letter bombs is really worse than blowing them off in any other way.)

Tan wrote that he was moving on to Ho's second base farther inside Indochina, where the Vietminh were more fully organized.

The population is now getting more anti-Jap than anti-French because with so many of the French locked up, organization is breaking down, with constant food shortages and disruption of transport and communications. So our life has become even more tough from the chaos. We have three small dwellings—if you can call them that: a little lean-to, built in the terraced rice fields, and two others built in the boughs of a tree overhanging a waterfall deep down in the valley. To get to either of these we have to scramble through the waterfall, and the rocks are slippery with slime so I constantly have a wet arse. We fixed up a "shower room" from the waterfall, but you have to watch out because our "house" is overhead and everyone pisses most conveniently. During the night when Mac wants to piss he doesn't get up, just shoves his Peter through a gap in the log floor and lets go.

Ho has now moved on to the forward base. His boys (and lots of girls, too) get up at 4:30 AM, sing patriotic songs, do half-an-hour of physical jerks and then cook rice for breakfast, after which some go off into the bush for firewood, some to find bamboo shoots, tender grass and leaves, etc., as substitute vegetables. There are plentiful wild deer and smaller animals as well as game birds but the summer grass is too long to find and shoot them. We also hear leopards or tigers, fighting or in the throes of ecstasy—what a din!

The gang all salute me and do everything they can to help us, and they worry if we can't eat their poor food. Mac is teaching them radio technique and says they all "love" him. They are very military-conscious and have military drill every day. The fact that we bought a sizable amount of guns [by "sizable" he meant two rifles, three carbines, a Bren gun, and a few six-shooters; all this had been his pet insistence] and ammo has really paid dividends. They say our weapons are much better than either the French or Japanese ones. They themselves have a few guns, such as Remington rifles dated 1904! And a "flintlock" where you have to strike a spark and another where you light a match to set off a fuse and then the gun goes off—you hope. Some are like shotguns but you have to load them from the front—put in the shot and powder, then tamp. Then you pull back a huge trigger and put a match head on the cap: looks like the guns the Pilgrims used to shoot turkeys with!

Such was Tan's description of Ho Chi Minh's first base. Twenty-five years later this old man stunned the world!

Invited to a movie at OSS I observed with some surprise that there were now hundreds of personnel, mostly in uniform; the enlisted men were getting woozy on beer, the officers on whiskey. A large crowd who had been operating in Burma was still bubbling over with various experiences. Were they talking about the carnage down there, the roar of gunfire, the blast of bombs, the swift ambush in the dawn's first gleaming, or perhaps about the tropic nights, the luxuriant jungle, and the pagodas chiming with wind-bells? They were like hell. What evoked the shrill voices, flashing eyes, and frothing at the mouth were the rate of exchange, the shortage of drink, and the high price of whores.

Before taking off for his drop-in, Humphrey asked for another cash advance, explaining that this was to be a marriage dowry for one of his sisters. Lily told me later that "it was his favorite sister, because they had the same mother. His father had four wives, two still living. My own father had five wives, and most of the time three at once. My own mother died when I was two, so after that I had three different mothers, each one worse than before." Poor Lily, it didn't bear thinking of!

The pilot now reported on the Tuei-Humphrey drop: "We made one pass to line up the site. On the second we threw out the containers. On the third the two boys jumped. Then we made a final pass to check. We saw the parachutes amid the brush but couldn't see the boys. In any case we had to fly off quickly to avoid attracting any further attention." Any further attention! Four passes must have alerted the Japanese for ten miles around!

A message from Simon said OSS had sent a big team down to the border to recruit and train Annamites for a full-scale SO raid into Indochina. "Jo-Jo was furious, because such an operation will bring savage reprisals from the Japanese and it will be Chinese civilians who will suffer!" This, alas, was typical of unco-ordinated operations.

Helen, joining me at breakfast during one of our quieter mornings, began chatting about her coworkers.

I thought at first Lilian was deceptive, but she isn't, she's merely secretive and hardly ever says what she really thinks. Not untrusting, not brooding, but just not communicative. She is the same towards everybody. She always makes a good impression on strangers. They think she is so friend-ly and easy to get on with. Then they find that even after a week, they are still in the same relationship as on their first meeting! She is very impetu-ous in her work, very anxious to learn. So anxious indeed that she doesn't listen properly and then gets things wrong. And she dashes through her work almost too cleverly and makes foolish mistakes through sheer impetuosity.

Susan is a wonderful girl, very intelligent, very industrious, and learns fast. It's hardly surprising that at school she got all the prizes. She never boasts or shows off, but something drives her to be always best. Then she thinks afterwards: "How silly, why should I want to be best? Is it just to prove that I'm not as stupid as some people think?" Because, you see, although she has a remarkable memory, never forgets anything, and can understand and anticipate a whole sentence before one says three words of it, there are times when she is in a dream and stares at you with wide-open eyes, almost as if petrified. She's often like that when you speak to her! And I can see her looking round as if frightened to tears and pleading with her eyes to any Chinese there to help her understand what this foreigner is saying—although as you know she understands English as well as any of us. Perhaps it's because she's so clever that she's so conscious of her limitations.

In the early days of her being here she used to remain in the office with a pile of work, practice typing, study coding, then do some French, then write letters, then study shorthand, and so forth, like a schoolwork list. One day I heard her murmuring some unknown language at great speed from a book on the desk. Then I discovered it was Latin! Yes, Latin! When I questioned her about it, she said, "Oh, it's terrible, I've forgotten almost all my Latin!" Yet there she was reading it at breakneck speed! And she's so methodical in her work that she'll sometimes spend half an hour to find the exact word in translating code messages, whether from Chinese into English or vice versa, or even dealing with French.

Another thing is, she's always so frank and open, never hides anything except from shyness or from sheer conviction that she's being stupid. Do you remember how, when she first came to the camp, she would go through the whole day in a dream and never talk to anyone, shuffling around with her hands tucked inside her sleeves, slowly, head down, and eyes fixed on a point just beyond her feet? Of course, that's the typical Chinese shuffle! Often enough at the start she would get so upset she couldn't eat or sleep and then would have to face the day quite worn out! [While Helen told me this, I could not help thinking how unobservant (or insensitive!) I had been to ignore what she saw so clearly. Often for days on end I would be too busy with work (or sometimes play!) even to pass a word with Susan, never mind be concerned about her. And sometimes when I did talk to her, it was only to give some critical comment about her withdrawnness!]

Liangski, who is always so kind and helpful to everyone, is now sick himself. And it's curious the way he resents anyone being kind to him. He simply refuses to take the medicine we get for him. He's as obstinate as a pig going to market. . . . Mac and Bob are just like small boys. But Mac is much cleverer than you would think. [How right Helen was! Mac later immigrated to the United States and did brilliant work in radiology and finally made a fortune in real estate.] Bob should have stayed in the job he first went in for, namely, acting. He just cannot help always giving a per-formance! Dick and Alex are good types, if a bit choosy: good minds, well educated, nice manners. They will certainly do a good job, Communists or not Communists, which is more than you can say for a lot of the crowd we've had recently. . . . Yip [in charge of transport] is a nice boy, but suffers from nervousness. That's a hangover from the time when the Japs caught him and because they thought he had some information they wanted, gave him a terrible going over. He's rather afraid of you, because his English is poor, and he fears to get things wrong. [Some years later when I was living in Hong Kong, Yip became my personal chauffeur, certainly lost any "fear" of me, and we became good friends.]

Ying [number two radio operator] is not doing his work very well just now because his wife is having a baby, and it is several weeks overdue. So that's why he's drinking too much. Although he never gets drunk, this affects his ability to think clearly.

Frankie Tan, of course, is a very special case! Quite clever, well informed, amusing, and usually good-tempered. It's only over Janet he comes a cropper. Right from the start he fell for her. This was in Luchow. And when Gordon set up the Lungchow headquarters, Frankie walked back the whole fifty miles to Luchow to talk her into taking a job in Lungchow, not knowing that Gordon had already given the job to me. But Frankie wouldn't rest until he'd got her down there, too.

So when Gordon and Bernard were away on business, and Frankie ran the show, he seized the chance to bring her in. Then he would be constantly finding reasons to call her into the office to do shorthand or take messages for cipher, or make sketch maps. Anything, whether useful or not, would be made an excuse to have her in there with him!

Janet played along on this until Gordon came back, and then she completely ignored Frankie and gave the big boss all her attention. Frankie would get raging mad with jealousy! At mealtimes and especially at dinner, he would sit there in a tight, gray fury and finally, unable to contain himself, would burst out with some cutting remark, whereupon Janet would ignore him with a disdain that Frankie could meet in only one way—the rum bottle. A single swig would make him drunk! And he would sit there turning purple while Janet watched with the withering contempt she puts on so well!

Gordon's attitude was that Frankie had to get over this absurd infatuation. First, he tried sending him off to work with Jo-Jo. But every day, rain or shine, Frankie would walk back to our place and hang around, pitifully pleading for a word, even a look. Then he would trudge back the long journey, often in the drenching rain. So this move having proved useless, Gordon then tried a kill-or-cure treatment by flirting with Janet himself, which as you'll have observed, she doesn't exactly resent from any VIPs. But poor Frankie would froth in despair and almost with tears in his eyes plead for Gordon not to do it!

Of course, Janet can't help the way she goes on. She was always the spoiled one in the family. I suppose she was born selfish. Our parents would try their best not to spoil her, but Janet would frustrate all their efforts. For instance, when it was a matter of presents they would always give us similar things so there could be no jealousy. But even when it was two bags of sweets exactly alike, Janet would insist on having that bag. Then as soon as I conceded, Janet would say, "No, it's the *other* bag I want!" I remember once when our aunt gave us a bag of oranges, we found upon sharing them out [that] there were thirteen, so my aunt said, "Helen shall have the odd one because she's the elder." Oh, my stars! What a fuss! Janet screamed blue murder! And when I gave her the odd one to shut her up, and my aunt praised me for being generous, we had another screaming fit; this was all a trick to get me praised, said Janet! So then she insisted on cutting the odd orange into two!

As for Bernard, you can't but admire him, always so methodical, over-cautious perhaps, never quite sure a thing is right, so feels he should improve it. Have you noticed that when writing a report he will change it and change it, not a bit like Gordon, who will think out a report early in the morning, dictate it as soon as we arrive, and never want to change a thing. And you can be sure it's just right! Bernard, like Liangski, is very kindhearted. But he's too blunt and often tactless. So he hurts people's feelings without the least intention of doing so. And then you can see how astonished he is at their reactions! . . . Well, I guess you know now what I think about everybody!

"Not everybody—you left out Gordon and me."

"Mr. Gordon's my boss, so I don't think it would be fair for me to make comments about him."

"Does that also apply to me? Come on, let's hear it."

"Too dangerous! You can sometimes be very sharp! In fact, sometimes I could throw the dictionary at you. But then I remember you'll feel better in a few minutes, and the sun will come out as usual. . . . Eight o'clock already! See you in the office, Lieutenant Fenn. Oh, I forgot again—Captain Fenn!"

She was twenty-three years old, educated in a mission school, had led a sheltered life, and Susan lamented her "trivial chatter." But what remarkable discernment this "chattering" girl revealed!

Lily, visiting me at the Commerce, showed some photographs of herself when she was a soldier in the Chinese army and had to shave her head to wear a cap. Very bizarre! She explained that the scars still evident on her face were caused by a shell fragment while fighting in Tuyen, and the large scar on her right forearm was caused by a Mauser bullet carelessly fired by another soldier. "Miss Chung wanted to join up, too, but she was too short. That's always been her handicap. With men it's the same—unless they're short, too. She's never jealous, but she thinks I'm so lucky to have you as a friend and is always wanting to know if we sleep together. When I tell her we're not she says, 'Then if you don't want to sleep with him, I do, so why not let me have him for a while? Otherwise you are being rather selfish, don't you think?' So then, of course, I had to admit you are sleeping with me. So then she said, 'As we are such good friends and share all we have, couldn't I have him for a night now and then?' Ai-ya! That set me back. So I finally said, 'We are good friends indeed, but we aren't that good friends!' In any case, her interest in you is not only for yourself, although of course that does enter into it, but because she wants to sleep with a foreigner."

"Really? Why?"

"Curiosity, mainly. Foreigners are supposed to be more virile, as well as more faithful than Chinese men, who want a different girl every night." (Surely a universal disease?) "There's a girl living next to me who's a 'pheasant' (prostitute), very high class, gets thirty thousand a night [then about U.S. $35.00], although, of course, she has to pay off both the Chinese and the American MPs. But she's very popular, always doing business. It's like living on the street with all the traffic to and fro because the boy opposite does some kind of massage, I don't know exactly what, but he has customers coming all hours of the day and night and must earn good money because the Chinese MPs also collect from him."

"But surely he's a—" The word "homosexual" not being in my dictionary, I tried to explain it. But it soon appeared that Lily had never heard of such a thing, could not believe it, and wanted an explanation of what possible sex men could have with one another. My Chinese was inadequate to meet this challenge.

I had promised to take her to a movie that evening. So we set off for the Golden Palace, a large matshead structure formerly a warehouse but now set up with rows of benches, torn silk drapes, and a well-patched screen. As we turned off along the street leading to this pleasure dome, a U.S. Army car with one occupant swerved across the road in front, perhaps to pick up a girl signaling on the opposite side. There came a screech of brakes and a thump as the car hit another pedestrian and skidded into a shop front. At once half a dozen other Chinese came crowding up to inspect the prostrate form. Then, crying, "Dead, dead!" they leapt furiously at the car, which the driver was frantically trying to back out of the shop front. But before he could make a getaway, they dragged him out and overwhelmed him with blows.

Promptly deciding this was no time to play hero, I dragged Lily into the shelter of a doorway. Two Chinese MPs now came running up with pointed Mausers and with threats and blows forced the attackers aside. The GI and the struck pedestrian both lay motionless. When a U.S. MP's vehicle arrived, its headlights picked us out like spotlights. But luckily their attention was so focused on the melee that we managed to slip off through the crowd and into the dark refuge of the Golden Palace, where we sat holding clenched hands as if to assure ourselves that we were still alive.

18

STRAINED RELATIONSHIPS

Unable to get further news from Gordon about our destiny, Bernard went off to Chungking to see Wedemeyer and get his okay for our transfer to AGAS, including my own services. I therefore began working more and more closely with Wichtrich. My immediate plan was to join Ho in French Indochina—less from the utility of such a move than from my desire for action, movement, travel, and adventure rather than sitting indoors at a desk! But when I suggested to Wichtrich that I should drop in, he immediately sat on the idea. "You're too essential here in headquarters to be spared for such a mission. As a matter of fact, I've already assigned Lieutenant Phelan for that job. But before we drop him in, I'd like him to stay round your camp for a week and pick up all the gen. You'll find him fairly knowledgeable already, since he's studied the layout pretty closely."

Study is one thing, but attitude is something else. Phelan was so far to the right politically that he even admitted he would rather have liaised with the French than with the Vietminh. What would Ho think about having such a reactionary officer foisted upon him? Another drawback to Phelan's character was that prevailing disease of snobbery inherent in so many of both OSS and AGAS personnel, who were all too often selected on the basis of family, wealth, education, or social elitism. Even regarding women Phelan was a snob! Having gotten himself engaged to a French-Hungarian girl from a wealthy family living in Paris, he let slip his opinion that American girls could be "kind of crude." He was, however, active, quick-witted, eager, good-humored, and anxious to learn: that gave a score above average.

Meanwhile, OSS had sent a Major Thomas to our camp "to inspect overall prospects" by going through our files. While he and I were having a preliminary coffee, Helen rapidly removed anything we did not want him to see. Thomas proved to be a pleasant, friendly fellow, and we left him happily plowing through the rest of the material. I will note here that Thomas was subsequently dropped into Vietminh and, despite initial prejudice, became a friend of Ho's and ultimately a lifelong friend of mine.

Pham, having been held up by various problems, called in to see me. He was much disturbed at hearing from Ho that OSS was sending down groups working closely with Frenchmen who were, in fact, more anti-Annamite than anti-Japanese. So what was our true policy? I told him that if operations were arranged through Tan, Bernard, or myself, Ho could rely on their loyalty to him. But we could not be responsible for what OSS might do. The AGAS people were more reliable, but even they were basically anti-Communist. We would shortly be dropping in an AGAS officer named Phelan. He was not my choice, and I wanted to warn Ho that he was sympathetic to the French. On the other hand, Phelan was essentially a pragmatist, and I felt he would adapt when he learned the real score. This proved to be true.

"You can be sure we'll give him a welcome—although I'm sorry it won't be you," added Pham as we shook hands for what we thought was definitely the last time. (We did meet briefly later—once in Paris when Pham was in a delegation at the French-Vietnam Peace Conference in 1954 and again in 1994 when he was prime minister.)

Two men from the Tenth Weather Group came to brief our teams on how to record and send in full data. Dear Helen, who had now become an almost "instant" translator, was nearly defeated in dealing with this technical material, not because of its intrinsic complexities but because the sergeant doing most of the talking wrapped up his explanations in long-winded diversions and pompous clichés. This disease seems endemic amongst specialists.

A courier brought a personal letter from Helliwell saying that OSS was finished with us unless we conformed to its requirements; we had three days to make up our minds. Was this the result of Major Thomas's visit to our camp? Had we left everything in the files, we might not have been given even shriving time! Because the letter was handwritten, I was able to assess Helliwell's character almost at a glance: clever, pompous, devious, energetic, ambitious . . . Beware!

The cook came in with a special request from the night-soil coolies who collected feces for the surrounding crops: could they collect our own contributions? As one of the Chinese night-soil coolies said when collecting excrement from the American Embassy, "All foreign shit better than Chinese, but American shit best of all!"

A package arrived for me from Tsung-wei, who had now gone with an OSS team to north China. Inside were wall rubbings from stones carved by the famous Wu Tao-tsu (Tang dynasty). One was of a seated Buddha, and the other depicted a winged horse hurtling through clouds over a mountain peak. These masterpieces took my mind off weather data, Helliwell, shit, and everything else until a knock at the door brought me back to earth: it was Bob Lee, full of himself as usual!

It seemed he had a plan for liaison with General Chung Fa-Kwei of the Fourth War Area. "The general is a friend of my father's. I've met the general, too, as well as his chief of staff, Colonel Wang. And I've got a lot of face down there, so they'll help me all they can. You see, an uncle of mine knew Stalin and Roosevelt."

"Stalin we can do without, and Roosevelt's dead. Haven't you any connections with President Truman?" I tried not to sound too ironic.

But nothing deflated Bob Lee. "Perhaps through a cousin who works in the Chinese embassy in Washington." I never did find out whether Lee had such connections or whether he lived in cloud-cuckoo-land.

Susan came back from a weekend in town with her hair waved in a kinky fringe that made it look like a scrubbing brush. This was considered "American style," but no one seemed to know why.

A courier arrived from Tan, having made the trip from their base in a record twenty days. In addition to Tan's report there was a letter from Ho. Written with a steel nib on rice paper, it read: "I will be very much obliged to you of taking care of our boys. I wish they can learn radio and other things necessary in our common fight against the Japs. I hope soon you will be able to visit us here, in our base. It will be great! Permit me to send my respect to General Chennault." The "boys" Ho referred to had stayed down in Ching Hsi. Jo-Jo had thought it better not to let them come farther north for fear of trouble with his own hierarchy, so Simon and his contact had somewhat reluctantly started training them.

With Tan's report were several photographs. He wrote, "One of them shows our group of 20 boys all armed to the teeth with our weapons plus some of their own ancient arsenal. In one snap you'll see the village 'meeting house.' One group is being taught to read, another about maps, a third about Vietminh principles. In the next room is a sewing circle where they make shoes, clothing and equipment for the guerrillas. Some of them are only fourteen but are as tough as nails."

When I told Lily it was goodbye because I was now giving up the room, she burst into tears. "Won't I see you anymore? Oh, Elder Brother, I so loved coming here, being with you, sharing everything!" And there was another flood of tears. Although she was but an incident in my action-packed life, I felt really sad to see her so upset.

Our radio transmitter was giving trouble, so Mac Young, a young lieutenant from AGAS, came to fix it and stayed on for dinner. A pleasant, extroverted youngster, he soon opened up about his thoughts and background. "In the final years of Prohibition, I earned my way through college by using my Lincoln Zephyr as fast transportation to run liquor from one state to another on behalf of a bootlegger. The old bus was covered all over with college labels and gag stickers so that everyone thought it was a big joke and never gave a thought to searching it. Each trip was worth a hundred bucks, and sometimes I did two a week. That's more than I've ever earned by honest toil! So I saved enough to buy this boat." He showed me pictures of a two-masted schooner. "Seventy feet. I keep it moored in Chesapeake Bay. And when I get back home, I intend touring the Caribbean for a start."

"Will you need any crew?"

"Why, sure! You want to come along? After we've done the Caribbean, we could tackle the Medi. Maybe a couple of girls if they could help sail. You've got some nice girls here, but I guess there's nothing doing? That's the problem with Chinese girls—always hands off! And I'm allergic to prostitutes. Neither do I go for chasing tail around the GI setups like the hospital or the Red Cross. Those stuck-up dames all think they're beauty queens. So a few months back I got myself a room in that little village west of here—you know it?—and eventually got friendly with a farm girl and was careful not to jump the gun. Stayed pals with her for several months, never made a pass until she got to trusting me. But I gave her lots of small presents! When in China do as the Chinese do, especially since it pays off! And what's more, I've been careful not to get her knocked up. 'Gather ye rosebuds while ye may,' but there's no sense in breaking down the bushes." I think one had to admit that Lieutenant Young's pragmatic solution to the problem of sex in China was an improvement on that of most GIs.

Helen came to tell me that two American officers were snooping around the compound. When I caught up with them about to enter the radio shack, they told me with a sick smile, "Colonel Heppner sent us to have a look-see. We asked the guard for you, but he doesn't speak English." This couple, it seemed, were only forward scouts. The next morning came a whole team under a major named Gasper (that really was his name). We gave them coffee and showed them everything—except those documents already tucked away.

It was certainly a big day, because in the afternoon came Colonel Williams of the Fourteenth Air Force, along with a colonel I did not know. After a good look around, Williams asked, "What were the terms on which the property was originally acquired?"

"All I know is that General Chennault's American Volunteer Group bought the land or leased it from the woman who owns this particular section of rice paddy."

"And would you know where she's located?"

"Yes, sir, she's over there in the paddy right now, planting rice."

But after a dubious look-see, he decided not to walk in his calfskin pilot's boots through the intervening four hundred yards of waterlogged paddy. We never did find out what all these visitors were really up to.

A wire from Simon said that OSS wanted him to go on a mission into Indochina led by Major Thomas: was there any objection? I wired him back: "None from me, but what would Gordon say?" So that was the end of it. But as per the ultimatum from Helliwell, we received no further funds or supplies from OSS. The money we had on hand would carry us on for only two more weeks, and we had seven teams out in the field and were sending OSS a weekly average of nine pages of intelligence—probably as much as they got from all other sources.

Included in our more recent funds were bags of twenty-franc gold coins in near-mint condition, although dated around 1900. Everyone succumbed to their fatal fascination as we counted them out *chink-chink-chink* on the table. They were issued to agents in money belts made in Rewi Alley's Chinese Industrial Co-operatives from handsome pigskin, with hand-worked brass buckles and twenty stitched pockets in which the coins stayed snug even when the belts were taken off. "Much too good for such riffraff!" sighed Helen whenever we issued a belt to an agent.

Gordon, having at last returned, had stayed over in Chungking, where Bernard now joined him for meetings with OSS, AGAS, the Fourteenth Air Force, the British Military Mission, the French Military Mission, and the whole Chinese hierarchy. "But OSS are the 'stars,'" Gordon told me when he joined us in Kunming. "Along the entire route from Washington to Chungking, they have the biggest funds, the biggest houses, the biggest cars, and women with the biggest tits. And in Chungking they bent over backwards to bring us in, offering both Harry and me commissions—on their own terms, of course, meaning they run the show. Whereas AGAS will let us do it our way. So I'm throwing in our lot with them."

The next morning came Betty M., ostensibly to get some lineage translated into Annamese. But she soon switched over to the subject of my hostility to Heppner. "Believe me, Charles, he's really a nice guy and wants to be friendly."

"And believe me, Betty, I've no quarrel with Colonel Heppner. I know he's on the level—it isn't his fault that I've been pushed around by OSS. Maybe it's my own fault. But that's beside the point. I'll do what I'm ordered to do. But I can't bring the GBT group into OSS because Gordon won't buy it."

But the worst thing was that my relations with Gordon also became strained. I was now mostly running the camp. The Ho operation and our seven teams in southern China had all been organized by me. So when Gordon had finished catching up on what we'd done, most of which he disapproved of, he found himself at a loose end, and he could not bear to be inactive. So frustration brought the inevitable outburst. "Charles, look at it this way! I brought you into the group and made you more or less a partner. Then I go away to get things straight with OSS, and when I get back I find everything's turned arse up! You've linked us up with an Annamite group whose real interest is to kick out the French, who happen to be my friends! One day they'll be killing some of those friends, and it's you I'll have to thank for it!" (All this proved only too true!) It was a heated attack, delivered with that force and clarity of which Gordon was a preeminent master. And what answer could I give? But at least I had to try.

"What you say is only half the story. While you stayed away all that time, Harry and I were forced to make decisions. It was the Annamites or nothing. You're a free agent, so you can afford to think of postwar Indochina and take action accordingly. I have to do what I'm told—more or less. So that's the way I've had to play it. I'm sorry it doesn't fit in with what you want, but there's nothing I can do to change it."

So we parted with, at best, a resigned recognition of the facts. But I soon discovered that the wounds still festered. At one point there was no jeep available for his use; at another he was issued with secondhand boots. Then I "resented his reading the wires first"! Or Bob Lee gave him sharp answers! And so on and so on. Animosity over such trifles, so contrary to Gordon's usual give-and-take, eroded the morale of the entire camp. I was both relieved and regretful when at last he told me huffily that he was leaving the camp and going to stay in the GBT townhouse.

But Gordon was never the sort to bear a grudge. Within hours of his departure he phoned to invite me for a drink. And for me it was never any problem
to take his hand of friendship. So we later on collected Susan and Helen for a
fabulous meal at the Cantonese restaurant, Gordon being host.

But the next day, we were, alas, back to square one. When he came to the
camp and sent Tan a wire ordering him to return, I registered a concerned
protest. Gordon slammed the desk—a rare instance of overt protest. "You'd better get this straight, Charles. Frankie works for me, not you. I feel responsible
for his welfare, and he'll get shot if he stays in that dicey setup. Apart from everything else, by working with anti-French Annamites, he's ruining his prospects of
getting a job with Texaco!"

"And threatening your own prospects, no doubt!" I was foolish enough to
retort. He and I shared similar bad tempers—sharp but always short. So only a
day later he was giving me in the most friendly way a report of his meeting with
Lieutenant Jean, a member of the organization known as DGER (Direction
Géneral des Études de Recherché). DGER, essentially a de Gaulle brainchild,
largely replaced the military Deuxiéme Bureau, which had long since become
pro-Vichy. DGER was the French equivalent of OSS (of which Sainteny, later to
become de Gaulle's personal emissary to Ho, was a significant member). Gordon
told the following:

> Jean told me the full story of the Jap coup of March 9th. The day previous
> it was already suspected by most of the French that the Japs were about to
> strike. The French were divided fifty-fifty as to whether they should put
> up some resistance or merely try to compromise. But even amongst those
> who wanted to take action, there was no agreement about what, when, or
> where. So when the Japs moved, there were only sporadic attempts at
> resistance, and a good many French were killed without anything accom-
> plished.
>
>   Then on March 23rd a declaration was made by Jacoby, minister of
> the colonies, and approved by de Gaulle, to come to an agreement with
> the Vietminh. And Jean amongst others had been frantically trying to con-
> tact them, quite without success. Through outside sources they finally
> learned that the Vietminh has rejected compromise and insists on full
> independence. But de Gaulle is convinced that compromise is always pos-
> sible. [Nowhere did de Gaulle exercise more of his resolution, energy, and
> skill than in defrauding the Vietminh of any genuine self-government, a
> trickery in which he was aided by the British, who employed similar

deceits to retain their own colonies; the Chinese, who were too busy loot-
ing to care what other nations did in Vietnam; the Americans, who were
too worried by Communist potential to give preference to any concession
in his favor; and, finally, the United Nations, at that time still an American
pawn. The weight of this united presence forced Ho into making concessions until he felt strong enough for a showdown, which occurred when
he, with Giap's masterly strategy, defeated the French at Dien Bien Phu.]

Jean offered an interesting sidelight: After the U.S. landed in North
Africa and set up Giraud to head "France-in-exile," he practically signed
over North Africa to the Americans—commercial treaties, port privileges,
duty preferences, personal status, the lot. De Gaulle resisted furiously but
then had no power. So he contacted Stalin, who agreed to back him and
really did so. The result was the assassination of Darlan, the ousting of
Giraud, and all his treaties with the Americans made null and void. But
the price for Soviet help was that de Gaulle had to sign the Franco-Russian
nonaggression pact, cede freedom to the Communist Party in France, and
recognize a large measure of colonial independence. I must admit frankly
that Ho is now the key figure in the Indochina scene.

He added, somewhat reluctantly, however, "I still think backing him was a mistake, because that's what really put him out in front." I could not dispute this
because I thought it was probably true.

Wichtrich asked me to get a clear understanding about the ownership of the
camp and if possible a written lease. So I maneuvered a path across the rice fields
and presented myself at the isolated shack where Mrs. Tong, the owner, lived with
her three small children, one of whom presented me a stool while the smaller ones
sought refuge in their mother's skirt. Mrs. Tong said she was quite agreeable to letting us have a lease as long as we protected her trees. It seemed that when the Flying
Tigers took over the site, they cut down six trees to make space for their buildings
and by way of compensation gave her the Chinese equivalent of one U.S. dollar! I
subsequently organized a written lease, but neither Wichtrich nor anyone else ever
arranged a final transfer.

Hearing me give one of our recruits a sharp telling off, Bernard commented,
"Charles, you might have given him a chance to explain. It's one of your foibles that you
can't be bothered to hear people out. It's as if you can't tolerate their low intelligence, inco-
herence, lack of facts, and noncomprehension of the obvious! You always expect everyone to think as fast as you do, and when they don't you first get impatient, then annoyed,
and finally contemptuous. And naturally people resent your assumption of superiority!"

I listened to this in some dismay. Coming from someone like Faxton, such obloquy I could ignore. But coming from Bernard, I knew it must be largely valid. So I promised to try to reform. Did I ever succeed? Does the leopard change his spots? But we are not leopards; we have will, awareness, and self-discipline! Alas, how little good such attributes are in promoting self-improvement!

The cook said there were "tigers" (meaning wildcats) living in the roof and eating our chickens, so would I kindly shoot them, or at least one, which would frighten off the rest. Remembering my one-day's slaughter in Africa (after which I had sworn never to shoot another wild creature), I resisted. But he kept nagging about the "poor chickens" (which he would subsequently slaughter!). So I finally agreed. While the staff beat around with sticks inside the roof, I stood near the opening where the wildcats went in and out. When one peeped out I shot it with my .38. For a moment it was poised there motionless, and then it fell plop on the ground, gave two kicks, and expired. I immediately regretted having killed this lovely creature. Gray and black spots along the back ran into delicate lines down the flanks and turned bluish silver at the belly, all the fur gleaming like silk. The cook's wife promptly cut it up, and the pan-fried fragments duly appeared on the mess table. I found myself right back in childhood, shunning the stewed rabbit my mother had killed. Everyone else ate some of the "tiger," including Susan, who had cried to see it die. She explained to me afterward that although her heart was "cracking," it was easier to face eating some than to be teased for not eating any!

Meanwhile, the cook had been keeping a pair of white rabbits. Just when they achieved plump adulthood, they disappeared. One of them was identifiable because of its broken leg. So when the cook was offered a pair of white rabbits in the market and saw that one had a broken leg, he claimed ownership. The seller indignantly denied it, and the case went before the local magistrate. Our statement, written in Lilian's beautiful calligraphy and suitably adorned with chops in red ink, no doubt swayed the magistrate into awarding us the rabbits. But when one of the boys went up in the roof to chase out the other wildcat, he found the remains of two rabbits, undoubtedly ours. But the cook would not lose face by returning the rabbits we had improperly acquired.

Doctor Lomas, the OSS health officer, called to check the hygiene of the camp. Was this a mark of renewed favor or to get the place cleaned up for new occupants? Lomas, an old acquaintance, assured us it was "merely routine." Later on, while sharing a coffee, he told us that the previous day he "delivered" a baby born to a Chinese woman while she was cleaning up the compound. "It simply fell out on the asphalt, and by the time I got there was barely alive. Because of brain damage and consequent idiocy, I decided not to try and save it. In such circumstances one never knows what's right. One of my first deliveries was a baby looking like a frog, and I thought it was kindness to let it die. So die it did. But afterwards I felt this was a wrong decision—you know our Hippocratic oath. And when another baby was born obviously bats, I did everything to keep it alive. This boy—a hopeless idiot—lived until the age of eighteen. There were no other children. The care of this one took every moment of the mother's time and a good deal of the father's income. Everyone used to say, "Poor Mrs. Goldeck, poor Mr. Goldeck, that child has wrecked their lives!" But when the boy died, the mother was heartbroken, declared she had nothing left to live for, became an alcoholic, and finally had to be sent to a mental home for a cure that never worked."

Lomas had brought me a postal package, which proved to be a birthday present from my wife: three new Simenons: what a bonanza! One superb story called *L'homme Qui Vit Passer les Trains* had me reading half the night. (I was introduced to Simenon's work [in French] by Ford Madox Ford, who said his succinct, lucid style was the peak one should strive to emulate. I have at least always *tried*!)

Helen mentioned that Gordon had written letters as from the Texaco Company offering both her and Janet jobs after the war. When Janet learned he had offered her less pay, she had the usual screaming fit. Later on, Gordon happened to show me a reply note he got from Janet, which included the phrase, "I'm so glad you offered a job to Helen too." "I'll bet like hell she was glad!" Gordon remarked sardonically. But apparently he did not know about the screaming fit.

Wichtrich having promised to clear my transfer to AGAS, I went to pay a courtesy call on Heppner and ask his release from OSS. It was my turn to get a "look." Was it pained or merely puzzled? "If that's what you really want—okay, providing AGAS will give us something in return"—not, of course for the troublesome Fenn, whom he must have been glad to get rid of, but for the desirable GBT and the even more valuable Ho hookup that, alas, went with troublesome Fenn!

A courier brought letters from Simon, Jo-Jo, Tan, and Ho. Although Simon as usual gave us useful intelligence, he also complained at having to teach the boys Ho had asked us to train, who were basically anti-French! Jo-Jo complained that OSS was still sending saboteurs across the border with no clearance either from him or from other Chinese officials. Tan complained in his letter (sent of course prior to Gordon's wire for his return) that these missions had also not been cleared with Ho so they would all be arrested on arrival in French Indochina. His letter also reported their difficult and dangerous trip to the second base. "At one point when we were completely surrounded by the Japs, some of Ho's boys created a diversion and drew them off so that we were able to practically slide down our arses one night along the river."

Ho's letter, written on a scrap of green rice paper, read:

> Mr. T and his second, Mac Sin, get on very well. We become a large family. I hope you'll come and visit us soon.
>
> Please, be so kind as to give this letter to my friend, Sung Minh Fang, of the Indochina café! Ten or 12 days after that, they will hand you a packet containing Allies' flags. I'll be very obliged if you'll send it to me by the quickest way.
>
> My best greeting to the great old man Chennault and to Mr. Bernard & all our friends. I wish you good health and good luck.

The courier who brought these letters spoke fluent French and during his visit revealed the following:

> While Ho had been off in Kunming all those months, some of the rival native groups had exploited his absence by promoting their own ends and belittling his achievements. It was spread around that he would never come back, that he was dead, that his mission to enlist American help was a waste of time, and so forth. When he did return, everyone was, of course, impressed that he had been flown to the border in an American plane! This certainly proved American friendship! Then it was learned that he had with him a skilled radio operator who would keep them in touch with the Americans and a Chinese American who carried powerful American weapons [Tan's Tommy gun and so on].
>
> Ho had arrived weak and very ill after his long and arduous walk, but when he was well enough he invited all the top men, including rival leaders, to a feast. Ho then explained that General Chennault had promised him personally to help their cause, and as proof of this he produced the signed photograph of Chennault ["Yours sincerely" meant much more when translated into Vietnamese]. And while everyone was examining this proof of friendship, Ho gave a Colt automatic to each of the rival leaders, saying, "The General wanted to send each of you a token of his regard."

You can imagine how this took their breath away! And after that there was never any question as to who was the leader!

This is perhaps an instance of the "contriving" I discerned in Ho's handwriting.

19
TRANSFORMATIONS

We were all up one night organizing the drop for Phelan. Changeable weather kept postponing the mission, and then our power gave out, so we lost radio contact with Tan. This had no sooner been remedied than the generator itself gave out. But at last all was ready, and the mission took off. But when the crew arrived at the point of the drop, they could not see the signal fires through the mist. Making a second difficult pass low to get beneath the mist, they saw the first signal fires, but because they did not spell out the letters as arranged, they might have been hill fires. (Due to the delay the wind had scattered the carefully structured pattern of the flames.) Coming really low they saw the sheets laid out, but there were six instead of four, which also had them worried: was this a mix-up, or was it some kind of warning? (It was merely an error in decoding our instructions.) So they circled around for half an hour trying to decide what to do. At last Phelan said, "Fires and sheets, it's too close to what we're looking for not to be right. I'll take a chance." Gutsy indeed! So he jumped and, so Tan (still in situ despite Gordon's instructions) wired us, landed in two feet of nice soft paddy, along with most of the ejected equipment.

"This grand spectacular," wired Tan, "had everyone spellbound!" And the next day, among more pertinent details, "Phelan seems an okay guy, hands out the same bullshit you do." This backhanded compliment left me guessing.

OSS, meanwhile, had been putting pressure on Simon to work with their Thomas group. So Simon had sent Tan a wire asking for Vietminh guides to take the group inside. When Tan checked with me on this, I warned him that although Thomas seemed okay, his team was pro-French and working with pro-French Annamites, and if Ho found we were cooperating with such, he would write us off. When Thomas and his team were dropped in, they were rounded up by the Vietminh, but with Tan's amelioration treated amicably. Thomas soon weighed up the odds and decided to work with Ho rather than the French.

Gordon told me that when he was en route to Washington, he wanted to send his GBT file and personal papers straight through so that he would not get involved in questions on the way, which might well hold him up. In Delhi, Dave Hunter offered to send them in the official OSS pouch, so they were duly sealed and receipted. When Gordon got to Washington, a friend in OSS tipped him off that the sealed package had in fact been opened and resealed after the contents had been duplicated for Donovan to go through. "Can you imagine that those bastards would go to that extreme?"

I probably gave him a skeptical look. "What I can't imagine is how you would suppose OSS would do anything else!"

"Ah, you're right. I must have been thinking there was honor among thieves."

Alec and Dick had returned from their mission with the Fourth War Area and were now scheduled for a job in the Communist north. But they came to complain that OSS had directed them to report to one of Tai Li's agents! "Obviously, we'll have to refuse this mission," said Alec, "because such a contact could get us shot even before we get started!"

When I mentioned this to Wichtrich, he said, "They are certainly right. OSS have already screwed up on this. When they sent the last team up there with the same prior contact, they were all taken prisoners, and some were actually shot. I suggest that if these boys aren't under contract to OSS, we'll undertake to send them directly to Mao." But, alas, they were still under contract, and despite their having refused this mission, OSS insisted on retaining them.

We had never succeeded in getting contact with Tuei and Humphrey Ho, so the mission had been written off as a failure, which hardly surprised me considering the inherent difficulties, not to mention the excessive caution of the pilot effecting the drop. What concerned me most was that I had risked their lives for such a long shot. It was therefore with hopeful relief that I had a message from the Fourteenth Air Force that someone claiming to be Humphrey Ho had crossed the border from Indochina and contacted their base down there. On our instructions they sent him up the line, and we brought him in. He looked very thin but brown as a chestnut and seemingly quite fit. Here is his story:

> I landed from the drop with a bump that almost knocked me out. Then I
> felt Tuei shaking me and came out of it. After burying our chutes we
> looked for the packages. But the shrubbery and grass were so thick that

even after hours of searching, we could find nothing. Late that afternoon Tuei gave a fisherman one hundred piastres to buy rice, but he never came back. Next morning, however, he got six or seven fishermen to help us with our search, and we finally found the package with the radio. No one knew anything about the eleven Frenchmen. And although we stayed around for three days making inquiries, we could get no news of them. One old fisherman became very friendly and got us new clothes because the ones we had were different from the local ones. He told us we should have to leave this area because everyone knew about the plane dropping parachutes, and the Japs had now got wind of it and were on their way. So he took us in his boat down the river towards Hué.

That night we slept in the hills and stayed hidden all next day. In the evening the fisherman got us some rice and said we'd better stay hidden until things settled down. He had made inquiries, but nobody knew anything about the Frenchmen. Then about five o'clock next morning he woke us up all excited and said we should have to leave fast: everyone was now talking about the "cloud spirits" who had come down out of the skies, and there were notices all over town saying: "Don't help the American fliers! Kill them or arrest them, and we shall pay you big money!" So there would now be plenty of people out to get us.

Before starting off the fisherman said it would be fatal to take the radio, which would be a dead giveaway. He wanted us to throw it into the river, and Tuei agreed, but I insisted on burying it against the chance we might retrieve it later. So we made a shelter with branches and earth amongst the thick shrubbery, and keeping only our piastres, money belts, and watches, we started poling back up the river. We'd hardly got going when a boat came down the river full of Japs! My cover story that I was a Chinese living there was useless—my skin was too pale. So when the Japs flagged us down, I stayed hidden, and after asking Tuei a few questions, they waved us on.

When we tied up around nine o'clock, another fisherman came to tell us that the river upstream was now all patrolled, so we should have to walk. Tuei decided that the only thing to do was head for Hanoi and get Vietminh help. So that day we walked almost nonstop to Quang Tri, which must have been nearly seventy kilometers! The fisherman said he couldn't come any further as he had to get back on his job. When we said goodbye he cried. I think he felt we had no chance, because here at Quang

Tri there was a Jap inspection station. But we managed to slip through in the dead of night. We got as far as Dong Da feeling done in and slept a bit in an empty hut. Next morning when the owner found us there, we shortly discovered that he actually worked for the Japs! But luckily he didn't suspect us of anything more than looking for work. Tuei gave it out that I was deaf and dumb, and I was always careful never to talk when anyone was around.

Tuei's plan was for us to get the train to Vinh, but when we tried to buy tickets we were told we had to have passes. So Tuei bribed the inspector to give us two. While we were filling in the forms a Jap soldier came up and started asking questions. When I acted deaf and dumb, he slapped me several times for not answering, but I went on acting dumb. That was a really bad time!

The station was full of Jap troops, and there were a lot more on the train. This one went as far as Dong Hoi, and we had to get off twice where bridges had been blown and cross in boats. There was a train each side to do a shuttle. On the ride to Vinh there were five bridges destroyed, with the same procedure. When we got to Vinh, Tuei said it would now be dangerous for him to be around with me—he didn't say why—and I should try and contact some of the Cantonese living there. So I went into a Cantonese restaurant, bought a bowl of congee, and asked a Cantonese boy working there if I could get a job, having just come from Quang Tri. Not wanting him to think I was a no-good, I said I had two hundred piastres to keep me going until I found something. I could see he was looking surprised, and suddenly he cut in to whisper, "Don't you know it's dangerous to talk Cantonese?" What was I thinking of? So when I had to admit I couldn't talk Annamese, he looked even more astonished. "Here, what's this? How long have you been here? Where's your identification pass?" Then it turned out that the one you got for me was a resident's pass, and since I knew no Annamese, I should have had a visitor's pass. So this boy said, "You're a wonderful person, and wonderful persons aren't popular with the Japs, so you'd better get going fast before we both come a cropper!" So there was nothing for it but to try and find Tuei.

Half the day went by while I searched and searched, not daring to be too obvious. At last I saw him at the end of a long street and had to run to catch him. "I'm in a hurry to catch the train," he told me. "What's your problem?" When I told him he tried to get me a tram ticket, but for some reason I couldn't understand, this proved impossible. But he finally found a truck driver who agreed to take us both to Hanoi for five hundred piastres—a very high price, but there was no way around it. When it was time to board, we saw several Jap officers sitting there on the benches in the truck, and the driver said, "Is it okay for my friends to sit in front?" Some of them said no, and we thought, "So that's it!" but one who was the boss finally said okay. At Than-Hoa these Japs got off. It was also the driver's home, so we slept there the night.

The next day he got us on another truck taking Annamite merchants up to Hanoi. Actually, we got off eleven kilometers this side of Hanoi where Tuei had some friends. It was also in Hanoi I saw Frenchmen for the first time, lots of them walking about the streets with their families. Around the outskirts of the town, there were dozens of corpses, some very decayed, and I was told they had simply died of hunger.

After a lot of coming and going, Tuei managed to contact some of the Vietminh crowd. They agreed to help me but were obviously more interested in going back for the radio! We were still talking about ways and means for both projects when someone rushed in to say that the Japs were on to us and we'd have to get going fast! Tuei had bought a bicycle, and we both got on it, he peddling and I sitting on the back. That night we got as far as Quang-Jan and slept there. Next morning Tuei was told by his friends that the Japs were on our track and [that] there was everywhere an alert for two men spying for the Americans. In case we were picked up we must get rid of everything incriminating, including my money belt and all my money except a thousand piastres and leave them in care of Tuei's friends. After doing this, we hid in a house for several days to let things quiet down, then went back to Hanoi to get the train to Laokay. In the Hanoi station there were Japs everywhere, searching people. While Tuei bought some passes, then the tickets, I kept edging out from where the Japs were searching, and we managed to get on the train before they reached me.

Although the train was packed, there weren't many Jap soldiers, and we weren't bothered. Five bridges had been blown, with the usual boat crossings. Tuei said goodbye at the end of the train journey and left me to complete this last part of the journey on my own. The big problem was to get across the river. As you know, it's a wide, fast river, and I can't swim all that well. In any case, Jap soldiers were patrolling, ready to shoot anyone who should try it. So the whole day I walked upriver until I found a spot not only deserted but where the current was not quite so strong. I took off all my clothes and bound them in my belt. After a struggle that nearly finished me, I managed to crawl up the bank on the other side! But immediately I was shot at by a Chinese soldier! When I kept shouting at him that I was Chinese, he came up to interrogate me and finally hauled me off to be further questioned. I knew you wouldn't want the Chinese to know I was working for you, so I told them I was SOS [U.S. Service of Supply] and that I had been into Indochina to see relatives. But they didn't swallow this, and I was badgered for days before they agreed to let me talk to the Fourteenth Air Force and so got through to you.

Although this mission was a total failure, Humphrey's story gave us some useful information, and considering what he had gone through I certainly didn't grudge him the money we paid (about U.S.$500 plus the twenty gold coins in his belt, then worth another hundred, which the Vietminh boys got the benefit of). And, alas, his sister died despite his help.

Because of confusion as to who was boss, morale in the office deteriorated even more. Gordon would occasionally show up and give orders that conflicted (more by accident than intention) with something I was trying to get done. Our staff then tended to form pro-Fenn or pro-Gordon cliques. And although neither he nor I encouraged such petty divisions, we could not prevent them. Bernard in his usual thoughtful way would try to mediate and even raised wages as a way to raise morale. But this cured nothing and almost emptied our coffers. When I applied for funds to Wichtrich, he said that was a problem until he got clearance. So there was nothing for it but to pester OSS, both for money and supplies. Everyone there would pass the buck, and I would sometimes spend a whole day cajoling this one and that one and came back to the camp exhausted as well as empty-handed. So finally thoughtful Bernard said, "Let me do the worrying" and kept badgering them until they finally coughed up immediate operating expenses. But it was clear that Gordon's refusal to be taken over by OSS would eventually bring us to a total halt.

A different sort of showdown came when Gordon asked me and Wichtrich to dinner at the GBT townhouse and casually announced he was transferring the property to Texaco. Because the payment had come from the British, this was none of my business or Wichtrich's either, but the colonel had no doubt hoped that this happy refuge would be transferred to AGAS along with the rest of the GBT setup. Although the atmosphere remained friendly, Wichtrich hinted that by such a move Gordon had transferred his interests from war activity to post-war. This touched a sore spot. "If I'm no longer wanted in AGAS," Gordon retorted, "I'll pull out, full stop. And that means Bernard, Tan, Simon, Liangski, André, Helen, and the rest of GBT will no doubt also pull out."

Wichtrich as usual played it cool. "Laurie, I never said you weren't wanted, indeed quite the reverse. You and your team have always been A Number 1. But we have to face up to facts. Wedemeyer insists that all operations in his theater come under his command. This means military control of all units. You were offered a commission but refused it on the grounds that you didn't want your outfit to be subject to outside interference. Also you object to our using men like Ho because you think he's anti-French—as well he may be. But Wedemeyer approves our using him. And so do I. Even de Gaulle now wants to rope him in! If you and your group want to pull out we shall certainly regret it. But it won't alter the facts." Then with that genuinely engaging manner Wichtrich was blessed with, he added, "If you won't run the show under our overall control, how about staying in as civilian advisor and running any activities that don't involve the Vietnamese?"

This gave Gordon a happy way out. "Okay, Al, on that basis I'd be glad to play along! As it happens I have a scheme right now for one of my French contacts down there to escort an American submarine to the coast below Hué and set up a base. Would you be interested in that?"

"Pack clouds away, and welcome day!"* was written all over Wichtrich's face. "You bet! And we'll certainly give you all possible support."

So, much to my relief we all parted friends. And a day or two later, Gordon again invited me to dinner, this time with an American colonel from the Fourteenth and two nice girls from the British consulate. Their stimulation plus a bottle of bourbon contributed by the colonel worked like magic to set me off on telling stories, shipboard stuff, the Burma war, and so forth, which afterward I would have thought excessive had not Gordon said how much they had all enjoyed my flow.

The following morning, walking across to the radio shack, I saw something glistening in the dust. It proved to be a blue diamond, almost one carat, no doubt a relic of the live-it-up Flying Tigers. It looked as though my luck had cer-

---

* Thomas Heywood, "Matin Song."

tainly changed! Guest now reported for duty, armed with a bottle of black-market Johnny Walker for which he had paid sixty U.S. dollars. I declined a drink with the usual "not before sundown" excuse. Not having yet found a way to use his services, I sent him into town to find a place we might rent to replace the lost GBT townhouse. He came back later shining with good news and alcohol. "I tracked down some rich Chinese crooks who showed me several places we could get! The sun's gone down, so how about a drink?" It was clear that Guest would warm up our somewhat subdued camp—but not too much, I hoped.

Despite discouragement from us, Simon several times cooperated with French anti-Ho groups, and I had to make some sharp protests. Either as a result of this or to liaise with Gordon, Simon shortly turned up in our camp. Because he wrote his usual excellent intelligence report, I did not question his motives. Meanwhile, Tan seemed to be still resisting Gordon's summons. Indeed, his wires indicated he was now dead keen on Ho. Even more surprising, so was Phelan! One of his wires read: "You misunderstand Vietminh attitude. They not anti-French merely patriots deserving full trust and support." Phelan's remarkable transformation might be the result of (1) his basic common sense and judgment; (2) Ho's convincing personality; or (3) the infectious enthusiasm of Ho's disciples.

When I called at the "townhouse," Gordon, who now spent most of his time there, was out, and the door was opened by a man named Hansen. Hansen headed up the Texaco Company and began chatting about future prospects. He said, "To be honest we're loathe to invest any money in either China or Indochina. There's no security in either place, and there will certainly be revolutions in both. So then we'll be thrown out. But the trouble is that meanwhile we have a pile of oil to sell, and we've got to sell it somewhere! Our only hope is to sell it before everything goes to hell. Otherwise, the Russians will move in and grab the business themselves."

His predictions were largely accurate. Although the Chinese Communists ousted Chiang's regime in 1949, and later the Vietnamese Communists ousted the American-Saigon forces, the Russians never actually moved in. They were always more concerned with suppressing internal dissidents than with commercial exploitation. Indeed, they had good reason to be more concerned! But our own preoccupation with Communism as a serious threat to our very existence was initiated and subsequently made gospel by that ever-dangerous combination of big business and the arms industry. This has cost us, among lesser misadventures, the disaster of Vietnam. One of the most curious delusions of humankind is that we learn from our mistakes. Yet even the most perfunctory examination of world history reveals that we never do. Our explanation for this, of course, is that each generation is convinced that it does not have to learn; it already knows, so from now on things will be "different"!

Arriving back at the camp, I discovered by chance that Gordon had called in to give Helen a radio message for Tan entirely concerned with Texaco affairs and confirming a Texaco job in Chungking. When I found Helen clandestinely coding this message, she admitted with embarrassment having been told not to let me see it.

When Chinese dollars declined to two thousand to one U.S. dollar, we offered to pay the staff in U.S. dollars to give them a measure of financial security. Helen was one of those who took up this offer. Meanwhile, Janet, who had gone to work with Service of Supply, was being paid in "rice," that is, according to the prevailing price of rice, which was another method of keeping up with the cost of living. Although both rice and U.S. dollars maintained a real value, they did not, of course, always coincide in value, so there was a constant rivalry between Helen and Janet as to who had the better arrangement. Only organizations with unauthorized funds, such as OSS and AGAS, could get away with paying in U.S. currency; some other U.S. units, not allowed to pay either in "rice" or U.S. dollars, paid an average black-market rate. Money-money became even more of a craving than sex!

Wichtrich offered his analysis of the GI in China:

There are five stages. On arrival he's a man of considerable knowledge about China, having read all the reports in *Time* magazine about politics, economics, history, and social relations. So when this newcomer meets the Chinese here, there is a lot of *kerchee* [ritual politeness] and fraternizing, and very quickly this GI knows and understands the Chinese as nobody ever knew and understood them before, so he'll spread the word how our relations with the Chinese could be so much better. The next stage comes about three months later when our man realizes that things are not quite as straightforward as he thought. He begins to see that all the equipment, supplies, financing, and most of the work comes from the Americans, and they really should be in the driver's seat, which they aren't. So he starts ordering the Chinese about, expects them to conform, and gets mad when they don't.

The third stage comes when he realizes the Chinese are defeating his driver's seat policy not by refusing to conform but by sheer indifference. So he decides to take a leaf out of their book and become indifferent himself: blasé, amused, ironic, but basically disillusioned. The fourth stage follows when he finds he can't keep this up and starts to get horribly frustrated, confused, and seeks escape in drink, opium, whores, and loud talk. So he is then sent home as "overtired." The fifth stage comes during convalescence, when he analyzes everything carefully, decides China was wonderful after all (although he can't think why), and is determined to go back as soon as possible and settle there for life.

To get on our Ho Chi Minh bandwagon fast, OSS asked us to get his help in a big drop of men and supplies for an anti-Japanese sabotage operation. Ho agreed to cooperate provided no Frenchmen took part. OSS promised "none." But Simon reported that a French friend of his was actually in on the deal, so I wired Tan to be sure to have this Frenchman and any others arrested if only for their own safety. Later on, when meeting some of Guest's "Chinese crooks," I discovered one of them was actually Simon's French friend, who indiscreetly boasted not only about this mission but about his inside knowledge of the Vietminh. "Ho is really dependent on an Annamite I know quite well who's actually quite pro-French, and when I get down there I can get the whole Vietminh working along with us." We warned OSS that this Frenchman was a nutcase, and after investigating for themselves, they withdrew him from the team.

Service of Supply (who next to the Fourteenth Air Force was the biggest U.S. group in China) was having a dance, so Guest persuaded me to go along with Helen and Susan. When we arrived we found Gordon there, too. The girls had come more on sufferance than for pleasure. Although Helen did her best to fit in, Susan sat there like a frightened rabbit until Guest persuaded her to have one small drink, after which, much to my astonishment, she got up and jitterbugged and even seemed to enjoy herself. The next morning she remarked in a pleasantly detached sort of way, "It's plain to see that Mr. Guest is a great one for the girls, even worse than you, and much less delicate in his attitude!" The shuffle, the slippers, and the cotton sack were all back in place, but had the contents really changed from Miss Simplicity to Madame Sophist? In any event, she had gotten us both weighed up!

The specter of disruption came to haunt us again. Whenever Gordon visited the office, Helen worked as his private secretary and willy-nilly kept his instructions secret. It was neither her fault nor his but just inherent in the situation. But when I heard her reporting to him some of my own actions, I grew too indignant to remain silent. After hearing my protest, Gordon said, "Very well. Perhaps it's better if I don't come to the camp at all since it riles you."

"You'll have to please yourself about that," I replied ungraciously.

Later on, Bernard tackled me. "Although it's an awkward situation, I think your protest went too far. Don't forget Laurie brought you into this show and made you really welcome. Now you do this and you do that and never even consult him, although you're utilizing all his setup, especially his picked associates. So I don't think you have any right, Charles, to question what he does." Because this rebuke was certainly justified, I went to Gordon and apologized. He at once put out his hand.

"No, it's for me to say I'm sorry. I know I've brushed off on you all the frustrations I've had to put up with myself, not only from OSS but even from AGAS and G-5 [Department of the Army] in Chungking. I suppose we're all as bad at heart, wanting to climb up our personal ladder more than anything else. I'm guilty of that myself, but I do try and put the war effort first if only because I want to end it and get on with my postwar life."

I suppose that was how I felt about it, too. But what really hit a chord was when Gordon added, "I can tell you honestly, Charles, if it hadn't been for your efforts to keep things running, I'd have packed it in long ago." And that was the last tiff we ever had.

Guest woke himself up every morning with half a pint of Indochina rum in a pint of coffee. Then he went out to shoot crows with his .38, rarely succeeding. Yet no matter how he behaved, everyone liked him, and he was always so keen to like and be liked that even bad-tempered Fenn seldom got really peeved with him. There were, however, occasional near misses. He often went off to town without letting me know. This usually did not matter, but on one occasion he was missing when Wichtrich sent for the pair of us, and I had to explain a full two-hour absence. When at last he got back, I found him in his room taking off his heavy GI high shoes, which he threw on the floor, exclaiming, "Holy smoke, but it's swell to get those damn things off!" I burst into laughter and then laughed and laughed, while Guest pressed me to explain the joke. At last I managed to spit it out:

"The joke is that now you've got those damn things off, you can damn well get them on again. We've been due at Wichtrich's for three whole hours!" Guest downed half a tumbler of rum and hurriedly put on his shoes.

Another mishap was more serious. To celebrate Helen's birthday, Guest organized a party. We borrowed dance records and laid in drink, and the cook fixed special food. Everything went swimmingly until Guest, in his customary easygoing fashion, gave Susan a playful slap on the bottom. It was the sort of familiarity an American girl would have responded to with a rebuke or at most an admonishing return slap. But Susan let out a yelp that reflected a combination of resentment, shame, and embarrassment. In China, such a gesture would be unheard of except as an insult. So I gave Guest the kind of dressing-down I thought he deserved. And he shortly disappeared.

The following morning when he did not show up for work, I was told he was sick in bed. When I subsequently looked in to see what was wrong, he was still in bed and looking dark eyed. "Hung over?" I asked him.

For a moment or two he did not answer. Then, as if reluctantly, he said, "I had a very bad night. But not from drink." He seemed loathe to answer my further questions, but at last blurted out, "If you must know, I felt absolutely suicidal!"

"Great heavens! Why?"

"First of all—the way Susan looked at me! A playful slap—good grief, who'd ever know she'd take it like that? And then when you bawled me out! In my whole life no one's every talked to me like that! Total contempt!"

"Oh, come off it! I was merely annoyed that you embarrassed her!"

"Much worse than that. You squashed me like a maggot!"

I tried to persuade him that my outburst was as much due to my bad temper as to his impropriety. But it took him the whole day to get over this shock. Nor could I understand why anyone, least of all someone like Guest, who had everything to feel secure about, should care that much about what I said. "Know thyself" exhorted several Greek philosophers. But we never do.

Tan wired us that the Thomas team was planning to blow up the railroad bridge on the line between Hanoi and Langson. But Ho said this would need armed protection because the Japanese would be onto them in battalion strength. He felt disinclined to risk this sizable encounter. Thomas then asked OSS for support. "Five hundred parachutists?" Tan had asked sardonically. But the OSS response was to start organizing a team of a dozen, with both French and U.S. personnel. Being informed of this Tan then wired, "The Vietminh will have hundreds of armed men ready to arrest all the Frenchmen." In a follow-up wire, however, he added, "Thomas is a great guy, already sold on the Vietminh and sending wires to OSS that they should work only with Ho and not with the French." What irony! A few weeks previously, only Bernard and I would risk backing Ho, and we got mostly abuse for it; now everyone wanted to get on the bandwagon!

A Captain Frisch of the FMM called in with a proposition that if we would bring Ho back to Kunming, de Gaulle would send a top French general with instructions to come to terms. "De Gaulle knows that the old days have gone for good. He wants to give the Annamites a fair deal and work with them, not against them."

Although I promised to put this to Ho, I offered FMM my opinion that he would not come. "It's my guess that at this stage it's more important for him to get his Vietminh fully established than to get French cooperation." This proved to be right. When I wired Ho the proposition, he wired back five words: "Sorry I cannot come now." Ho was, of course, right. De Gaulle never had any intention of real cooperation. He would make promises and even concessions, but the intention was to keep real control in French hands, as later became constantly evident. Starting with nothing, and for many years having little enough, the Vietminh slowly but surely took over until in a final confrontation at Dien Bien Phu they totally defeated the final French bid for control. In Russia, and in China, Communist-inspired have-nots had also achieved power after starting with nothing. How was it achieved? Ho put his finger on it when he once told me: "Determination, determination; with that you can achieve anything!" Of course, there was a lot more to it than that. First, one must have a population deprived and exploited, largely peasantry and necessarily energetic; a code, bible, and war song (Communism); an inspiring, tireless, and effective leader; and finally an opposition disintegrated, corrupt, uninspired, disunited—all or any of those.

When a jeep drove into the compound, I looked out to see a little bearded Chinese farmer dressed in faded blue climb out from the seat beside the driver. How odd! And when this farmer yelled out in English, it seemed even more peculiar! Hurrying outside I stared and stared. Could it be . . . ? Surely it couldn't . . . ? But it was! Frankie Tan in person. We fell into each other's arms, and then I heard *all* about it. Fortunately, Gordon was not there to hear Tan's hymn of praise for Ho and the Vietminh, and I warned him to lay off this eulogy when they did meet. But Tan was irrepressible. "Laurie will have to face the facts. The French in Indochina are as good as finished. When the war ends the Vietminh will certainly take over. And meanwhile Ho can do a lot to help us finish it! Intelligence, pilot rescue, and sabotage for OSS if they don't screw it up. I've brought back sackfuls of documents that will prove it!" For a whole hour I could not stop his flow. Here is one story that I noted down:

One of their boys, a marvelous swimmer, fine physique, looking just like Sabu [the exotic star of *Elephant Boy*, a recent movie] used to dive into the swirling torrent of the nearby river and leap in and out amidst the rocks like a porpoise. The river was full of fish, and when we threw in a hand grenade, you could then grab the stunned fish as they floated downstream. But the big fellows lurked under the rocks where they were safe. So this boy begged for a grenade, dived in amongst the rocks, then came up minus the grenade and laughing his head off. Almost in the same instant there came a muffled explosion and up shot a column of water ten feet high! After which he dived back in and came up with a large fish in each hand and one between his teeth! I'm not kidding! Better than any Hollywood stunt I've ever seen!

Tan also brought me a letter from Ho:

I want to write you a long, long letter to thank you for your friendship. Unfortunately I can't write much, because I am in bad health just now. (Not very sick, don't worry!) What I want to say, Mr. Tan will say for me. If you see Messirs Bernard, Vincent, Reiss & Carlsen [of the Information Office], and our other friends, please give them my kindest regards. Pham said that you will come here. We are ready to give you the heartiest welcome. Do come as soon as you can.

As previously mentioned, Ho had been very much shaken by his walk to the first base. Tan said that on the second walk to his advance base at Thai Nguyen, he arrived really sick. At the time he wrote the above letter (in which he is anxious that I should not worry about him!), he was so gravely ill that his closest friend, the military leader Vo Nguyen Giap, subsequently wrote in his recollections: "For hours he lay in a coma. . . . Every time he came to he would murmur his thoughts about our work. I refused to believe he was imparting his dying thoughts. But afterwards, looking back on the scene, I realized that he felt so weak that he was dictating his last instructions to me." This makes it obvious that had we not flown Ho to the border, either he would have been unable to make this further journey in time for it to be effective, or he would have died from the added strain.

20

UNCLE HO AND
UNCLE SAM

Tan's final report began:

> The immediate necessity of utilizing Indochinese natives was precipitated
> by the sudden silencing of our French radio set after the Jap coup of
> March 9th, 1945. Although we were not entirely without ideas as to where
> and how to contact reputedly reliable representatives of the different native
> parties in Indochina, it was Lieutenant Charles Fenn who made the best-
> considered contact with agent "Lucius" (Ho Chi Minh) who claimed to
> represent the Vietminh League of Indochina.

I could not help wondering how Gordon would react when he read this particular tribute! But fortunately he had now become immersed in plans for his
submarine scheme. As usual, this combination of imagination, possibilities, and
practical application released him from frustrated idleness, so the usual good-
tempered Gordon was restored. Having Tan back, of course, greatly helped this
transition. He even suggested we might arrange for some of his French friends
inside French Indochina to meet Ho and work out a scheme to cooperate!

Finding personal relationships thus straightened out and our work flowing
smoothly, Bernard, having done three years without a break, decided he might
justifiably resign and go home. Although no one deserved a break more than
dear Harry, I soon missed him badly, not only as a friend but because of his efficiency in office routine as well as with technical stuff such as transmitters, generators, vehicles, and electrical circuits. Many U.S. personnel (far less deserving)
were also going home, certainly not because of overwork or because the war
looked like it was ending (the Japanese were, indeed, more strongly entrenched
in China than ever) but because of the "China disease" Wichtrich had spoken of:
frustration, disillusionment, boredom, and sheer inability to cope, the combina-

tion of which drove them over the edge. This, of course, never applied to either Bernard or to Chennault, who also went home at this time (no doubt to get his private airline organized), or to Kasy, who not surprisingly went to America the same week. What did seem surprising, at least initially, was her offering me the use of her house rent free. I later realized this was less from generosity than in the hope my occupation would protect it from vandals and thieves. I then discovered she had also offered it to Guest, who now invited me to drinks there and dinner at a restaurant with two girls from the FMM. "*Mais pour l'amour de Dieu,* don't tell our boss!" they implored us. Mlle Raymond, who had recently been liberated from German-occupied France, told us some grim tales of those years during which she and her mother invariably had Germans billeted on them.

"Although often arrogant and bullying, they were usually fairly well disciplined and only made advances when drunk. But one sergeant we were landed with proved menacing and even violent when I rejected his advances. So one night mother and I stoked up the fire, closed the windows, and went off to sleep in the barn. When the sergeant was found dead next morning, the kommandant made a terrible fuss, and we were badgered for days on end. But fortunately nobody could prove anything." She was a sweet girl, but I could not help observing (now an ingrained habit!) that she cut up her portions of duck as if she were carving up a bullock.

With real or well-feigned regret, the girls turned down our solicitation to stay the night. "To spend an evening with Americans is bad enough, but to share your beds, mon Dieu—that would be a crime worse than murder!"

"But we'll get you back before daybreak," Guest pleaded. "So no one will be any the wiser."

"*Ah, cheri, tu plaisantes* [Ah, darling, you're joking]! That's one thing our 'intelligence' is sure to find out!"

On the way to the FMM we were passed by a jeep at a very fast clip. Either through indignation or wanting to show off, I felt an aggressive impulse to overtake this jeep and flag it down. When I did so and bawled the driver out for reckless driving, it was only then I observed that he was a captain and his passenger a full colonel! And they were naturally put out at being barked at by someone in a nondescript uniform (fortunately nonidentifiable) transporting two girls! Strong words ensued, but luckily the colonel was apparently in a hurry and did not argue further. I drove off feeling decidedly foolish, but fortunately for my ego the girls, having understood almost nothing of our English, seemed to think I had administered a well-deserved reproof. And Mlle Françoise kissed me good night with such fervor that I thought she might easily commit a "crime worse than murder" if only the war went on long enough.

———

The "tiger's" mate having now been chased away, the cook bought six white baby rabbits so endearing they made your heart leap! But from day to day they got dirtier and dirtier and more and more stepped on; one died from injury and another from dysentery. At last I rebelled. "Either look after them properly or get rid of them; that's an order!" The next day they appeared on the luncheon table swimming in sauce.

We had had several bad storms with such torrents of rain that our little river became a raging cataract and the camp an island amid vast floods. Then one night lightning blew the generator. With no Bernard to help, I was trying to fix it when Susan came to assist. "Thanks, hold the flash," I told her. Then came another terrifying crash of thunder, and she dropped the flash and threw herself into my arms. I assumed this was only out of fright, but then I heard her whisper, "I love you." I think this astonished me more than anything else that happened during the entire war! In these days of women's lib, we take women's overtures for granted. But at that time, for a Chinese girl who had never had an affair to throw herself, literally as well as figuratively, at a foreigner was almost unthinkable. Fright, of course, partly accounted for it. Also, we were all living under pressure, and Susan in particular had been thrown into an environment so divorced from her traditions that she had probably changed more in the past few weeks than in the past ten years.

One day in town I saw Lily coming down the street. Now involved with Susan, I would have gladly avoided a meeting. But then I thought that would add insult to injury. Seeing her unhappy look, I thought it best to ask her into Kasy's house rather than have a confrontation in the street. This proved a mistake; we had no sooner sat down than she burst into tears. When this had partly subsided, she told me she had heard from Lao that I had "another girl." "Lao keeps wanting me to marry him. But I can't bear that he should even touch me!" Her tears soaked down into her faded blue dress and made a dark patch, spreading, spreading. "Man's love is of man's life a thing apart, 'Tis woman's whole existence."* This hyperbole is at times devastatingly near to the truth.

I relate these details only to emphasize that the ordeals of war are by no means limited to danger and discomfort or even to deprivation of an environ-

* Lord Byron, *Don Juan.*

ment and pattern of existence that had become part of our very nature. In addition to these ordeals, there are the afflictions that lead us (as a way of escape) into drunkenness, drugs, violence, moral corruption, mental breakdown, xenophobia, whoring, and (perhaps above all) the penalties and miseries inflicted in one way and another on the populations among whom the war is fought, injuries not limited to shot and shell but resulting from our own behavior.

This was indeed one of those times, fortunately rare, when guilt and compassion so weighed me down that not even my usual anodyne—dear Bach, beloved Mozart—could lift me from the pit. Then—bang! It was one of those times when, had I been religious—devotedly religious!—I might have thought God had taken pity on me! An AGAS officer whose name I didn't know came bursting in with the astonishing news that two "atom" bombs had been dropped on Japan with overwhelming effect and that the Russians, having simultaneously declared war, were already sweeping into Manchuria! This announcement banished my gloom in an instant. And a later news flash that the Japanese were ready to surrender left us all flabbergasted.

The FMM now tried frantically to organize a mass reentry into their former colony, collecting cars and equipment, recruiting personnel, requisitioning, printing up forms, and sending wires, all in a mad scramble that was promptly frustrated by the grim ultimatum that Chinese troops were crossing the border en masse while preventing the disorganized French from sending in a single man!

Wichtrich then informed me, "The whole of FIC [French Indochina] is to be divided north and south, with the Chinese temporarily occupying the north and the British the south. This is not anti-French, it's just the reality; they themselves have no troops, no equipment, and no cohesive organization. Meanwhile, Charles, we want you to persuade Ho to come up here and negotiate with us collectively."

"He'll never come. Why should he?"

"The French are ready to talk turkey. All the big shots will be ready to meet him. And Wedemeyer will see that he gets a square deal."

"What kind of 'square deal'? Down there he's in the driver's seat, with most of the country behind him. Here he'll get nothing but empty promises."

"But the Chinese and the British are taking over with large-scale troops and sophisticated armament. Ho has nothing to stand up against that."

"Although the British troops may hold the south, the Chinese troops will care about nothing but loot. So Ho will sweep the board north of Hué." (This forecast proved correct. In south Indochina, however, British troops might not have prevailed had the unspeakable Major General Douglas Gracey not reinforced them with rearmed Japanese. He subsequently declared himself delighted with the discipline and fine military qualities of this former enemy. "Thoughts that do lie too deep for tears"!*)

"How about if Wedemeyer sends Ho a personal wire?"

"Colonel! I doubt if Ho has even heard of Wedemeyer! Chennault's gone home, but even he would get nowhere now that Ho is in the driver's seat. However, I'll certainly ask him to come."

When I sent Ho a wire explaining all the big-shot reception he would get, he wired back, "Very sorry impossible come now."

The pressure to get Ho to a "conference" was of course merely to halt his further expansion. At the Yalta Conference between the Allied powers, it had already been agreed that colonial powers, including the French, would get back their colonies. Roosevelt had opposed this return to what he considered the "bad old days, doomed to failure by incipient revolution." (How right he was!) But the collective vote had forced him to swallow it. In French Indochina, however, events had moved too fast, and in order to halt Ho's further progress toward self-rule, he was to be flimflammed with a pretentious conference!

When I reported Ho's final turndown, Wichtrich said (almost with relief), "Okay, we did our best. Now I have another job for you. The immediate task for AGAS is to comfort and, if possible, aid the prisoners of war, who are, of course, still held in the camps in horrible conditions. So teams are being organized to that end. There are no American prisoners in Indochina, so we can write that one off. Because you're also well posted on the South China area, I want you to handle the Canton–Hong Kong mission we're flying in."

He then explained the setup by which a plane loaded with a dozen or more mixed personnel (American, British, and Chinese) plus immediate relief supplies would fly to Canton and Hong Kong and arrange with the Japanese to contact the prisoners, mainly to declare our intention of immediate relief and (we hoped) rescue.

It was only because the bulk of the prisoners in that area were British that our contingent included British personnel. Among these were a colonel and two majors. Although I was officially in command, this outranking was in itself embarrassing. But much worse was the fact that two of them had escaped from

---

* William Wordsworth, "Intimations of Immortality."

the Hong Kong prison camp, which made them liable to execution! Although the war was over, could we count on them now being safe?

On landing in Canton very warily (on a reportedly unmined strip of a mined airfield), we were all immediately arrested by the obviously hostile Japanese, and I, as commander, was marched off to face the Japanese commanding general. Although I had an interpreter, the general spoke fairly good English, having once lived in America for a year. He explained, courteously but very dryly, that although he himself, after the exchange of several wires to Tokyo, was satisfied that Japan *had* surrendered, he could not convince his army that this astounding fact could possibly be true, because here in China they were still winning! He could therefore not guarantee our safety. But he had secured the promise of his leading officers that they would allow us to fly off unhindered if we went immediately. Otherwise, he could not guarantee our safety.

I had been ordered to stay regardless of difficulties, but this extremity had not been anticipated. The difficulties and indeed dangers to all of us were extreme, but the real challenge was, of course, to those British officers who had escaped from the Japanese and whose lives were at risk. To make this the excuse for cut and run seemed rather too easy, but as I came out to the open field I was quickly warned by one of my team that without any decision by me, the British were already agitating for cut and run (as who could blame them!), against a not-too-earnest protest from some of my own team that we had been ordered to stay. And I was warned that the Japanese had signified their awareness of this dissension by a further increase in their hostility. I solicited a quick vote and suppressed a sigh of relief when it registered "go." Upon my signal, the general's aide-de-camp circulated the word. A somewhat angry buzz was followed by some equally angry orders that to my relief calmed the hoi polloi to a mere sullen buzz. We were already climbing into our plane, the engine was roaring, and the props were whizzing. The door slammed, and we were off.

It was only when we soared aloft that the copilot came to inform me privately that before we reached Luchow (where we had taken off), it would be dark, and because that field was unlighted, we could not land but would have to fly on to Kunming. Moreover, the pilot could not be sure there was enough gas, so we might have to jump! He assured me, however, like a kindly, if long-suffering, uncle, that he would let me know in good time for us to get on our chutes. Wow! But one thing you learned in OSS was never to show your feelings. So, having checked with him our estimated time of arrival, I settled down amid the racket in the plane and wrote in my diary, which the pressure of events had made me neglect for almost a week. As we got nearer and nearer to the time of arrival, I had to admit feeling a certain small tension. The jump in itself might not have bothered me (who knows?), but it was now pitch dark, and there below us lay a chaos of largely uninhabited mountains where, even supposing one survived the drop intact, one would almost certainly perish from drought, starvation, cold, or hungry wild animals! So when at last I heard the engine decline through a series of diminishing bursts to a final ploppity-plop, with the plane simultaneously dropping, as it were, into space, I could not but think what a fool I had been not to accept Japanese incarceration rather than fly off. But I had to look calm, unafraid, in charge, the boss. I so well remember—it's the trivialities that the mind camera records—screwing on the cap of my fountain pen, clipping it into my uniform pocket, standing up, and half shouting, "Attention, everyone!" when out rushed the copilot calling, "It's okay, just switching"—he had gotten this far when the engine started up with a gurgle that instantly leapt to a roar— "over to the emergency tank! We wanted to use up every drop in the main tank first!" My God, what a relief! And ten minutes later we landed with a bump on the Kunming airfield.

I received one final letter from Ho.

> The war is finished. It is good for everybody. I feel only sorry that all
> our American friends have to leave us so soon. And their leaving this
> country means that relations between you and me will be more difficult.
>
> The war is won. But we small and subject countries have no share, or
> very small share, in the victory of freedom and democracy. Probably, if we
> want to get a sufficient share, we still have to fight. I believe that your
> sympaty [sic] and the sympaty of the great American people will always be
> with us. I also remain sure that soon or later, we will attain our aim,
> because it is just. And our country get independent. I am looking forward
> to the happy day of meeting you and our other American friends either in
> Indochina or in the USA!

Ho spent the remaining twenty-four years of his life struggling for that independence, dying four years short of that final "victory of freedom and democracy" he wrote about. The "democracy" was perhaps nebulous, but the victory was certain enough, and it was achieved not only against the French (despite their having been partly restored to power by superman de Gaulle) but also against the "great American people" Ho truly admired and befriended and would have gone on admiring and befriending had not our subsequent policy and behavior transformed him into an enemy. It was, indeed, a supreme tragedy for America that with Roosevelt's death we inherited a series of presidents incapable of evaluating America's true interests, which should have been concerned more with developing friendly relations with existing democracies and promoting democracies elsewhere than with promoting an almost religious campaign against Communism, a campaign that, as with all antidogma crusades, served only to provoke and hence promote it.

It is true, of course, that these American presidents reflected the creed of a considerable proportion of Americans, including almost the entire business world. Perhaps even Roosevelt might not have prevented the sharp right turn America took when the Soviet Union ceased to be a useful ally and became, as formerly, what was considered a dangerous enemy. And the Soviets had, indeed, emerged from the appalling carnage inflicted on them by the Nazis a united empire second only to the USA in global power and, from the American viewpoint, dangerously supportive of Communist insurgency everywhere. But events proved that we made nothing but mistakes in trying to prevent this movement. First, in China we supported the Chiang regime, a disastrous failure that left us daggers drawn with China for decades—an almost childish quarrel with what was, after all, a world power! Then in Korea, we maneuvered the United Nations into an anti-Communist war that established in the southern half of the country a regime as totalitarian as the Communist northern half and even less representative of the population. Finally, in Vietnam, we suffered, through our own folly, the worst failure and most humiliating defeat in our entire history. It must, however, be admitted that our ceaseless "cold war" against the Communist Soviet Union did largely help to bankrupt that empire, although this result has disastrously affected the world economy.

How did Vietnam achieve these two incredible victories, one against a European power, the other against the world's superpower? First, there was Ho's iron will, dedication to the cause, and magic leadership; second was the military genius of Vo Nguyen Giap; and third was the extraordinary resolution of the Vietnamese people in achieving freedom.

Neither France nor America had any similar assets. De Gaulle was, of course, a great leader, but his concentration of purpose was divided. America had no great leaders, either political or military. Nor did the American Army in Vietnam care what it was fighting for. Survival became the objective; danger and hardship were to be avoided; in place of the will to victory was an urge to get out fast and in one piece.

The declared purpose of America in fighting the Vietnam War was to suppress Communism, a political creed that had been anathema from its establishment in Russia in 1917. When I asked Ho whether he considered himself essentially a Communist or a nationalist, he declared himself to be both: Communism was the means and nationalism the end. It was not until I wrote about his life (*Ho Chi Minh: A Biographical Introduction*) and had to explore international politics in depth that I discovered what he meant by this. Political revolutions are not won by throwing bombs or spouting on street corners. First they require, as I wrote in the biography, "a logique, a verbalizer, a frame, a unifying philosophy to serve as a raison d'être, a proselytizer, a guide and above all a dogma by which to exclude deviationist groups and concepts." Ho found this in the cause, analysis, and inevitability of revolution as expounded by Marx and in the application of Marxian theory to successful practice. The more one investigates this theory and development, the more one understands why it succeeded in transforming whole nations.

The first mistake America made was in not understanding it and supposing Communism could be suppressed by supporting the nationalist group who opposed it. Had this group been efficient, united, and strong, they might have successfully opposed it on their own, whether in Russia, China, North Korea, or Vietnam (to name countries where revolutions succeeded). But armies employed in civil wars must be given both a very strong lead and a very good reason to fight against fellow citizens: the Communists were dedicated and ready to die for their cause; their opponents were largely conscripts who had little interest in their cause and only wanted to survive. This was fatal to success in each case. (A half success was established in South Korea but only at the cost of installing a corrupt dictatorship.)

The subsequent failure (subversion, decline, adaptation) of Communism in the past decade has been due not to its deficiency as a system (it has never been faithfully or efficiently developed and utilized) but to the inherent and repeated failure of the human race to live up to its ideals. Surely nothing could be more desirable for humanity as a whole than to share and share alike; to have equal rights; and to receive honors, praise, and promotion instead of monetary gain, because money, if not the root of all evil, comes close enough: indeed, in this present world the pursuit of money (materialism) has now exceeded all other human interests.

But returning to facts: Ho was indeed a Communist linked to Soviet Russia. And the big question is: Would he have remained as friendly to America as he was to those Americans with whom he worked so loyally during World War II? I think he probably would. His relationship with the Soviet Union never involved a military alliance. More than any other world leader of the period, Ho was internationally minded and broadly envisioned, having been a global traveler, extensive linguist, political theorist, diplomat, head of state, humanist, and even a poet. Nor has time subsequently clouded his image with revelations of faults, decline, or misdeeds as happened to many other world leaders. Even when becoming world famous and his name a battle cry for resurgent youth, he remained the same simple and unpretentious Uncle Ho who so admirably personified the creed that all men are brothers.

My initial attempt to relieve the POWs in Canton and Hong Kong having failed, I successfully accomplished this mission a week or two later when the Japanese military conceded defeat and our consequent entry. There were no American prisoners in Canton and only a few in Hong Kong (the bulk having been repatriated earlier on an exchange basis). Their identification and clearance required reference to documents in the American consulate. It so happened that the Japanese military in Hong Kong, having considered the embassy strictly a civil enclave outside their own jurisdiction, had simply locked the door, awaiting instruction or the arrival of a civil official who never came. As I mentioned in the first chapter of this book, thanks to OSS training, I had not much difficulty in picking the lock. I found the consulate in perfect order and, having located the required documents, relocked the door.

Despite the failure of the initial POW mission, I was adjudged to have handled it with both courage and skill and was consequently awarded America's highest peacetime award, the Soldier's Medal for Valor.

For my services to OSS and AGAS in South China and Vietnam and particularly for my recruitment of Ho (curious irony!), I was awarded the Bronze Star.

For meritorious services to the Republic of China, I was awarded the Breast Order of the Cloud and Banner with Ribbon. This was signed by Chiang Kai-shek, a fact that sufficiently established the neutrality of my political stance during World War II.

For services to OSS I received a tribute from General William J. Donovan, head of OSS: "A special citation awarded Charles H. Fenn in appreciation for his invaluable work in AGAS during World War II."

After my routine discharge from the Marine Corps at the end of World War II, I reenlisted in 1947 with continuing rank as captain.

I list these various credentials merely to emphasize (in view of what follows) my loyalty and services to the United States.

In 1952, when I was beginning my ultimate career as a writer (which happened to be initially in London theater), I received a letter from the American consulate requesting me to call in with my passport for a checkup. (This seemed odd because the passport was still current.) At the consulate, when I presented my passport as identification, it was taken to the consul, and when I was myself shown into his office I saw it lying on his desk.

After some polite chitchat, the consul announced that the passport would now be reissued only for return to the United States. Very surprised, not to say taken aback, I said I did not at this time wish to return because my first play was opening in a small London theater the week after next. The consul looked briefly thoughtful and then suggested that I might return a week or two subsequent to that event. Suddenly, I caught on to the possible reason for this odd behavior. The London theater world had recently welcomed a number of significant U.S. actors who had left America for political reasons. I had not until that moment given much thought to this fact, but now it struck me that both their exodus and the peculiar ultimatum I had received from the consul were connected with the political investigations by U.S. Senator McCarthy that I had read about in the news and that my sponsorship of Ho Chi Minh had now caught up with me.

Upon this revelation, my OSS training prompted me to make a grab for my passport. But this gesture needed some stretching on my part, and the consul, having the advantage of proximity, was quick to knock the passport onto the floor at his feet. So obviously we were now daggers drawn! Having told the consul, reasonably politely, that my work just then prevented my return to America, I said goodbye and left.

During the next few months the consulate put further pressure on me to return and finally gave me a deadline, with a warning that if I did not conform, my passport was subject to cancellation. The loss of the passport had already been an unpleasant handicap, because in addition to writing and producing my own play (and, I hoped, "plays" in the plural), I represented a Swedish theatrical group for whom I found other writers' work suitable for production in

Scandinavian theaters. This required occasional trips to Stockholm and Gothenburg. It was only after much red tape that I succeeded in getting from the British Home Affairs office a travel document that did, indeed, enable me to travel, but only at the expense of hard looks, many questions, and frequent obstructions.

When it came to a showdown regarding the cancellation of my citizenship, I was so indignant with what I considered this disgraceful ultimatum presented to a U.S. citizen formerly adjudged a hero that I made no further protest and thus became stateless. I then proceeded to apply for British nationality (necessarily repudiated when acquiring U.S. citizenship), my eligibility for which was endorsed by five British friends of eminence in various fields.

I was subsequently asked to call in at Scotland Yard, where a series of questions getting more and more unpleasant at last drew forth an accusation that my answers were "untrue." It then became clear that I had been spied on for the past few months and certain events given a twist or exaggerated to distort reality. For example, although I had actually met (at a party given by Kingsley Martin, editor of the *New Statesman*) a woman member of Parliament named Monica Felton, who was a "dangerous Communist," I had nevertheless denied knowing any Communists! So although this meeting was a two-minute chat, I had told an "untruth." Even my friendship with Kingsley Martin, Harold Laski, and Lord (Fenner) Brockway (all respectably left wing at a time when the British government was very right wing) was twisted into "political agitation"!

Not surprisingly, my application was refused. When Harold Laski, who was an MP, inquired through channels for the reason, he discovered that because my left-wing opinions and associations were not considered sufficiently harmful enough to ban me, it was actually American pressure that mostly affected the decision to turn me down. But Laski suggested that the UK was now moving slightly left and that I should reapply in a few years time. When I did so I was again interviewed by a Scotland Yard official, with further evidence of their spying (nobody could be more aware of the technique than I myself!) and was again turned down.

Circumstances later took me to live in Ireland, where after five years' residence and with excellent Irish sponsors, I applied for Irish citizenship. When this also was refused, one of my Irish sponsors learned that the Irish government, having discovered that the Americans had canceled my citizenship and the British had twice turned me down, had no wish to take into their own nest someone so curiously shunned.

After being stateless for eighteen years, with exasperating difficulties when-ever my work (or occasionally my pleasure) required me to travel, an American friend who happened to hear of my problem expressed his astonishment that I had not learned or been informed that I could now get back my U.S. citizenship merely upon application. He explained that a wealthy German woman who had been deprived of her own U.S. citizenship on similar grounds pursued her case all the way up to the Supreme Court, which ultimately declared that no American citizen could be deprived of citizenship. I had only to apply to the Dublin embassy for a passport with evidence of my former status, and my citi-zenship would be promptly reinstalled. Although I thought he was romancing, I followed his advice and did indeed get a U.S. passport within a few weeks.

In recent years I have been several times invited and much welcomed to sev-eral OSS and AGAS conferences and have indeed received effuse thanks for my contributions to the proceedings. But I never received any official apology for this earlier lamentable duress. I was, however, favored not only with further OSS and AGAS hospitality but with a special boost from the British Broadcasting Company, which produced a television documentary titled *Uncle Sam and Uncle Ho,* which received an Emmy Award for excellence and in which the director was kind enough to designate me as the star. In this program, widely shown on both sides of the Atlantic, the representation of Uncle Ho was impartial, accurate, and consequently (in view of his true character) sympathetic. The representation of Uncle Sam was also impartial and accurate but, in view of the facts, not quite so sympathetic. As Tacitus reminds us: "A leader's error is the nation's guilt." By and large, however, America has been a world benefactor. One cannot say that of many nations.

ABOUT THE AUTHOR

Charles Fenn was born in London on June 19, 1907. He began his working life as a bellboy on the Cunard Line. After five years at sea, he emigrated to the United States, became a textiles salesman for Cannon Mills, and subsequently became an American citizen.

An officer in the U.S. Marine Corps during World War II, Fenn was assigned to the Office of Strategic Services (OSS), and subsequently to the Air Ground Aid Services (AGAS), where he engaged in the rescue of downed pilots and liaison with prisoners of war. He received invaluable help in AGAS work in southern China from Ho Chi Minh. In connection with these various pursuits, Fenn was three times decorated for services and valor.

Professionally, he is a writer of plays, novels, and some nonfiction. In 1973 Fenn wrote *Ho Chi Minh*, a short biography that was published in several countries and highly rated for its insight and accuracy. His novels include *Tropic Zero-3*, *The Golden Rule of General Wong*, *Crimson Joy*, *Floating Pagoda Boat*, *Pyramid of Night*, and *Journal of a Voyage to Nowhere*.

Fenn moved to West Cork, Ireland, in 1963 to live near his daughter and her family. Charles Fenn died in May 2004.

The Naval Institute Press is the book-publishing arm of the U.S. Naval Institute, a private, nonprofit, membership society for sea service professionals and others who share an interest in naval and maritime affairs. Established in 1873 at the U.S. Naval Academy in Annapolis, Maryland, where its offices remain today, the Naval Institute has members worldwide.

Members of the Naval Institute support the education programs of the society and receive the influential monthly magazine *Proceedings* and discounts on fine nautical prints and on ship and aircraft photos. They also have access to the transcripts of the Institute's Oral History Program and get discounted admission to any of the Institute-sponsored seminars offered around the country. Discounts are also available to the colorful bimonthly magazine *Naval History*.

The Naval Institute's book-publishing program, begun in 1898 with basic guides to naval practices, has broadened its scope to include books of more general interest. Now the Naval Institute Press publishes about one hundred titles each year, ranging from how-to books on boating and navigation to battle histories, biographies, ship and aircraft guides, and novels. Institute members receive significant discounts on the Press's more than eight hundred books in print.

Full-time students are eligible for special half-price membership rates. Life memberships are also available.

For a free catalog describing Naval Institute Press books currently available, and for further information about joining the U.S. Naval Institute, please write to:

Membership Department
U.S. Naval Institute
291 Wood Road
Annapolis, MD 21402-5034
Telephone: (800) 233-8764
Fax: (410) 269-7940
Web address: www.navalinstitute.org